Jeremy Whittle is a cycling corre[...] has been writing about European c[...] acclaimed author of *Bad Blood: The Secret Life of the Tour de France* and collaborated with David Millar on his best-selling autobiography, *Racing Through the Dark*. Both books were shortlisted for the William Hill Sports Book of the Year award. Jeremy is also a former editor of *Procycling* magazine, a PPA Awards nominee, and has contributed to the BBC, Sky, CNN, *L'Équipe* and numerous other international media.

Praise for *Ventoux*

'A really excellent book.' **Richard Williams**

'An intense hit. A must-read.' **Ned Boulting**

'Heart–stirring and jaw-dropping.' **Tim Moore**

'A terrific book.' **Matt Dickinson**

'Highly recommend Jeremy Whittle's *Ventoux* – a fascinating and expert insight into the mountain and into the current state of pro racing.' **Peter Cossins**

'My favourite sports book of this year. Really textured, well-written, atmospheric and intelligent.' **Ed Pickering**

Ventoux

SACRIFICE AND SUFFERING ON THE GIANT OF PROVENCE

Jeremy Whittle

**SIMON &
SCHUSTER**

London · New York · Sydney · Toronto · New Delhi

First published in Great Britain by Simon & Schuster UK Ltd, 2017
This paperback edition published by Simon & Schuster UK Ltd, 2018

5 7 9 10 8 6 4

Simon & Schuster UK Ltd
1st Floor
222 Gray's Inn Road
London WC1X 8HB

www.simonandschuster.co.uk
www.simonandschuster.com.au
www.simonandschuster.co.in

Simon & Schuster Australia, Sydney
Simon & Schuster India, New Delhi

A CIP catalogue record for this book
is available from the British Library

Paperback ISBN: 978-1-4711-1301-7
eBook ISBN: 978-1-4711-1302-4

Typeset in Bembo by M Rules
Printed and bound by CPI Group (UK) Ltd, Croydon, CR0 4YY

For my parents

Contents

Introduction   1

    I: *13 July 1967 . . .*   3

PART 1

Winter   9

Kilometre Zero   13

Carpe Diem   36

    II: *I first started riding . . .*   49

Foaming at the Mouth   53

    III: *You never forget your first Tour de France . . .*   77

PART 2

Summer   81

    IV: *I was bowled over . . .*   95

Eddy   97

    V: *Eddy's a great rider . . .*   100

    VI: *I love Corsica . . .*   124

Golden Years   127

The Accidental Grand Tourist   132

The Americans   149

PART 3

    VII: *Marseille*   195

Gone in 60 Seconds   197

The Light That Never Goes Out   266

    VIII: *White sky above me . . .*   282

Autumn   286

Acknowledgements   289

Bibliography   291

Glossary of Names   295

Index   301

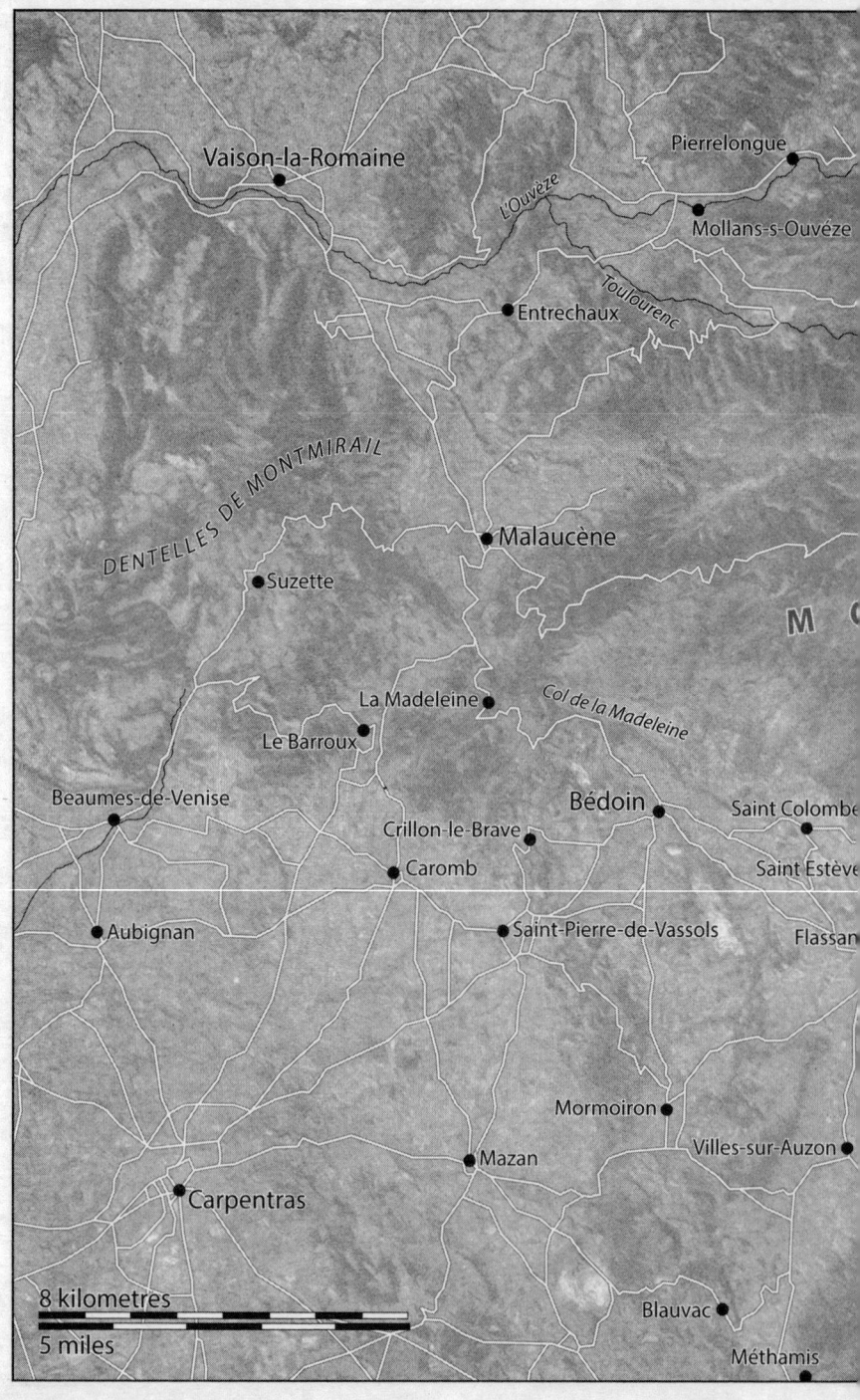

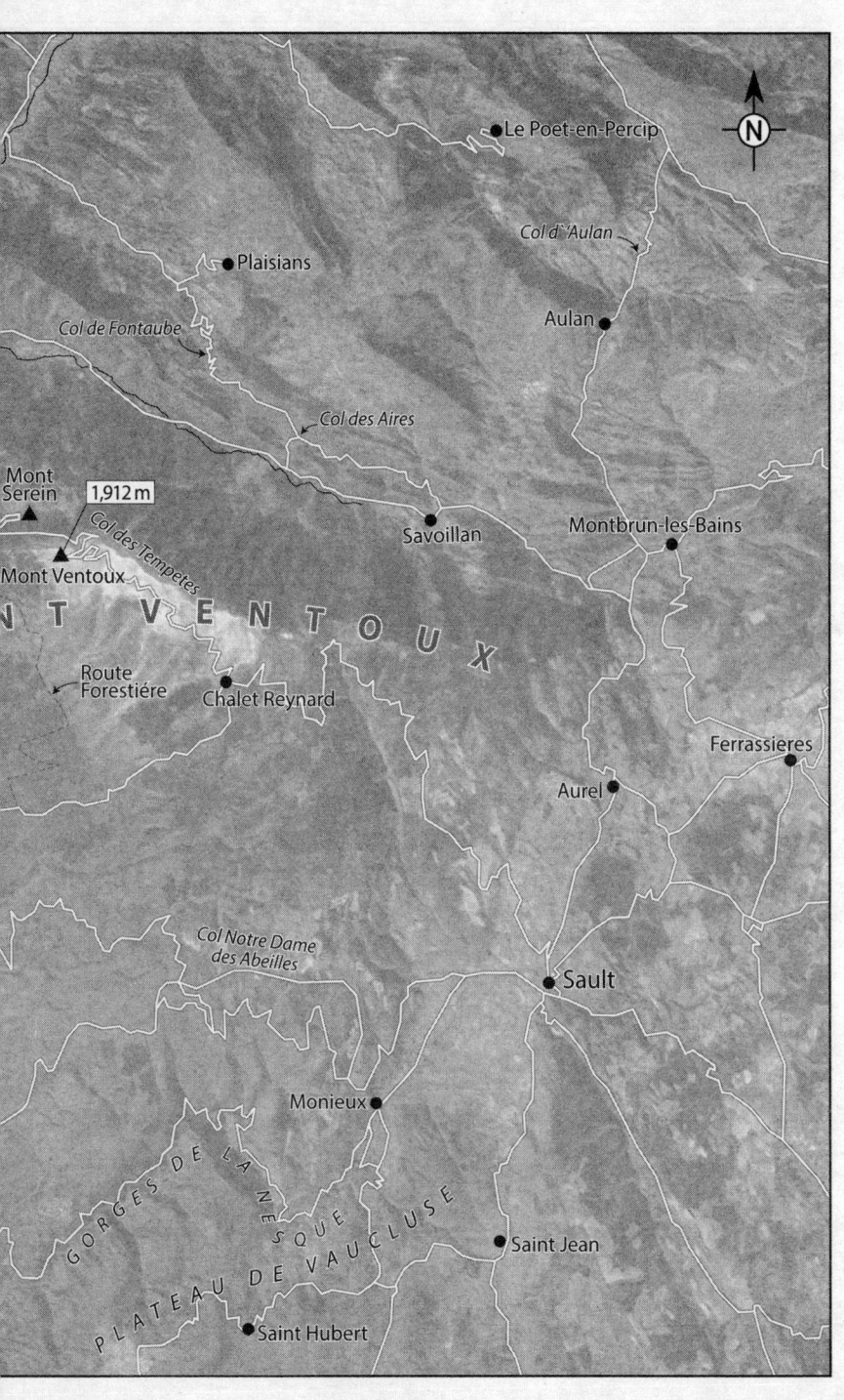

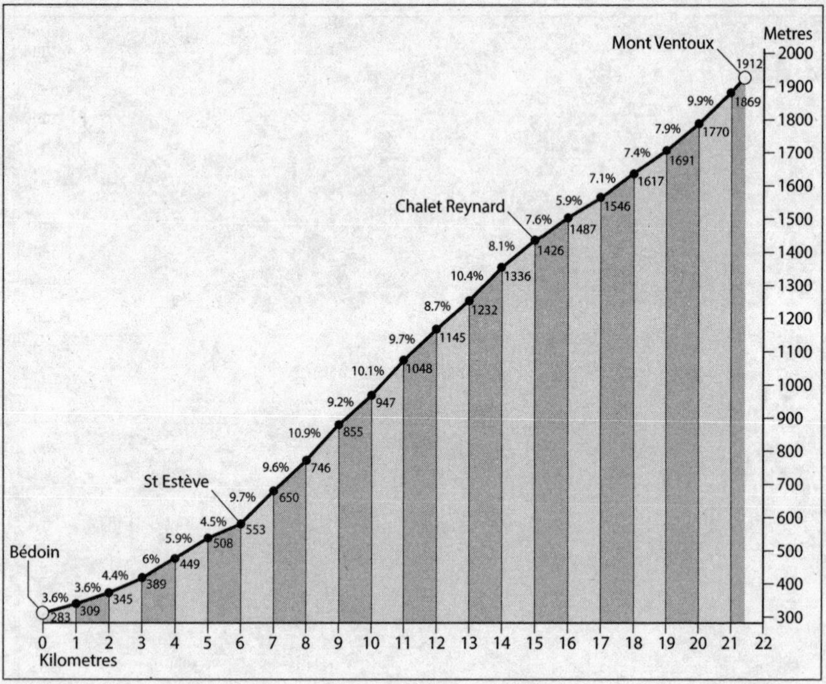

Chart 1 — Bédoin to Mont Ventoux

Mont Ventoux — 1912

Chalet Reynard

Km	Gradient	Metres
	9.9%	1869
	7.9%	1770
	7.4%	1691
	7.1%	1617
	5.9%	1546
	7.6%	1487
	8.1%	1426
	10.4%	1336
	8.7%	1232
	9.7%	1145
	10.1%	1048
	9.2%	947
	10.9%	855
	9.6%	746
	9.7%	650
	4.5%	553
	5.9%	508
	6%	449
	4.4%	389
	3.6%	345
	3.6%	309
		283

Bédoin

St Estève

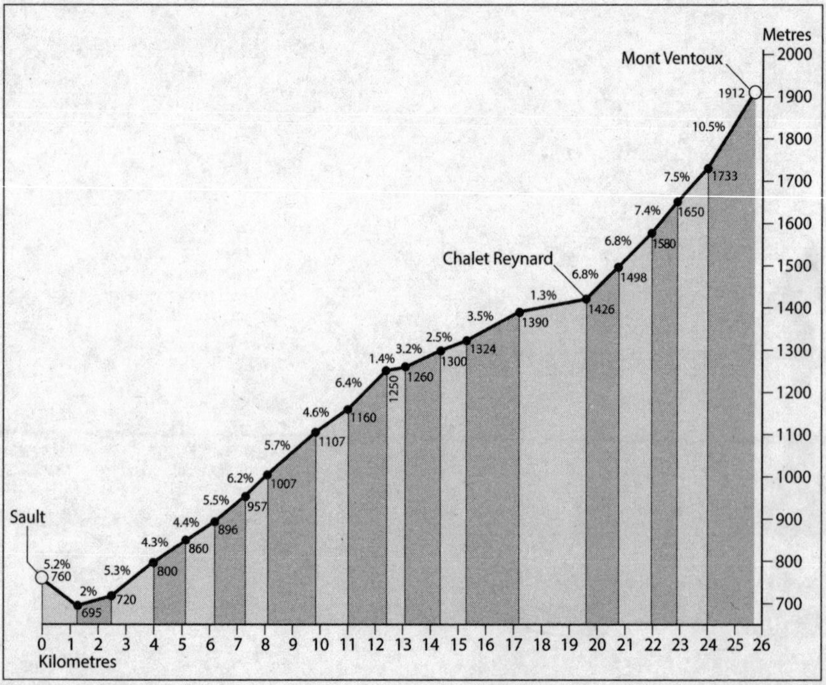

Chart 2 — Sault to Mont Ventoux

Mont Ventoux — 1912

Chalet Reynard

Gradient	Metres
10.5%	1733
7.5%	1650
7.4%	1580
6.8%	1498
6.8%	1426
1.3%	1390
3.5%	1324
2.5%	1300
3.2%	1260
1.4%	1250
6.4%	1160
4.6%	1107
5.7%	1007
6.2%	957
5.5%	896
4.4%	860
4.3%	800
5.3%	720
2%	695
5.2%	760

Sault

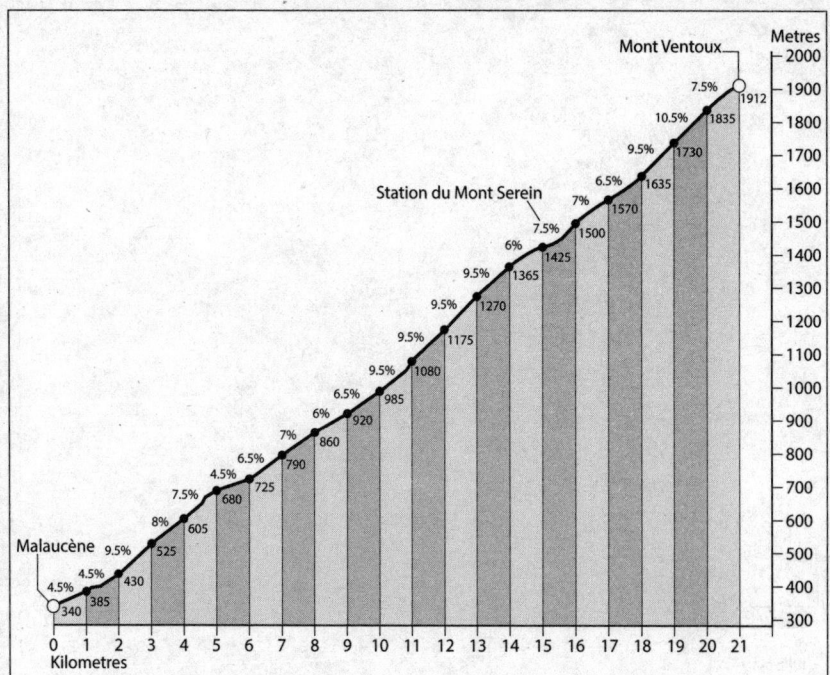

Introduction

Visible from the Alps, from the Pyrenees and from 35,000 feet, Mont Ventoux is a mountain so singular, so identifiable, that pilots flying south towards Italy and the Côte d'Azur use its bleached summit as a reference point. The vast, unmistakable bulk of the 'Giant of Provence' dominates the rolling landscape of the Drôme and Vaucluse regions of the south of France. The gruelling ascent has become one of the most feared and revered climbs in cycling.

This is a history of the significance of the Ventoux, to the development of professional cycling and, more intimately, to those whose lives, like my own, have been enriched, defined or shaped by their experience of it. It is based largely on collective memory, on conversations and recollections, encounters and interviews. It is a personal interpretation of events and histories, some public, some private.

Some of those histories are well documented, some passed on by word of mouth, some by rare photography and some, too, preserved digitally. In this book, parts of that narrative are accelerated, other parts slowed or paused and revisited in greater detail. As such, it is subjective – a snapshot, a single frame, taken from one perspective.

That is particularly relevant with the dramas that have been provoked by its brutality and by its part in the death of British cyclist Tom Simpson in July 1967. The debate over how

Simpson should be remembered – as flawed but courageous hero or as another example of professional sport's ongoing ethical malaise – will continue long after this book has been digested. His story is not the *raison d'être* of this book, but the Simpson tragedy – in an era of naivety and lawlessness – ensures that, of all the mountains in cycling, it is the Ventoux that casts the longest shadow.

Of all the renowned climbs in cycling, it is the Ventoux that is both inspirational and intimidating; it is the Ventoux that has the richest history; it is the Ventoux that most embodies both the grandeur and the darkness of professional racing.

That is why my fascination with the Giant is so enduring.

I

13 July 1967

White light. The bleached sky pulled taut by the heat. The bleached sky, taut like a drum.

There's no blue any more, not up here. Not like the blue down by the sea, on the beach, all kids screaming, ice creams and cold beers. Up here, it's just white. Like I'm on the Moon or something.

There's salt crusted around my lips, baked onto my face, salt in my eyes. No sweat any more, just salt. Maybe it's too hot to sweat. That's funny, eh? Too hot to sweat, you reckon, eh, Tom?

It's too bloody hot to do anything, let alone ride up the sodding Ventoux. I should be on the beach in Corsica with Helen and the kids. Anywhere but here. I hate this bloody place. So bleak. Just salt and dust, like in a desert.

I've been here before, but it's never been this bad, never been this dry. So much noise buzzing all around me, a right din. Bloody shouting, bloody helicopters, bloody motorbikes, bloody buzzing insects.

'Come on, Tom!'

'Allez Tommy . . .'

Leave me be. I'm fine. Just keeping it going, pushing on, turning it over.

How much longer?

3

Maybe five minutes, or so, maybe a bit less if I can keep this going. Keep this up, then chuck it down the other side sharpish.

One last push, tick the bastard off, then get down the other side, get back on the front. I'm rapid going down – I'm quick enough, I'll catch back on.

Why am I not sweating? I should be sweating cobs – five miles to the gallon, pouring into my bloody shoes, soaking my socks, like that time I had to wring them out in the sink.

Blow me, though, my guts. I've had it with feeling this rough, day after day. I thought they'd be sorted out by now. But it's always the same on the Tour. My guts, my breathing, the salt in my eyes, the salt in my mouth, and then there's my head, banging like a drum.

Nothing left in the bottles either. No more of anything. All gone, ages ago. Now I need water. No bars up here, though, Tom, no bars on the bloody moon.

Keep it going, keep pushing. How far have I got left now? Up here, you can't really tell. Probably a bit over two, then down the other side, bastard ticked off, into Carpentras, job done.

Just keep it going. Get it over with. Forget that bloody drum.

I know they're all watching me, waiting for me to crack. They've been waiting for that to happen for days. In the cars, on the motorbikes, Plaud in the French bloody team car. Now even Aimar's staring at me! Is he mad?

'Take it easy, Tom! Are you all right, Tom? Have some water, Tom!' – blah blah blah, like I'm struggling. Like I'm bloody done for.

I can hear it all, all the bloody buzzing around me. And I can still just make them out up ahead, the hunched, rocking shoulders, just up this godforsaken hill.

Don't you worry – I'm keeping tabs, keeping it ticking over.

But I can't breathe, can't see anything – just the white rock, the white light. And the white sky above me, as white as the skin of a bloody drum.

The drum banging inside my head.

~

PART 1

'The mountains provided a mythic kingdom, an alternative world in which you could reinvent yourself as whoever you wanted. Nonetheless, it didn't matter how you imagined yourself or the mountains: the landscape could still kill you.'

— ROBERT MACFARLANE,
Mountains of the Mind

Winter

During the night, the freezing rain that pelted down on the cat-black autoroutes and deserted retail parks of the Rhône valley fell delicately and silently above 1,000 metres, as gigantic snowflakes blessing holy ground. The next morning, as a low sun struggled to break through, the Giant's summit was icy white, dusted with snow, from the tree line to the barren frozen summit.

Far below Mont Ventoux, I sat drinking bitter coffee in a village café, clad in layers of thermals, my toes already frozen, wondering if I really wanted to reconnect with the suffering that had typified all the previous mornings and afternoons I'd spent toiling on those slopes. And I wondered too, as ever, if I was really ready, once again, to ride the road that killed Tom Simpson. I knew, deep down, that over the years I never really had been.

At least, for once, there was no wind.

Wind and the Ventoux are old mates, old muckers, old bed-fellows. That unrelenting whipping wind, that loathsome Mistral, it drives you mad they say – whips away your placemat, knocks over blackboard menus, blows campervans off mountains, blows cyclists off the Giant. If the heat doesn't get you, the Mistral – the wind that picks up, builds to a frenzy and then dies at a moment's notice – will.

I drank the last of the coffee, pulled my thermal mufflers

tighter still around my extremities and set off, from Bédoin on the road that put paid to Tom, that put Eddy Merckx in an ambulance, that forced a crazed Ferdi Kübler to quit, that made Chris Froome run. This then, is the climb of *L'Équipe*'s 'killer mountain'.

It's not so bad at first – really, it's not. You start to wonder what all the fuss is about. The views of the Vaucluse in winter are beautiful as you climb up from Bédoin past the hamlets of Les Baux and St Colombe. On this winter morning, it was all woodsmoke, low sun, silhouetted vines, churned earth and morning-blue hills rolling south towards the distant Luberon.

The first real pain – shocking to the mind as well as the body – comes at St Estève, on a steep left-hand corner as famous for slaloming Porsches, Abarths and BMWs as for the sudden crippling degeneration in morale of a million Lycra-clad wannabes. It's a brutal bend, one that the French poetically describe as '*un petit enfer*' – a little hell. It is a bend so savage that it immediately fuels self-doubt. This is the bend of which Eros Poli, stage winner over the Ventoux in 1994's Tour de France, said: 'I thought I was dying.'

I hate this bend.

I hate it because it immediately highlights limitations. It takes your vanity, your silly dreams, and hurls them heartlessly to the tarmac. And as you turn through it onto the steep ramp, you can look up, almost vertically, craning your neck to take in the distant, pitiless summit. Perhaps a sadistic road engineer thought to himself: 'One day Eros Poli, the biggest, tallest, heaviest man in cycling, will ride here thinking of glory and wealth and his heart will drop out of his chest and onto the very road itself when he sees what I have created!'

Famous climbers – Fausto Coppi and Charly Gaul – have been pictured here, as have many two-wheeled donkeys, of which I am the latter. If a photographer had been here this clear and icy morning his lens would have captured me, swathed in thermals and wearing a Munch-like expression, open-mouthed and wide-eyed in appalled horror.

I steadied my nerves and winched myself uphill. Thankfully, I was alone, or at least had thought I was, until two women in Dutch colours skipped past me, out of the saddle as the road reared up, riding like twins, elegantly matching each other's swaying pedal strokes. They moved ahead and out of sight, dancing on the pedals, light as feathers.

After St Estève, there is no pleasure to be had: the ride becomes purely about pain management. I plodded on, deep into the thick forest, bright winter sunshine overhead, snow melt trickling down the gutter as the interminable ribbon of steep tarmac stretched ahead.

I hauled myself up and through the 12 per cent hairpin of the Virage du Bois. Unlike so many other famous climbs, the Ventoux's south side has few bends. Hairpins help a cyclist in distress: the gradient eases momentarily and the novelty of ped-alling through 180 degrees fuels the sense of momentum. Unlike the multiple hairpins on the climbs of Alpe d'Huez, or the Stelvio, the Virage du Bois doesn't really do that. In fact, it offers false hope, because within seconds you are staring at another runway of vertical road and battling the gradient again.

I rode on, watching trees sprout leaves faster than I could turn the pedals. My breath formed clouds in the icy air. I knew I had a few more minutes of pain to manage. I knew that the road would be closed by snow beyond Chalet Reynard, where I would stop at the old café to refuel and warm up with coffee and homemade *myrtille* tart.

Melting snow plopped off overhanging branches onto the road ahead. My mind wandered as I turned the pedals against the gradient. Just keep pushing, I told myself.

I thought of the one time I'd come up here with my parents,

on their last foreign holiday, the autumn before my mother was lost to dementia and before caring for her around the clock put paid to my dad. Dad never understood my fascination with cycling. He was an architect, who emerged from London's post-war East End with a roll of drawings and a burning need to right social wrongs. The exotica of the Tour de France was as familiar to him as the carnival in Rio.

Once on holiday, after a long lunch in Malaucène, we'd driven round to Bédoin and headed up the mountain.

'Did you really cycle all the way up here?' he'd asked quietly as we passed a weaving rider close to the summit.

'Yes, Dad – a few times,' I said.

He took in the barren scene.

'Goodness me,' he said. We never talked about the Ventoux again.

I slowed to a halt in front of Chalet Reynard, altitude 1,426 metres, the café-refuge first opened in 1927, and straightened my back. I settled in front of the fire, toes tingling and peeled off layers of sweat-soaked Lycra, hanging them over a wooden chair to dry. The *myrtille* tart, freshly baked and warm, crumbled as I bit into it.

Kilometre Zero

'Don't leave Provence without enjoying the tour of Mont-Ventoux – altitude 1,912 metres – the Giant of Provence,' proclaims the old poster, now to be found on the wall of every holiday home, gite, hotel, chambre d'hôtes, restaurant and bar within a 50-kilometre radius of 'Windy'.

I still sometimes refer to the Ventoux as 'Windy'. It's an old habit.

Yes, there's a rather tedious argument over the origin of the name Ventoux that says, 'Ah, just because *vent* means wind it does not follow that Ventoux derives from that word' – and more of that fascinating debate later tonight on Radio 4 – yet the pass just below the top of the Ventoux, although rather confusingly not actually the summit itself, is also called the Col des Tempêtes.

That would suggest that windiness, and stormy weather generally, *are* connected to the mountain's name. For me, windy mountain, famed for blowing over campervans and cyclists, works perfectly. In late autumn and early spring, when the summit is hidden by clouds, and the Mistral rattles shutters and doors, '*Vent-oooooh!*' has real resonance.

The gushing prose on the art-deco poster, originally produced by Les Frères Rulliere in Avignon, continues further extolling the delights of a day out on the Ventoux.

'The most beautiful panorama in Europe,' it states. 'Visibility as far as 275 kilometres, from the French and Italian Alps to the Mediterranean Sea.

'And that's without mentioning the famous culinary specialities of the Hotel du Mont Ventoux – proprietor Raoul Vendran, reasonable prices, no more or less expensive than in the valley – with modern comfort and a Provençal atmosphere.'

The building is still there, just 250 metres from the summit. Now it's the Café Vendran, closed in the winter, when snowfall usually blocks the road up from Chalet Reynard, but open in high season for hikers and bikers needing breakfast, lunch, cognac or coffee.

The café – and the summit itself – has mixed reviews on TripAdvisor that are at odds with the romantic prose churned out in praise of Ventoux by French sportswriters (and these days, some British ones).

'The summit of Mont Ventoux is a fairly grim place,' reads one, 'where hordes of weary cyclists and disappointed tourists stumble around the rocky wastes wondering why they came.'

Another review, written in French, really puts the boot in:

'... there are no public toilets at this world famous summit, frequented each day by hundreds of sportspeople. The men can go and relieve themselves in the wilderness, but what about the women?'

True, French men often relieve themselves alfresco, although there are no bushes to hide behind and, anyway, it would be foolhardy to do so in a gusting Mistral.

'There are a few stalls selling sweets and sugary treats, but nothing healthy for an athlete. One restaurant, the Vendran, has toilets that are dirty – I've known cleaner toilets in Turkey! – and without toilet paper ...'

This, then, is a book about the mountain of my dreams. It's horrendously steep and appallingly windy, desolate and forbidding, sells overpriced tat, is streaked with windblown piss and, even worse, there's no toilet paper.

It's probably haunted too, not just by Tom Simpson, Ferdi Kübler, Fausto Coppi, Laurent Fignon and the other legends of the Tour de France who have done battle here and lost, but also by the numerous touring cyclists, walkers, hippies and day-trippers who failed to properly respect it. And forgot to go to the loo first . . .

Mont Ventoux is the final Alp, the last peak before the pines give way to the arid thickets of maquis and, eventually, the salted humidity of the Bouches-du-Rhône and the Mediterranean. Ventoux is the last giant ripple in a rumpled geological quilt.

It exists in other-worldly isolation, an aberration of nature, a child's fantasy mountain of strange flora and fauna, dark forests and wild animals, eerie deserts and astral winds, topped off with a cartoonish meteorological observatory that looks like Tintin's rocket to the moon.

It has a schizophrenic, wilful climate that can be bestial, hateful and brutal. It is a climb so severe that it has brought Tour de France champions to tears and delirium, as both Fignon and Kübler testified. Most notoriously, it can kill and does so on an alarmingly regular basis.

There are many clichés used to describe an ascent of the Ventoux. I like to think of it as cathartic, liberating, cleansing, redemptive. For others, however, it is, by turns, forbidding, monstrous, diabolical and murderous. Google 'Mont Ventoux' and within a few seconds the search spits out descriptions of it as the 'death climb'. Nepal has Everest and the 'death zone': Provence has Ventoux and the 'death climb'.

Jean Bobet, the brother of triple Tour de France champion Louison Bobet, and also an accomplished writer, described the experience of approaching the Ventoux in the heat of July 1955 as 'a lingering death'.

'Nothing is more impressive than a silent peloton. Nobody says a word, nobody laughs. Lifting your head slightly, you can make out the shape, in the distance, of the Ventoux. You can smell the fear of the men going to a lingering death,' he wrote.

In fact, so treacherous is the mountain that fatalities are almost commonplace – it is a playground but it can be a dangerous one. 'Every year there's a few people who die on the Ventoux,' says Éric Caritoux, one of France's best-known cyclists during the 1980s, who grew up and still lives in Flassan, at the very foot of the mountain.

'Between the hikers, the cyclists, the motorcyclists, the quad bikes and everything else, it's about ten people who die on the mountain, each year.

'There's a lot of people who climb it now, maybe more than before. Now there's people making bets at the restaurant or the bar – "I bet you can't make it to the top of the Ventoux" – and, of course, if you haven't trained, you can't climb the Ventoux just like that.

'It's not something you can do on a whim – "Oh, I'm going to climb the Ventoux" – just like you'd drink a glass of wine . . .'

In August 2013, a cyclist and a motorcyclist collided three kilometres from the summit on the climb from Bédoin and were killed. In May 2012, a 43-year-old Belgian cyclist died after climbing the Ventoux, suffering a heart attack at the summit. Pierre Bellier, a 59-year-old from nearby Orange, disappeared on the Ventoux in June 2014. Six days later his body was found, with a fatal head injury, at Alazards, near Beaumont du Ventoux.

In September 2015, a 64-year-old cyclist collapsed and died as he climbed the north side of the mountain. The same month, a 29-year-old Belgian cyclist from Flanders was killed as he descended the Ventoux towards Malaucène.

So there is always drama on the Ventoux. In fact, it is almost expected. If it's not the heat, it's the wind. If it's not the wind, it's the gradient. Sometimes, it's just the sheer excitement of experiencing this alien world. Once, however, the group I was riding up with saved a life.

In 2010, I rode up from Malaucène with old friends celebrating a landmark birthday, climbing through autumnal drizzle to emerge, above 1,500 metres, into perfect blue skies and warm sunshine. The climb from Malaucène is underestimated and underappreciated. The final kilometres, from Mont Serein to the summit, really bite. Ahead of my slow progress that morning, sports photographer Bryn Lennon was hanging around at the summit, having already climbed to the top. And as he waited for the stragglers, Bryn found himself drawn into a life-or-death struggle – and, no, it wasn't mine.

As I rode wearily through the final hundred metres, I barely clocked a Lycra-clad figure slumped, Simpson-like, against the rocks. 'That's not funny,' I thought, assuming that the huddle around him signified some kind of misplaced re-enactment of the 1967 drama. I wheeled breathlessly to a halt at Bryn's feet.

'You see that bloke over there pretending he's Tommy?' I blurted.

'He's just had a heart attack actually, Jez,' he said calmly.

Later, over dinner, Bryn told me the whole story.

'We were waiting for you guys to come up and then saw this rider had collapsed. I only really spotted him lying there because, when he fell, he landed on my camera bag – if he hadn't done that I probably wouldn't even have noticed.

'I realised we were watching him die. We started running around shouting "doctor, doctor". But he'd got lucky because there was a Swiss doctor there, who'd just hiked up. He rushed over and started working on him, pumping his chest. The first time didn't seem to get anywhere and then, second time, he slowly came around.

'By the time we left to go down, he was sitting up and the ambulance was there. But that was 45 minutes later.' The ambulance had driven to the summit from Carpentras.

After all that, the high-speed descent should have been uneventful. But coming down the Ventoux can be just as heart-stopping as going up. My rear tyre blew as I passed the Simpson monument, at something close to top speed. I got lucky too, managing to hold the bike upright on a straight section of road and avoiding being flattened by the campervan I'd only just overtaken. If I had been cornering, it could have been disastrous.

I've always loved descending, as much because it is payback time for those who, like me, struggle uphill, as for the speed and exhilaration of swooping downhill, slaloming through hairpins. The rush of riding downhill, at 50 or 60 miles an hour, is intense, and the closest I've ever come to flying.

The descents from the summit of the Ventoux, either to Malaucene, Sault or Bédoin, are not for the faint-hearted. The north side soon slings you through a succession of tight hairpins, where it's necessary to almost come to a halt, before accelerating again. The first couple of kilometres downhill track back and forth across the white rock, an expansive view north towards the Drôme and the distant Alps distracting your eyes away from the road, the bends rushing up to meet you.

Further down, past the ski station at Mont Serein, the road surface improves and the 12 per cent ramps become runways. This is where, in 1994, Eros Poli's downhill race speed exceeded 100 kilometres an hour and where Marco Pantani, seeking better aerodynamics, slid his rear end off the saddle and hung it delicately over his rear wheel.

Descending towards Bédoin is just as quick and just as

dangerous, but with more traffic coming towards you. From the summit, the road is laid out in front of you, winding downhill across the bleached scree through fast sweeping bends, with plenty of space and options for taking the racing line. But with no landmarks or trees, beyond intermittent snow poles, it's easy to forget just how fast you are moving.

That changes once you pass Chalet Reynard and find yourself picking up speed through the forest, the tree-lined road narrowing, the rock walls coming alarmingly close as traffic comes up the mountain towards you. Once through the steep bend at the Virage du Bois, the speed gets even higher, the long straight ramps throwing you towards the right–left–right sequence of bends leading to St Estève.

There is, of course, a third way down. The road from Chalet Reynard to Sault is probably the least stressful of the known routes off the mountain, barely losing any altitude as it leaves Chalet Reynard, but then accelerating through the forest and finally looping down onto the upper reaches of the Plateau de Sault at 800 metres.

The road eases off steadily as it crosses the lavender fields, past the Champelle lavender farm and then crossing the Nesque river, before one final short sharp climb into Sault. Relatively speaking, it's the 'easiest' descent, but it is still fast enough to allow for rapidly overtaking cars and campervans, my own personal benchmark for risk-taking.

It's not just cyclists who are at risk as they climb and descend the mountain. There's a lot of hunting on the Ventoux and in the nearby foothills. In fact, there's a lot of hunting in France generally, particularly in the Vaucluse *département*, where Ventoux's humpback profile dominates the surrounding landscape.

On 8 December 2012, a hunter was shot in the head by his own teenage son, as they pursued wild boar on the slopes of the

Ventoux. The man died 24 hours later. In January that year, during a cold snap of ice and snow, a wolf was found shot dead in the woods at the foot of the Ventoux.

Coincidentally, Jean-François Bernard, who won the 1987 Tour de France time trial to the summit of Ventoux, the day of my very first experience of roadside Tour-watching, is an enthusiastic hunter. When I tried to arrange to meet him, 'Jeff', as he is known, wearily tossed me his business card before shrugging: 'You can call me, but you'll be lucky to get hold of me. I'll probably be hunting.' And, as it turned out, Jeff always was.

Ventoux is also the home of documented mountain climbing. It is widely accepted that Petrarch, with brother Gherardo, made the first documented ascent in April 1336. Petrarch's musings contrast starkly with the pages of first-world whingeing on TripAdvisor. Firmly aligning himself with the cathartic, liberating, cleansing and redemptive school of Ventoux diarists, he wrote a suitably poetic account of his ascent, describing his climb to the summit, 'as if suddenly wakened from sleep'.

The mountain is a very steep and almost inaccessible mass of stony soil. But, as the poet has well said, 'Remorseless toil conquers all.' It was a long day, the air fine . . .

We found an old shepherd in one of the mountain dales, who tried, at great length, to dissuade us from the ascent, saying that some 50 years before he had, in the same ardour of youth, reached the summit, but had gotten for his pains nothing except fatigue and regret, and clothes and body torn by the rocks and briars.

In his rapture, Petrarch, keen to discover 'what so great an elevation had to offer', describes with remarkable clarity the view of the mountains towards Lyon, the Bay of Marseille, and the 'waters that lash the shores of Aigues Mortes'.

The brothers came down the mountain in the gathering dusk, which must have been even more dangerous than their ascent. They stopped at an inn and Petrarch wrote his account by candlelight.

> With every downward step, I asked myself this: If we are ready to endure so much sweat and labour in order that we may bring our bodies a little nearer heaven, how can a soul struggling toward God, up the steeps of human pride and human destiny, fear any cross or prison or sting of fortune?

The first road from Bédoin to the summit was opened in 1882 and by September 1903, *excursionnistes* as they called them, were racing their automobiles from Bédoin, haring up the climb in less than half an hour. The lack of efficient gear changing held cyclo-tourism back until the early 1900s, when French cycling sage Paul de Vivie – already a veteran of the Galibier and Furka passes – decided to ride from St Étienne to the Ventoux.

His became one of the epic assaults on the Giant. Despite announcing his summit attempt in his own publication, *Le Cycliste*, under his *nom de plume* of 'Velocio', only two others joined him on the St Étienne start line at two in the morning. They rode the first 200 kilometres in ten hours and after a pause in Orange, headed on to Carpentras. There, de Vivie was met by two subscribers to *Le Cycliste*, who had ridden up the Rhône valley from Marseille to join him. At St Colombe, at the foot of the mountain, de Vivie's party was joined by a Monsieur Albert, Velocio's old friend.

Moustachioed, beret-wearing and be-tweeded, the group began the climb. Within minutes, the gradient forced them to walk. Worse was to come when, after 10 kilometres of the ascent, a violent storm broke over their heads. They rook refuge in a farmer's hut or *cabanon*, and then, as night fell, descended through torrential rain to Madame Vendran's hotel in Bédoin.

Tweeds and beret dried at the fireside, Velocio, undeterred, was back early the next morning, climbing through low cloud. Later, he wrote melancholically of the slog to the summit, of the 'monotony of the lunar landscape'. Monsieur Albert, riding a heavier machine weighing close to 20 kilograms, was left so far behind that he missed lunch at the Vendran's hotel, just below the summit. Velocio was back in St Étienne by the next evening, having broken the journey home at Loriol-du-Comtat.

That was the first recorded bike ride to the summit of the Giant. One of Velocio's companions, Adolphe Benoît of *La Provence Sportive* newspaper in Marseille, was seduced by the Ventoux.

His enthusiasm for the new climb led to the inaugural Marathon du Mont Ventoux in 1908, when Jacques Gabriel rode to the summit from Carpentras in two hours and 29 minutes. Velocio returned in 1903, this time for a round trip of almost 400 kilometres, ticked off between a Wednesday afternoon and a Friday morning, that included a three-hour climb to the Ventoux's summit. He climbed the Ventoux for the last time in 1929, when he was 76.

Once the second road, climbing from Malaucène, was opened in 1932, cycle racing on Ventoux became well established, with races such as the Circuit du Ventoux, the Tours du Sud-Est and of the Vaucluse all using the mountain as a venue, as well as higher-profile and ongoing events such as the Dauphiné Libéré and Paris–Nice.

But Ventoux owes its greatest contemporary notoriety to the death of British cyclist Tom Simpson, a world champion and, long before the production line of British cycling success stories, a sportsman so popular that he became BBC Sports Personality of the Year. On 13 July 1967, Simpson collapsed below the summit in furnace-like conditions during stage 13 of the Tour de France.

Simpson's collapse and death, forever depicted as a 'doping death' although heat exhaustion, dehydration and illness were also contributing factors, is the mountain's most famous tragedy. His story was expertly documented by William Fotheringham in his book, *Put Me Back on My Bike.*

Since Simpson's death, however, cycling's gladiatorial brutality, its doping demons and ongoing ethical struggle, and the demands of the Ventoux have become inextricably linked. Half a century on, that ethical struggle continues. Every victory is scrutinised. Every champion is subject to trial by Twitter. Anti-doping, underfunded and underpowered, remains behind the curve of medicine in sports science and, in cycling's leading teams, sports doctors retain an unnerving degree of autonomy.

July 2017 is the 50th anniversary of Simpson's collapse, yet the Tour's parent organisation, Amaury Sports Organisation (ASO), now so wary of any adverse publicity, has studiously avoided marking that pivotal moment. So there will be no anniversary visit to the Ventoux. Yet, when I asked him, Tour director Christian Prudhomme said, 'There's no fear of the Ventoux at ASO. The feeling for me is that the Ventoux has to be used rarely.' The Simpson drama, he says, 'was a long time ago now'.

'After all, the Tour came back to the Ventoux, only three years later, in 1970, when Eddy Merckx won. And you have to put things in perpective. Things have evolved. It is history.'

But the notoriety of the Bédoin ascent has also been at the expense of the beautiful northern side, made famous in the post-war 'golden age' of Tour racing and also by numerous subsequent visits during the week-long Dauphiné Libéré race. This gruelling road, climbing up from Malaucène, is my favourite ascent, and I'd happily debate the notion that it is that much 'easier' than the climb from the south. It winds through pine trees and limestone cliffs to a high corniche, with views over the Drôme and the Vaucluse, before long ramps of 10–12 per cent lead to the Mont Serein ski station, at 1,400 metres.

There, from the wide bend overlooking the nursery slopes at the admirably named Chalet Liotard, which serves good *prix fixe* lunches, the road narrows and ramps up once more towards the summit. Those final kilometres, emerging from the last stands of trees onto vertiginous hairpin bends, may not be as disorientating, but they are just as demanding as the finale to the south side. Better still, on a clear day, as you round the final few bends and near the summit, the French and Italian Alps emerge above the hills of the Drôme to dominate the distant horizon. Then, as you turn right to reach the summit, the views towards the Mediterranean, concealed throughout, are suddenly panoramic.

Yet for all the Ventoux's dramatic televisual appeal, Prudhomme remains a little cool towards it. 'You have two climbs above all the rest,' the Tour's director says, 'the Galibier and Tourmalet. Then there is Ventoux and Alpe d'Huez.'

Double Tour champion Bernard Thévenet, a stage winner on the Provençal mountain in July 1972, describes the Ventoux as a 'mountain of drama' and Alpe d'Huez as a 'mountain of happiness'. Prudhomme seemed to agree. 'The Ventoux is different. Alpe d'Huez thrives on its regularity, the Ventoux thrives because of its rarity. It's something else.'

But the Tour director's rankings of the top climbs doesn't quite tally with that of Eddy Merckx, who took a lone victory on the Giant in July 1970. 'There's Galibier, Tre Cime di Lavaredo, the Gavia,' Merckx says, 'but Ventoux is in the top three.

'It's difficult to say which is the hardest. Sometimes the Ventoux feels harder than the Galibier. It depends how you feel.'

Prudhomme, meanwhile, waves away any suggestion that it is the Tour's ever-growing logistical demands – for power lines and parking, hotels and hospitality, combined with the mountain's exposed summit and potential problems for the Tour caravan and media coverage – that have made ASO steer clear. 'That's not it, not at all. You remember what Ferdi Kübler said back in the 1950s? Ventoux is not a climb like any other.'

Then he leans in, smiling, and prods me in the chest. 'Ever been up the Ventoux on a bike?' he asks.

'Me . . .? Y-e-s,' I say, a little defensively. 'A few times actually – mostly when I was younger.'

There's a pause. 'How about you, Christian?' I ask.

'No, never,' Prudhomme replies.

But I'm left struggling with the Tour's fixation with the climb from Bédoin. Surely the ascent from Malaucène, made famous in the 1950s and 1970s and used so often in classic stages of the Dauphiné, is just as appealing, particularly as a new generation of cycling obsessives have yet to really discover it?

'*Non,*' he says bluntly. 'Bédoin, always. It's a magnificent climb from Malaucène, but for me it's always Bédoin. It works on TV, it's a stadium of cycling, it's incredibly beautiful. And the Ventoux, part forest, part desert – it's always compelling.

'The exploits are magnified by the surroundings,' he says, spreading his arms expansively and launching into a romantic treatise. 'The setting makes them even more magnificent. The great history of the Tour lives on thanks to the champions, but it also lives on because of the places too.'

And since 2014, Yorkshire, so it seems, is now as big a feature of the Tour. 'Yorkshire is now part of the legend. People in France were blown away by the Yorkshire Grand Départ in 2014.'

Bernard Thévenet, now director of the Critérium du

Dauphiné, says that the 'Ventoux is essential for any mountain stage race'. Yet it has not been included in the week-long June race since 2009, the summer before ASO took over full ownership of the event.

That's in stark contrast to the frequency with which the mountain was used under former director, Thierry Cazeneuve, the nephew of race founder and former Resistance fighter, Georges Cazeneuve. Now, however, with ASO's increasing need to test logistics for stage finishes, the Dauphiné has at times morphed into a dress rehearsal for the Tour, rather than an event in its own right.

The Ventoux, so it seems, has become less essential, a casualty of that commercial imperative. In the decade prior to ASO buying the race, the Ventoux was included in the Dauphiné's route no less than seven times.

But Thierry Gouvenou, the Tour's sports director with a specific responsibility for route design, says that the absence of the Ventoux from the Dauphiné (now known as the Critérium du Dauphiné) is a question of candidacy. 'The Ventoux region hasn't put itself forward as a candidate for a Dauphiné stage for a few years now,' he explained. 'It's not that we're against having it in the Dauphiné . . .'

And taking the Tour up the mountain from Malaucène?

'I don't think we can go up that side,' Gouvenou says. 'It's not really possible coming up that way; there's nowhere for the *zone technique*.

'And anyway,' he says, agreeing with Prudhomme, 'the climb from Bédoin is the mythical side.'

But the man for many years responsible for the sea of finish-line logistics that outweigh almost every other concern suggests that the north side is also too dangerous for the modern Tour. Jean-Louis Pages, until late 2016 the Tour's director of sites, knows his car parking and traffic calming. He knows every mini roundabout, every plant pot and every sleeping policeman – or *ralentisseur* – from Paris to Poitiers, Marseille to Montmartre.

For many years, he owned the finish lines, shepherding, pushing and sometimes hurling the media – particularly photographers – out of the way if they disobeyed. He knows how many cars can be parked in every suburban Palais des Expositions or Salle des Fêtes, how wide each finish-line boulevard needs to be, the turning circle of each team bus and the proximity of the nearest hospital, airport and police station.

Pages argues that the Ventoux's north side is not as good, or as safe, for spectator viewing – 'there's not as much room at the side of the road on the way up,' he says.

'Yes, I know it's still spectacular – the views of Mont Blanc and the Alps are incredible – but when you get further up, especially near the top, the road's on the edge of a ravine.'

He's got a point, but then a lack of fans didn't stop the Tour from climbing the single-track-width Lacets de Montvernier in 2015. And, I say pointedly, when Thévenet won in 1972, climbing up from Malaucène, did anyone fall over the edge? Emboldened, I suggest my grand plan for the 50th anniversary of Tom Simpson's death: that the race climbs to the summit from Malaucène, then descends to Sault, before looping over the Col Notre Dame des Abeilles and climbing back up from Bédoin to a summit finish.

'*Et voilà*,' I say, 'that's an epic and mythical stage, surely?'

Jean-Louis throws his head back and laughs. 'You think so? Well, then you can tell the riders. You can tell Mark Cavendish!'

In June, July and August, Lycra-clad and slick with sunscreen, cyclists descend on the Vaucluse and teem over the mountain's three ascents like demented ants, refusing to be daunted by the challenge of the 'killer mountain'. Of the three routes up – to the north from Malaucène, the east from Sault and the 'Simpson route' or 'race side' – it is the Simpson side that draws the crowds and Bédoin that has become the base camp. Afterwards, dehydrated, drained and burnt by the sun, the riders come down from the mountain and lounge listlessly in the pizzerias, bars and cafés of the three villages, struggling to recover, gasping like beached fish in the warm evening air.

Bédoin has become the focal point for Ventoux obsessives. Here, a seasonal industry, spanning March to October, has sprung up of kit, bikes and memorabilia. The most long-standing bike shop is the hangar-like Routes du Ventoux, just as you exit the top of the village and head away from Bédoin, towards an avenue of plane trees, leading to the foot of the mountain. There are pictures of past visitors, Sean Kelly, Johan Museeuw and Chris Froome, pinned on the wall behind the counter.

A few metres away, in the old fire station on the other side of the boulodrome, former professional and *L'Équipe* journalist Jean-Michel Guerinel runs the Ventoux cycling museum, the Expo Cycles Bedoin. His fast-growing collection includes Tour-winning bikes dating back over a century, and Ventoux stage-winning bikes, original and rare racing jerseys, numerous racing caps – or casquettes – and an extensive library.

Most of the museum's exhibits belong to local collector, Lino Lazzerini, from nearby Cavaillon. Lazzerini's collection is the fruit of a lifelong fascination and brims with the energy and eccentric enthusiasm of the obsessive. As Lazzerini's Cavaillon man-cave started overflowing with cycling artefacts, Guerinel stepped in with the ideal solution – the old *sapeurs-pompiers* garage at the bottom of the Ventoux.

The museum, initially a short-term pop-up for the summer of 2015, has become a fixture on the tourist itinerary. 'We get a lot of foreigners coming here,' Jean-Michel tells me as he shows me around. 'The Ventoux fascinates them. It's legendary, probably because it's the only climb where a rider has died riding uphill.'

But the collection doesn't dwell on the Simpson story. 'We have bikes from Tour winners, four of whom won on the Ventoux. Louison Bobet's from 1955, Raymond Poulidor's in 1965, Merckx from 1970, and Thévenet's from 1972.'

There is further memorabilia too, and rider postcards and team calendars from the pre-digital age, characterised by the cheesiest portraits imaginable, cover the walls. Here, gathered under one roof, are some of the worst examples of team launch photo shoots ever to see the light of day. Some of the old woollen trade jerseys stand out too, as much for their heavyweight characteristics as for the vintage fonts and retro logos painstakingly stitched in.

Guerinel continues to source further additions to Lazzerini's collection. 'We're hoping to get Marco Pantani's bike from 2000,' he says, 'Chris Froome's from 2013, and Virenque's from 2002.' The bike he covets, more than any other, is Charly Gaul's from the 1958 Tour's time trial to the summit of Ventoux. 'It may be a little difficult to get our hands on it.'

There are younger and female Ventoux-philes too. Belgian cyclist Betty Kals is the latest of a crop of extreme Ventourists and holder of the women's record for the most Ventoux ascents in 24 hours. Although she only started cycling in 2010, Betty's obsession quickly took hold. Now, she says, she knows the Ventoux 'by heart'.

Betty admits that until she started riding she was known as a party girl. 'I was always partying, I smoked, hung out with all my friends. But then I wanted to stop – overnight. So I took up cycling. I had an old mountain bike, which I took in to be fixed and the mechanic lent me a road bike. I rode 300 kilometres that week – on my own. After that, I was addicted.

'When I arrived in France I climbed all three routes up the

Ventoux. I was really attracted to it, as if I wanted to tame it. One day I began thinking about doing it ten times and of beating the record for the number of successive climbs from Bédoin. It's a bit of a crazy idea, but my record for the eight climbs also became a women's record for vertical distance in 24 hours.'

Betty, used only to the short sharp hills of the Belgian Ardennes, was thrown a curve ball the day before her 2015 Ventoux record bid. 'I only knew the day before that I had to do both the climbs and the descents by bike. I'd planned to come back down in the car. I was supposed to do nine climbs by bike and nine descents in the car.'

Descending by car would have afforded Betty valuable recovery time, to rest, nap and eat. Now she had no choice but to ride down Ventoux, in the dark, whatever the conditions. 'The rules were only made clear to me the day before, so I was rushed. I decided to go for the record for vertical distance covered in 24 hours by bike.'

She left the start line, just in front of the Routes du Ventoux shop, at five in the morning on 14 May 2015, needing to surpass 11,000 metres of climbing in 24 hours. At first the conditions suited her. It was warm and sunny throughout the day, but as night fell on the mountain, the weather changed. 'I'd done seven climbs and that took me to 11,200 metres so I'd already broken the record, but even though I felt OK, I stopped the eighth climb at Chalet Reynard, because a huge storm had come in.' By that point she'd ridden 331 kilometres in 24 hours, and climbed 12,336 metres.

Talking about her ride a year later, Betty has no great sense of achievement. 'Mont Ventoux seems to me to be relatively easy,' she says. 'I can't really explain this. For people who've never climbed it, it can definitely be very difficult. For me, it just seems normal. I like the last two kilometres before the summit because I get an adrenaline rush. Maybe because it means the pain is over, and I like getting up there quickly. It's the adrenaline that pushes me to the top.'

Betty's status, as the Ventoux's Queen of Pain, is rivalled perhaps by the members of the Cingles du Ventoux, a growing but select club formed of those who've completed all three climbs to the summit – from Sault, Malaucene and Bédoin – in one day. Obviously 50 per cent of the total distance of 135 kilometres is descending, which doesn't sound so bad, until you look at achieving an altitude gain of 4,300 metres in just 67 kilometres. According to fitness, this can be as little as a seven-hour day, or almost double that, and involve riding from dawn to dusk.

There is a fourth climb, too, which begins in Bédoin but diverts to the little known track of the Route des Cèdres, to be found on the left of the road, about three kilometres above St Estève. This is a *route forestière*, winding across the southern slopes to meet the climb from Malaucène, just above Mont Serein, at approximately 1,500 metres in altitude. The track is closed to traffic and in parts is potholed, rocky and fractured. If you complete all three climbs and still have the energy for the Route des Cèdres, you can become a Galerien, having ridden 187 kilometres and climbed 6,052 metres.

Alastair Campbell's obsession with the Ventoux dates back half a lifetime, to his days working as a journalist in Fleet Street. Since then, the mountain has become a fixture in the rhythm of his life. 'Fiona and I have been going down there for 30 years now, every summer since the kids were born,' he says of his annual family visits to the Vaucluse. 'At first, I viewed the mountain as a piece of striking scenery. I was a latecomer to cycling and only really got into it when I took up triathlon in 2005.'

But it's also been a refuge during the difficult times. 'When I had a breakdown in the 1980s, I went there for the rest and recuperation I'd been told I needed. It has been an important part of our lives. I like the climate, the scenery, the people.'

Now, with an entrenched love of cycling, as well as a friendship with both Chris Froome and Dave Brailsford, Campbell, a man who lives life intensely, has joined the growing band of Ventoux obsessives. 'I tried to climb up by moonlight once, but had a massive asthma attack a few miles up. Fiona seemed to sense that it was a crazy idea and drove up to find me gasping at the roadside.'

Ever competitive, he has taken to racing his son Rory to the summit. 'He is a much faster cyclist but we have developed a handicap system. He gave me a minute's start for every year older and every kilo heavier. So I set off 57 minutes earlier and was well over halfway by the time he left – I was convinced I was going to win. But he caught me on the last but one bend and had barely broken sweat.'

Campbell's relationship with Tony Blair was cemented in a holiday home in Flassan village, hidden in the rolling landscape stretching south of the Ventoux. This is the Comtat Venaissin, now a land of milk and honey, of holiday homes and character hotels, of heady wines and runny cheeses, fertile figs and fecund fruits, where the water sways lazily in the pool at sunset and a haze of barbecue smoke thickens the twilight.

The region flourished under the Romans – the architectural vestiges of these five centuries can be found in Carpentras, Orange and Vaison-la-Romaine and across the Rhône valley in St Rémy-de-Provence – and by the 14th century, had become the seat of Pope Clement, who divided his time between Malaucène, Carpentras and Avignon. The Popes enjoyed the wines, cheeses and figs just as much as the Romans had before them and Comtat Venaissin remained a Papal state until a bloody dispute during the French Revolution.

High above the Comtat, the Ventoux's summit stands

sentinel, and awaits the next day's obsessives. By night, the mountain is quiet, except perhaps for some wide-eyed, spliffed-up students, shivering in their sleeping bags as they wait to welcome the sunrise over the Italian Alps.

But under darkness, even unseen, the Ventoux dominates the landscape, presiding over it. There are no lights on the deserted mountain. Only a winking red beacon, above the summit, on top of the observatory – a warning to low-flying aircraft to steer clear – gives away its presence.

Bédoin is where Tom Simpson slugged his last apocryphal gulp of cognac in July 1967. On any morning in high summer, the Lycra tribes from across Europe congregate here, before they make their pilgrimage to the deadly slopes.

They pedal under the plane trees, past the pavement cafés and bakeries, estate agents and gift shops, some stopping for a caffeine hit at the café-restaurant du Mont Ventoux, others purposefully speeding through, big-ringing their way past, before turning right towards the mountain.

Some, like Betty Kals, are sleek, Froome-thin climbers, with an elegant pedal stroke, who you know will find a regular cadence as they climb through St Estève, the Virage du Bois and on past Chalet Reynard towards the summit. Others, some on borrowed bikes and in borrowed kit, egged on by their mates, look less well suited to the demands of the Ventoux. These are the ones Caritoux spoke of, the ones you fear for. These are the ones who buy the sugary treats. These are my people.

A few ignore the mountain, pedalling towards the winding Col de la Madeleine, which meanders lazily over the Ventoux's foothills and leads north to Malaucène and then beyond, into the deserted Drôme. Others bypass the start of the climb and take the rolling road over to Flassan, dropping down towards Villes-sur-Auzon before heading into the grand and spectacular Gorges de la Nesque.

There are numerous sportives or challenges on, close to and around the Ventoux. There have been time-trial challenges up the Gorges de la Nesque, combined with full-blown sportives the following day. Then, of course there is the Étape du Tour, the Tour organisation's own mass participation ride following the *parcours* of a selected Tour stage each July, although that too has had a chequered history on the Ventoux.

Maybe it's the connection to the dramas of the Tour de France, but the extreme conditions of the Ventoux have, as they always seem to, played a big part. In July 2000, the Étape to the summit of the Ventoux, which included Greg LeMond and Alain Prost in the field, was effectively abandoned after numerous riders suffered hypothermia, due to near-freezing temperatures in the final kilometres of the climb.

A couple of days later, in the Tour stage itself, Lance Armstrong and Marco Pantani raced frenetically through buffeting crosswinds to their infamous denouement at the summit of the Giant. The Mistral was so strong that day that the Tour organisers curtailed their usual post-race presentation and associated showboating, which may have been just as well given the bitter atmosphere between the two riders.

The 2009 Étape du Tour, from Montelimar to the summit, was variously described as carnage, chaos and catastrophic. Heatstroke, a lack of water at feed stations and the relentless route saw many riders suffering from exhaustion as they tackled the mountain, with some walking, others vomiting at the roadside and others in a state of collapse. That may have also been partly down to the nature of the Étape, which attracts its fair share of have-a-go weekend warriors, Mamils and corporate teams, some better prepared than others. Certainly, anyone who may have thought it was a bit like tackling an upmarket London to Brighton but in the south of France endured a baptism of fire.

There are plenty of other sportives in the Vaucluse, some more intimate and less prone to the 'lifting your bike above your head at the summit and posting it on Instagram and the company intranet page' mindset of the average Étape-iste.

There's a succinct report on the Velo101 website – a useful source for all fans of French regional cycling news – of the GFNY world series *randonnée* on the Ventoux in July 2015. The event was one of a series of sportives around the world, with legs in Spain, Italy, Brazil, Mexico and New York. Ridden in a *canicule* – a heatwave – entry to the GFNY Ventoux cost 75 euros. For that, the riders got a jersey, a bottle of local red and, handily, a lavender sachet.

Weaving its way through the foothills north of Ventoux, the route took in the Col de la Péronière, the Col des Aires, the Col de Macuègne, the Col de l'Homme Mort, and then the Gorges de la Nesque before arriving at the foot of the mountain. As in July 2009, the Ventoux was, according to Velo101, a furnace that day, provoking numerous withdrawals due to heat exhaustion. Greater disappointment for some came at the afterparty in Vaison-la-Romaine. The post-race meal, *daube de boeuf à la provençale*, was 'really not seasonal', says the report a little huffily, before stating that it would have been better to adapt the buffet to the 'climatic conditions'.

But then I've come down from the summit of Ventoux in high summer, dazed by heatstroke, sapped by exhaustion, burnt by the sun. And on those baking afternoons, not even the most expertly adapted buffet would have accelerated my recovery from the ravages of the Giant.

Carpe Diem

It's hard to remember exactly where we were on the Ventoux when my mum's ageing Mini Metro decided it had suffered enough. I do know, however, that it wasn't on the way up the bastard, in the airless and claustrophobic woods that shroud the mountain's lower slopes. Instead, my mum's car confronted mechanical mortality on the way down.

Back then, in the mid-1980s, Mont Ventoux was road cycling's Everest, unattainable, tainted by a half-remembered tragedy, a backwater of the Tour's past and relatively little known to non-Francophiles. I first read about it in long-gone French magazine *Miroir du Cyclisme*, sometimes available in a specialist newsagent's in Old Compton Street, in the heart of Soho, and only then after painstakingly translating a flowery and overwritten description of the mountain's torrid past.

Riders – bamboozled by the gradients, the sunlight, the fierce winds and swirling mists, the intense and relentless heat – lose their minds up there, the feature claimed, voyeuristically. Look at this, the picture captions read, here's Ferdi Kübler zigzagging at walking pace and, also in 1955, Jean Malléjac, lying like a drunk at the side of the road, and see over there – there's Simpson, in '67, spreadeagled on the rocks, breathing his last.

As a gauche ingenu with a woollen jersey, a Chas Roberts steel frame and a copy of Bernard Hinault's *Memories of the Peloton* under my arm, cycling up the Ventoux – because only fearless demigods such as Fausto Coppi, Eddy Merckx or Bernard Hinault dared venture there – was totally out of the question. Today, like Everest, some of the fear has gone and it is within almost everybody's reach – even, absurdly, on a Boris bike. You can attribute that to e-bikes and triple chainsets, performance clothing and cheap flights, and the plethora of books documenting cycling's arcane and wacky history, not to mention its many iconic climbs.

But, in the September of 1986, shocked by the tragedy of Tom Simpson and fascinated by the notion of the Ventoux as the ultimate mountain climb, my friend Andy and I had driven a three-door, 998cc Mini Metro, with beige velour interior, all the way from Cheshire to the south of France, to visit The Mountain That Killed A Cyclist. It was a thousand-mile journey that, through the studious avoidance of motorway tolls and driven at average speeds, sometimes in excess of 45 miles an hour, induced a thousand-mile stare by the time we finally reached the south of France.

Eventually, as we pootled along towards the banks of the Rhône, we saw the 'Giant of Provence' rise out of the midday heat haze. Our reaction was appropriately one of shock and awe. We stopped and got out to take in the view. My right arm was as burnished as chorizo, my Ray-Bans had moulded to my forehead and we were in chronic need of a launderette.

'Wow,' I said.

'Looks really like snow on the top,' Andy said.

'It isn't, though,' I said, a little smugly.

'Yeah, I do know that,' he said. 'Just really looks like it.'

Until then we had thought that the pinnacle of climbing was the Horseshoe Pass, Holme Moss or Ditchling Beacon. Now the scales fell from our eyes – this was a real mountain.

We drove through Carpentras and then into Bédoin, pausing for a cold Coke. Then we began the approach to the climb, grinding through the gears until we found that second just about assured a steady progress, rolling up through the vineyards and olive groves and finally onto the ramps heading up through the dark forest.

'Shit,' Andy said, as the Metro's luxurious interior filled with horseflies and hornets, 'it's ridiculously steep.'

'Bastards,' I hissed as one bit me on the thigh.

Ahead of us, we saw a lone rider, hunched over his machine, riding at five, possibly six, miles an hour, his lean, mahogany-brown legs slowly turning his lowest gear. We pulled alongside and gurned admiringly as sweat rolled off him.

'He's brilliant!' I exclaimed. 'Do you think he's a pro?'

We eased ahead and pulled over on the verge, jumping out in readiness for our man to pass.

'*Allez, allez!*' we shouted as he studiously ignored us and stared, dead-eyed, at the long ramp of tarmac ahead.

His lack of acknowledgement puzzled me. 'Is he Italian? Maybe he doesn't speak French?'

'*Forzaaaa!*' I bellowed hopefully at his back as he plodded on. 'Go on ...! You can do it!'

Only higher up the mountain, as we saw many more riders clad in local club colours, climbing and descending, did the banal normality, for locals at least, of riding the Ventoux finally sink in.

'I mean, they can't all be pros,' I said hesitantly.

'They're probably just, you know, really great amateurs – or on a club run,' Andy suggested.

'Still, they're all really good, though. I bet some of them could have been pros,' I concluded as we ground on towards the summit.

A kilometre or so from the top, we spotted what we'd come for. I pulled over, the little red car a tiny speck on the sea of white rock.

There's a slightly morbid tradition of laying cycling para-
phernalia at the foot of the memorial to Tom Simpson,
marking the site where the British rider finally collapsed to the
ground. This was the spot I remembered from the grainy
black-and-white pictures in *Miroir du Cyclisme*. This was where
they battled, vainly, to resuscitate him, even as his rivals rode
on.

I took in the mess at the foot of the memorial. Some of it was
respectful, but some was literally just rubbish. What did leaving
a water bottle or a racing glove signify anyway? And why would
you leave an old banana skin there, for God's sake?

*Here's to doping in cycling? You died so, er, we could ride (or some-
thing similar)? Here's to amphetamines . . .?*

Or just, *I'm so sorry that it all ended this way for you.*

I didn't understand at that time why the memorial felt so
unsatisfying, yet at the same time I knew we had to leave something, that after such a long journey we had to make some
gesture of remembrance. In the absence of wild flowers, I rum-
maged in the boot and then rather pathetically draped an old
inner tube over the plinth of the statue.

When Simpson had collapsed that day, he had been surrounded by a crowd, battling to revive him. Now, late on this
autumn afternoon, with the Mistral picking up and whipping
across the rocks, it seemed a particularly eerie and desolate place
to die.

We got back in the Metro and crawled, whinnying in first
gear, through the eye-popping final bend to the summit, before
breathing a cartoon-exhale in front of the Tintin observatory,
with all of Europe – so it seemed – laid out at our feet. We hung
about, taking pictures, until the gusts of wind were too strong.
Then we set off on the descent. But by then Mum's
Ventoux-conquering Mini Metro, like Ferdi Kübler in 1955,
had got cocky, believing it was 'not a Metro like the others'.

We breezed downhill, picking up speed, and began careering through the bends on the dramatic and beautiful road towards Malaucène. You can't do donuts in a Metro, but on the crazed descent towards the valley, the warm air rushing up to meet us as we left hot rubber on each and every hairpin, we came pretty damn close. We plummeted towards another hairpin and I pressed on the brake pedal. Nothing. The tyres squealed in complaint. We sped on down a 12 per cent ramp towards yet another sweeping bend. I pumped the brake pedal harder. Still nothing.

I was sitting in a tin can, far above the world, hurtling at 100 kilometres per hour from the Ventoux's moonscape towards a precipice into space. Planet Earth was blue and there was nothing I could do.

'We're going to end up like Tommy!' wailed Andy.

'They'll have to put up a memorial!' I yelled as the rear end fishtailed and I stamped hopelessly on the brake pedal once more.

'Change gear!' Andy shouted.

I fumbled frantically and changed down. The engine screamed in distress. We slowed momentarily but then reached another steep ramp and picked up speed once more. Over a thousand miles under our wheels – the plains of Cheshire and Shropshire, Spaghetti Junction, Watford Gap, the Home Counties, Normandy, the arid Ardèche and eventually the grandeur of the Rhône valley – only for it to end like this . . .

Just in time to save us from plummeting towards the valley, a run-off lane appeared. We ploughed joyfully into the warm, soft sand, the Metro mercifully shuddering to a halt. I flung open the door and collapsed onto the sand. Andy got out and muttered something about needing his own space. He sat on a rock, head in his hands, on the opposite side of the road.

Somewhere up on Ventoux, close to the summit, lost in the

gathering cloud and gusting winds, Ferdi Kübler's eerie cackle echoed off the bleached rocks:

'Le Ventoux, alors – c'est pas comme les autres . . .!'

Nine months later we were back, but this time, prepped by repeated weekends in the Cambrian mountains, we'd come to ride. And a week after that, we would watch, because on 19 July 1987 the Tour de France was to climb the Ventoux in an individual time trial.

Six of us – Andy, Peter, Martin, Mark, Gil and I – had entered La Tom Simpson *randonnée*, or sportive, run a week before the Tour stage, organised to mark the 20th anniversary of the Briton's death by something called 'Ventoux Sports' and supported by the local Comité des Fêtes in Carpentras. Over 163 kilometres and in 3,500 metres of climbing, the route took in two ascents of the Giant, climbing first the Gabelle col, above the edge of the Gorges de la Nesque, before dropping down through the familiar lavender fields to Sault.

Then, from Sault, we would climb to Chalet Reynard and on, past the Simpson memorial, to the summit. After descending to Malaucène, the route looped around, over the Madeleine climb, into Bédoin and back up and over the mountain, before swooping down the descent once more and back into Carpentras.

The afternoon before the sportive, we paid 80 francs and signed on – using a hastily fabricated club name, VC Pif Paf – blithely assuring the chap in the tourist office that our British racing licences were fully in order and that we had thoroughly prepared for the event. We studied the impressive list of event sponsors as we stepped out of the air-conditioning to be met by the stifling afternoon heat. RoyalDine cafeteria and restaurant, the Grimaud Peugeot dealer on the route de St Didier, Mondial Cups, the trophymakers for all sporting occasions, and the Hotel du Théâtre on the Boulevard Albin Durand, were all supporters of La Tom Simpson. Hanging around outside, in the shade of the plane trees, was an elderly Englishman, who heard our voices and spoke to us briefly.

'You'll be fine with the right gears,' he said, letting slip that he knew the Ventoux pretty well.

'You've been up it before?' I asked him.

'Well, I was Tom Simpson's manager in 1967,' he explained.

We left our gite on the far side of the Col de Murs at six the next morning, in time to see the dawn illuminate the Ventoux's unmistakable profile. An hour later, at exactly seven, we rolled away from the Allée des Platanes in Carpentras towards Mazan. People had turned out to watch and we were astounded by the numbers standing at the roadside. Kids in pyjamas, mums in dressing gowns, old blokes clutching an invigorating morning Pastis as we rode past pavement tables. Some of them cheered and clapped.

The event organisation was impressive: there was a police escort, Mavic mechanical assistance from hovering cars and motorbikes, a local TV crew and Barry Hoban – Simpson's former team-mate who'd subsequently married his widow, Helen – had fired the start gun. But within minutes the pace was so high that we were fighting to hang on, even to the very back of the 400-rider peloton. As we headed towards the Gabelle climb, silver paper fluttered through the morning air towards us, the detritus of the *'chaudières'* up at the front – the riders 'lighting up' on amphetamines.

We clung on but eventually had to let them go and, as the sun climbed higher, plodded on, over the Gabelle, down to Sault, through the lavender fields and then onto the slopes of the Ventoux itself. The climb from Sault to Chalet Reynard is 20 kilometres, the final section a sweeping high-altitude corniche offering glimpses of the limestone desert above.

We stopped at the feed zone in front of Chalet Reynard, where the D974, climbing from Bédoin, meets the D164 from Sault, the lesser-known approach to the junction. I glanced back at the point where the two routes converged and suddenly understood, very clearly, that the climb from Sault is for sensualists, the road up from Bédoin for masochists.

Only six kilometres then remain to the summit, but they can be six kilometres that question your mental resilience, and, if it gets really bad, flag up the futility of human endeavour. As Lance Armstrong knows well enough, there's only ever one winner on Windy (and it's never him).

By now, far behind the leading riders, our lack of knowledge, experience and power were very evident. We hadn't eaten enough, we hadn't drunk enough and we hadn't prepared well enough.

We left Chalet Reynard, and soon afterwards, a police outrider passed us. A few minutes later, the lead group, now on its second ascent, rolled by at speed, a cavalcade of cars and motorbikes in its wake. Within moments they were through the next bend and out of sight. Humbled, we pushed on. The six dots on the desolate landscape, cut adrift on the humpback mountain, pedalled on, but seemingly without any real progress.

I don't remember much about the final kilometre, but I do remember that I was sadly lacking in the adrenaline rush that so motivated Betty Kals.

At some point before the summit, close to the Col des Tempêtes, there was a French chancer with a camera – who no doubt usually touted his talents to bikini-clad girls on the beaches of the Var – sprawled in a deckchair at the roadside. I crawled past him and there was the click of a shutter and then the sound of him jogging breathlessly alongside me as he stuffed a business card into the pocket of my jersey.

As I rode around the penultimate bend, it happened again.

No card this time, but the sound of a shutter and a shouted greeting in French, which I didn't catch due to the pounding in my chest and the rushing of blood in my ears. Then, almost unexpectedly, I was round the last bend and up there, dancing on the ceiling, at the top of the Giant, gawping up breathlessly at the Tintin rocket, looking down on France, spread out below me.

We staggered to the feed zone, ate bananas and slugged Isostar, chewed some 'sugar pills' and then had a crumpled copy of a local newspaper stuffed down our jerseys. *'Pour la descente!'* they told us. We rolled away from the summit and quickly picked up speed. These were the 1980s – we all wore racing caps, not helmets. Helmets weren't cool. They made you look like a dork. Hinault never wore a helmet. Only Americans wore helmets and what did they know about cycling?

Within a few kilometres, the hot air of the valley had warmed us up. I didn't need a newspaper under my jersey to keep out the chill any more. At 55 miles an hour I took one hand off the bars and pulled the folded copy of *La Provence* out of my jersey. The wind immediately tugged it out of my hand and it wrapped itself around the face of the Frenchman descending just behind me. I heard a distant cry of 'Putaaaaain!' float away on the wind as I braked into the next sweeping bend. We sped on down the thrilling 21-kilometre descent to Malaucène, racing each other, taking bends on the wrong side, acting like idiots, overtaking cars, taking far too many risks. We were down in 20-odd minutes, mercifully intact.

Or so we thought.

Peter, with us when we had left the top, wasn't with us when we reached the bottom. We waited, first a few minutes, then a quarter of an hour, which became half an hour, but still no sign. We sat on a wall, and watched more *chaudières* sweep past on their way to the finish. Then we moved to a café and drank coffee. And then an hour had passed and we got really worried.

Eventually, freewheeling anxiously into view, we saw him. The first few bends of the descent, overhanging the Ventoux's vertiginous north face, had done for him. 'Vertigo,' he said. 'Just had to stop and then walk. And even walking was bad.' Shaken, we set off again for Carpentras and the finish.

As we reached the edge of town, we found ourselves mixed in with faster, stronger riders, coming off the Ventoux for the second time. Wearily they rode to the finish line, while we – now well rested – slipped into the dead air behind them.

Slumped at the finish in the shade of the plane trees, Peter recounted his tale of woe. Too terrified to ride any further, he'd taken off his racing shoes and walked much of the way down from the summit, even as passers-by, assuming he had punctured or crashed, stopped to offer him a lift. It was hardly Kübler-esque and, unlike Fignon, we hadn't cried salty tears, but for a first experience of the Giant it had been a harrowing enough day. Yet when the results came out, some time after we'd crossed the line, we were somehow placed in the top 50 riders.

Our game burst of sprinting to the line, allied to some eccentric timekeeping, had mixed us up among the elite amateurs who had climbed the Ventoux twice, just as quickly as we had once. The good people from Ventoux Sports came over, shook our hands with beaming smiles, offered 'Felicitations!' and presented us with bottles of red wine and stylish Eddy Leclerc branded cap-sleeve racing jerseys. None of us said anything.

The bottles of Côtes du Ventoux – labelled 'Le Bidon du Cycliste' – depicted a rider heading up towards the Ventoux's summit, angelic wings fluttering on his back. 'Le vin qui donne les ailes' it read – the wine that gives you wings. Maybe we should have drunk a bottle each before we started.

*

A week later, we were again up before dawn, leaving our scruffy little tumbledown gite with bad plumbing and only one toilet, just off the road near Murs, our white Citroën Safari with GB plates parked outside. We took blankets, flasks, bread, ham, cheese, water, beer and wine. We drove over the Col de la Ligne, up through St Hubert and then to St Jean-de-Sault, dropping down to Sault and pausing briefly to wolf down coffee and croissants in the still, warm morning.

The road up from Sault to Chalet Reynard was already busy, cars and cyclists making their time-honoured pilgrimage to the route du Tour. Gendarmes waved us past, as walkers strained to lug their cold boxes and hampers. When we could drive no further we pulled over and parked. Then we walked, wrapped in blankets, through the cold mountain air, past the big bend at Chalet Reynard and higher, maybe a kilometre or two, until we could see the road winding up from below and then snaking on across the rocks above.

We settled down at the roadside. I pulled on an ANC Halfords cap and switched on my Walkman. Kate Bush 'Running Up That Hill'. Kate Bush, over and over.

We scoured the Tour classifications in *L'Équipe* and decided that Stephen Roche would, almost inevitably, win the time trial to the top of the Giant and take the race lead. 'Jeff' Bernard was hotly tipped as well, but beyond his Frenchness, we didn't know much about him.

Then we sat and waited.

It was odd to see famous riders – Luis Herrera and Fabio Parra, from Colombia, Marc Madiot of France, American Andy Hampsten, Phil Anderson of Australia and Norwegian Dag Otto Lauritzen – characters only before glimpsed in highlights packages on Channel 4, so close, grimacing and gasping as they raced towards the summit. I remember seeing Roche ride past and Charly Mottet, struggling to hold onto the *maillot jaune*.

But, most of all, I remember Italian sprinter Guido Bontempi's lumbering style, producing a cadence so leaden that Peter had time to jog alongside the burly Italian and yell: 'Gertcha Guido, my son!'

When Jeff Bernard came past, there was a palpable sense of expectation among the crowd. He looked like he was dying, his face pulled into a spasm of agony, spittle decorating his chin and shorts. But he was visibly faster than any other rider we'd seen. Yet, as Bernard's star rose even higher, left flailing to retain his status as French cycling's top dog was Laurent Fignon, once Bernard Hinault's great rival and our existential hero, due to his professorial look and rakish, insolent style.

Fignon, Tour winner in 1983 and 1984, often appeared to be brimming with barely suppressed rage, both on and off the bike. That afternoon, however, he was filled with desperation, as yet another comeback attempt failed to achieve lift-off. In his auto-biography, *We Were Young and Carefree*, published shortly before his premature death from cancer at just 50, Fignon describes the Ventoux as a 'majestic theatre'. Yet that afternoon it became the theatre of his nightmares, rather than his dreams.

'In front of a hysterical crowd, I had decided to give it my all,' he wrote. But, he continued, 'nothing happened – nothing at all'.

'There was emptiness, nothingness. I'd had too much emotional turmoil, too many troubles to deal with. I was sixty-fourth, more than ten minutes behind Jean-François Bernard. I was appalled by my performance.'

Fignon's son had been born 24 hours earlier, during the rest day in Avignon. Some of those at the roadside had heard the news. 'Allez Papa!' they called as he churned painfully up the mountain.

Yet even that failed to inspire him. 'It was savage. I simply couldn't move. It hurt all over. Such was Mont Ventoux.'

After he had finished the stage, Fignon, overwhelmed by self-doubt and contemplating quitting, broke down. 'I cracked. "I'm never going to make it," I thought. Away from prying eyes, I wept for a long time.'

Oddly, though, that collapse, or *défaillance*, at the summit of the Ventoux was the making of his Tour. 'I have to go deep into distress before climbing back out again,' he once said. Three days later, Fignon appeared resurrected as he joyfully won the ski station stage finish to La Plagne.

At the time, French riders still dominated the Tour and their rivalries were intense, bitchy and sometimes self-destructive. Fignon, desperate to reassert his star status, was instrumental in the derailing of Jeff Bernard's hopes of overall success the after-noon after his fellow Frenchman had won on the Ventoux.

'The next day we decided to skip the *ravito* – to race through the feed zone – while the other guys slowed up,' Fignon said. Bernard, surprised by the move but also too gauche to think through the dangers of such a scenario, hesitated to take up the pursuit. Thirty years later, his indecision still haunts him.

'It was when he lost the race for good,' Fignon, always the king of '*franc-parler*', said in his autobiography, adding with characteristic ruthlessness, 'It was a basic error.'

II

I first started riding a bike when I was 12. We used to race this old bone-shaker around the block. I loved it. After I joined Harworth Cycling Club, all I thought about was riding. I got a delivery-boy job, so I could get a better bike. I saw it as a target, a milestone to be reached. I liked that.

I think I learned that from my dad really. He was always a grafter, he didn't shirk. Even after he'd had his accident down the pit in Durham, he got a job in a glassworks in Harworth. I wasn't much good at other sports, like football or cricket. I couldn't catch a ball, so it was always cycling for me.

Early on, I was always lagging behind on the club runs, left behind on the hills every time. I was still scrawny back then and the other lads took the piss – 'Four-stone Coppi' they called me – ha bloody ha!

I showed them in the end, though.

When I was 16 I won the club's 25-mile time trial. After that, I was pretty pleased with myself. I got cocky and developed a bit of a swagger about it, which didn't go down too well. In the end I left, which, in hindsight, was inevitable.

By then, I knew I wanted to make a career in cycling. By the time I was 17, I was winning races, right, left and centre, reading about all the big races on the continent, like the Tour. Looking back, I can see I was obsessed. Cycling was all that mattered to me; winning was all that mattered.

But my ambition got me in hot water once or twice. I was suspended from road racing for six months after I rode through a stop sign and got pulled over by a copper. It was a real blow and for a while I was pretty low. I thought I was done.

I still had my dream, though. I rather fancied myself as the British Hugo Koblet. They called him the *pédaleur de charme*, always dapper, very handsome. He was the lad who used to comb his hair before he crossed the finish line! He was always well turned out, had a nice car – and a pretty girl too.

If I wanted to make progress, I knew I had to get to Europe, get a chance with a team, learn French, and become one of 'them', one of the top guys. How the hell was a cash-strapped miner's son from Durham ever going to manage that?

I'd spent a long time racing on the track, before I realised that my heart lay in road racing. After I was selected for the '56 Olympics in Melbourne, it felt like the world was my oyster. But when we got to the team pursuit semis, I made a right fool of myself. It was embarrassing and I never forgave myself really, because everyone knew the Brits would have been the favourites for the gold.

It was my mistake: I did a lap flat out, but just blew up. Next time it was my lap, I had nothing left. Afterwards, I cried my eyes out. I felt so bad for the other British lads. I shall always blame myself for letting the country down and for the loss of that gold medal.

By now, I was growing used to the travel. It always felt very cosmopolitan, arriving at an airfield and flying off to some far-flung corner of Belgium, Germany or France to race. I think I developed a bit of a taste for the high life!

I could have carried on racing in England, I suppose, but once I'd won the Nationals, I knew that it wouldn't have stretched me like racing on the continent would. So I had to get away. When I finally received an offer from France, it was too good to refuse. It also ensured I could steer clear of national service – in fact, my call-up papers arrived just after I left.

'Good luck then, lad,' Dad had said, bidding me farewell. I'd saved up £100 and set off for Brittany with two suitcases and a spare pair of wheels. I stayed with the Murphys, at their butcher's in Saint-Brieuc, which turned out to be all right.

It was a right pain not speaking French, though. I used to try but I lost my nerve and couldn't really speak to anyone. If it was going to work out I knew I had to speak French, otherwise I'd never be accepted. And I wanted to be part of it all; I wanted to be accepted.

Although I picked up some wins, at £35 each, which wasn't bad going, I didn't have that much cash. But then I got lucky – I was offered two contracts, Mercier or St Raphael-Géminiani. I chose St Raphael – on 80,000 francs a month. I still needed to win races, though. The salary alone wasn't enough. Not if I wanted some sharp suits and an Aston Martin – and I do love cars.

There's something else though. I want to clear up all this stuff about me being a draft dodger. They came after me about my call-up in January 1960 but, the thing is, I knew that my professional career could be wrecked. In the end, I had to go for one of those interviews, to get cross-examined.

'So you're a special case then are you, Simpson?' they said.

I told them that I was racing as a pro now, that I had to get back to France for the first training camp. I left the very next day. They still sent the call-up papers again, even though they knew I was in France. It became an almighty fuss. The German papers said I was the man 'who would not fight for his Queen'. I mean, as if, after all my hard graft, I'd let the bloody Germans, of all people, put me off my career.

Anyway, I raced through that spring, but I kept hearing that they were after me. In fact, I even cancelled a trip to race on the Isle of Man. Just as well as it turned out because the military police were waiting for the plane when it landed. I got fined for that too, £25, but it was worth it to save me from 18 months' national service. God knows how things would have turned out if I'd done it.

Back home, after that, there were always people stirring it, calling me a draft dodger, but that really wasn't the case. It was just that cycling always came first. So I got stuck in to my racing. I wanted to make my mark. I managed it at Paris–Roubaix. I went off on my own, but ran out of steam five kilometres from the velodrome.

That day, I got more publicity even than the winner. It was the first time a Classic had been televised live. Later, they told me that people had been crying when they'd seen a lone rider get caught that close to the finish.

~

Foaming at the Mouth

I have a tattered old booklet that I once picked up, possibly from the shelves of the late lamented Sportspages bookshop in Cambridge Circus, called *Fabulous Fifties*, documenting what many still regard as the golden era of cycling. The rough typeset and romantic prose betray a kitchen-table labour of love. This was produced, clearly by a fan, and one with a very old typewriter.

The few poor-quality photographs, of gaunt, slick-haired, olive-skinned riders, spare tyres wrapped around their shoulders, capture their agonies on the rough roads of post-war Europe, like the most melodramatic El Greco.

Fabulous Fifties was one of a series of booklets 'written by well-known personalities in the cycling world', which sprang from the 'high-class' magazine, *International Cycle Sport*. Delve deeper and pioneering sages like Jock Wadley, Noel Henderson and Ron Kitching emerge from the pages as the driving forces behind this publishing revolution. Touchingly, for me at least, having once had a hand in both, the wiki references section cites *procycling* and *Cycle Sport* as spiritual successors.

Yet there's no doubting the hero of Henderson's potted history of the post-war peloton: as you leaf through the pages, 'Gem' – Raphaël Géminiani – jumps out as the star, the rough diamond from the Auvergne, the outspoken catalyst for the great exploits of Koblet, Bobet and Coppi.

'There was drama, comedy, even tragedy wherever Géminiani went,' Henderson writes. Gem was, says Henderson, not the greatest rider of the fifties (he never won a major tour), but 'there could be none whose career was more passionate, more turbulent, more fascinating, more heroic or more amusing'.

Such adoration stems principally from the fact that, rather winningly, Gem didn't bother trying to hide his inner chimp. His behaviour was 'unspun'. He could be arrogant, rude, provocative, uncouth and disrespectful. The fans loved him.

He attacked spectators, repeatedly dunked a star team-mate's head in the bath, likened his national team boss to a donkey, and described his more successful compatriots, Louison Bobet and Jacques Anquetil, as 'les Judas'. His moods blew with the wind, and all too often when you were riding against or alongside Géminiani, that wind was a 100-kilometre-an-hour Mistral.

He was one of a generation of new stars in road racing who came to prominence as Europe emerged from wartime austerity. These leading lights – Géminiani, Fausto Coppi, Hugo Koblet, Bobet – luxuriated in a new-found freedom. They flaunted the trappings of liberation: trench coats, cigarettes, Brylcreem, Studebakers – even, in Coppi's case, adultery. You can almost imagine them selling stockings and sausages on the side. The images of them all from that time exude style, confidence and a hint of resurgent post-war sensuality.

Louison Bobet's brother, Jean, wrote in his memoir, *Tomorrow We Ride*, that the four superstars – Coppi, Kubler, Koblet and his brother – 'were not just winners, they had style. They plumped for fine hotels, fine restaurants and large cars. They lived like stars as befitted their rank.'

These elegant, proud men, captured on mountain summits, and at dining tables, their fans and admirers gathered around them hanging on their every exploit, stare back at the camera, coiffed and clear-eyed, firing the dreams and aspirations of French, Belgian and Italian fans, drained and exhausted by the Second World War. Clear-eyed perhaps, but often wide-eyed too. There is little mention in *Fabulous Fifties* of the prevalence of speed in the peloton, of the rampant use of amphetamines, even though their use was well known and, through that decade, became even more of a concern.

Mont Ventoux's arrival on the route du Tour in 1951 played a significant part both in cycling's post-war renaissance and in the spread of pill-popping. The Giant was a suitably daunting and dramatic stage for theatrical heroics, which coincided with the Tour's first years of TV coverage.

As they lined up in Montpellier's Place de la Comédie on 22 July 1951 for the first ever Tour de France stage over the Ventoux, the riders were justifiably nervous. There had already been drama that July, more than enough, in the build-up to the Tour's inaugural visit to the 'bald mountain'. A grief-stricken Coppi, debilitated by the death of his brother, Serse, had almost abandoned the Tour the day before the Ventoux stage, while a few days earlier, Wim van Est, wearing the yellow jersey, had come close to death in the Pyrenees.

Van Est's tumble, from the '*balcon*' of the Soulor, the Cirque du Litor, is one of the Tour's great stories. Holland's first-ever *maillot jaune* dropped into space descending the Col d'Aubisque and was rescued from a small ledge that saved him from falling into the valley below. 'A metre left or right and I'd have dropped six or seven hundred metres,' he said later. But it was the manner of his rescue that came straight out of the Tour's comic-book legend.

As the traumatised and sobbing van Est clung to what was more a grassy knoll than a ledge, a rope, tossed down the mountainside to haul him up, proved too short. As their panic grew, his rescuers improvised. Desperate to reach his stranded rider, team manager Kees Pellenaars joined together the rope and the team's supply of inner tubes. 'They got 40 tubulars, knotted them and threw them down to me,' van Est, once imprisoned for smuggling tobacco, said. 'It was all the tyres they had.'

Eventually, watched by a crowd so stylish themselves that they looked as if they had stepped out of a Rapha catalogue photoshoot, van Est was hauled back up to the road. In an effort to calm his shattered nerves, they plied him with cognac. Maybe, in the light of his extra-curricular activities, he'd rather have had a fag.

'After that,' he said, 'I couldn't go on.' Nor, their inner tubes stretched to breaking point, could his team. This being the Tour, though, there was marketing capital to be made from his near-death experience. A couple of days later, quotes from van Est featured in an ad campaign for watches. 'My heart nearly stopped on the mountain – but not my Pontiac watch!' it exclaimed.

So it was a depleted peloton that rode to the foot of the Ventoux that hot Sunday. Pre-race favourite Coppi was a shadow of himself and Hugo Koblet of Switzerland had already determinedly stamped his personality on the race, seizing a series of swaggering stage wins, including the previous day, in Montpellier. Koblet admitted that his swashbuckling riding was a deliberate ploy. 'That's the way I'm playing it,' he told *L'Équipe*. 'Ride at the front, not in the bunch. My tactic will always be the same: don't let my rivals steal any time.'

But Koblet had fatally wounded his rivals long before the Ventoux stage, winning the 85-kilometre time trial to Angers and then producing a performance now synonymous with cycling's coveted panache and which inspired that sobriquet of '*pédaleur de charme*'. On the stage from Brive to Agen, Koblet slipped clear after only 37 kilometres. One rider, Louis Déprez, followed him, but by the 64th kilometre Koblet was alone, time-trialling clear of the peloton and into the Tour's folklore.

His rivals – the Italians Coppi, Magni and Bartali, and the French, led by Géminiani and Bobet – gave chase. But their combined efforts had no impact. Meanwhile, the gap kept growing. After 77 kilometres, Koblet led by more than a minute and a half, and by 120 kilometres a virtually uncatchable four minutes.

As he entered the finishing straight, Koblet relaxed and took his hands off the handlebars. In a gesture that immediately made him a star, he reached for a comb and coiffed his hair before celebrating the success of his 140-kilometre lone attack. Then he wheeled to a halt and pointedly checked his stopwatch, as he awaited the arrival of the peloton.

It was a performance of such arrogance and style that his rivals were aghast. 'I'm getting another job,' said a crestfallen Géminiani after crossing the line, two and a half minutes later.

Gushingly described by *Miroir du Cyclisme* as looking 'closer to Clark Gable than a racing cyclist', Koblet became an over-night heart-throb. By the time, a week later, that the peloton rode out of the Place de la Comédie, there was little doubt, even with the Ventoux looming in the distance, on the final outcome of the Tour.

On a cloudless summer's day, the route to the Ventoux took the convoy from the Camargue, over the Rhône via the bridge at Beaucaire–Tarascon, crossing the Durance at Pont de Rognonas, through Avignon and then to Malaucène, the side of the mountain now relegated to history by the modern Tour. French news reports of the time babble excitedly of stifling heat and huge crowds flocking to the roadside to witness the first visit of the race to Ventoux. 'The public clapped, their cries of joy growing louder,' said one.

And so, through the afternoon heat haze, the relentless white noise of the cicadas reaching a crescendo, the Tour peloton arrived at the foot of the Ventoux and entered the unknown. Swinging right in Malaucène, they began the long climb. Soon after passing the source at Grozeau, where the gradient first kicks in, Manolo Rodríguez, of Spain, attacked, a dozen riders moving clear with him.

The road, only completed in 1932 and still gravel-strewn and rough in places, steadily took its toll. The riders plodded on, some seeking the few patches of shade, and many visibly wilting in the heat. By the time the leaders reached Mont Serein, at 1,432 metres, where the Chalet Liotard hotel and restaurant now overlooks nursery ski slopes and dominates a broad flat hairpin, the front group, their spare tyres wrapped around their shoulders, had reduced to Géminiani, Bobet, Bartali, Lazaridès and the peerless Koblet. These were the '51 Tour's 'royals'. Those scattered behind on the rocky road to the top of the Giant were the also-rans.

With three riders from the French national team – Lazaridès, Géminiani and Bobet – all in the front group, their manager Jean Bidot's sole aspiration was to prevent Koblet taking more time. As they left Mont Serein, and the road reared up again, Bobet faltered, as Géminiani, hunched and frowning, redoubled his efforts to drop Koblet. Under a burning sun, a huge crowd, crammed in across the steep white scree, lined the final ladder of hairpins to the observatory. Bobet slipped further behind and Géminiani still battled to break Koblet, but without success.

Yet it was a man born in Athens, adopted Frenchman Lucien Lazaridès, who accelerated and led over the top to become the first rider in the Tour de France to reach the summit of Mont Ventoux. His brother, Apo, passed the observatory four minutes later. 'Lucien is a rider for severe but consistent gradients,' Apo, sounding like a team PR, had told French journalists before the Ventoux stage. Clearly, he knew his brother's strengths well.

But although he lost ground on the climb, Bobet was not out of the picture. Just over a minute behind Lazaridès at the summit, he launched himself into the long descent, plummeting past Chalet Reynard and down through the forest, through the *virage* at St Estève and on into Bédoin. He raced across the plain towards Avignon. By the time the Frenchman had reached Carpentras, he and five others, including Lazaridès, had joined forces. As they closed on the finish line in Avignon's Allée de l'Oulle, Bobet, of little interest to Koblet who only had eyes for Lazaridès and Géminiani, attacked to win the stage.

Bobet's success drew a mixed reception. His stage win was scant consolation for what had in fact been a forgettable Tour for him. He had been criticised for his poor climbing and his personality had little traction with the fans. He was also developing a reputation for moods and anxiety. His relationship with the loud, irrepressible and sometimes bombastic Géminiani, who insisted on truncating Bobet's first name to 'Zonzon', was not easy.

For Coppi, the first ascent of the Ventoux in the Tour had been another humiliation, as he oscillated between '*campionissimo*' and catastrophe. His schizophrenic nature was highlighted 48 hours later, when he broke away after 50 kilometres of stage 20 and rode alone over the mighty passes of the Vars and the Izoard to win in Briançon. Such a turnaround may have had something to do with Coppi's self-confessed affection for pill-popping. His own banal acceptance of amphetamine use – *la bomba* – was famously documented in one television interview.

After admitting to taking *la bomba*, 'whenever it was necessary', Coppi was asked how often this would be. 'Almost all the time,' he replied, with a pragmatism that has become legendary.

Whatever the fuel behind Coppi's Alpine resurgence, Koblet's overall advantage by then was such that he didn't care. By the time his Tour ended in victory, he was a post-war superstar, a romantic hero, a suave, seductive and glamorous figure, comb at the ready, car keys in his hand, a glint in his eye.

The Zürich baker's son made the most of his success and fame. He bought sports cars, was – obviously – sponsored by a comb manufacturer and married a model. He had, it seemed, got it all. But 1951 proved to be his peak: he never completed another Tour de France. As rapidly as it had ascended, his star was extinguished.

Such was the success of the Tour's inaugural Ventoux visit that the 1952 Tour included a second ascent, this time from Bédoin. But Koblet, Ferdi Kübler and Bobet were not on the start line. In a Tour peppered with long mountain stages and three new summit finishes – at Alpe d'Huez, Sestrières and the Puy de Dôme – Fausto Coppi expected to shine.

But the enduring and resilient Géminiani, second overall to Koblet in 1951, was still there as well, and still sounding off. Renowned for his temper tantrums, his delight in intrigue and gossip and his arrogance, Géminiani was the post-war peloton's big mouth. When I first met him, more than 40 years later, he hadn't changed.

On my first European race, the 1994 Paris–Nice, he was more than a little irritated to be asked to chaperone me, a random British journalist, when I pitched up with a backpack at a start village in St Étienne.

'Do you not have a car?' asked race organiser Josette Leuillot, incredulously, after I had put myself at her mercy.

'Er, no,' I said.

I didn't have a car, I didn't have any hotels and I only had about 200 francs to last me the entire race. But I was blessed: the Leuillot family's generous hospitality was fully extended to me.

I watched as Josette toured the start village and asked the clannish French media if they had space for me. Finally, she had a word with Géminiani, then working on the race as analyst, in-house bon viveur and generic old cove. There was an explosion of disbelief and protest, a spitting of breadcrumbs, red wine and forestier pâté and – it may have been a contractual obligation – a theatrical mini-storming-off.

Josette watched him go, shrugged and walked over to me. I smiled hopefully.

'Get in with Gem,' she ordered sternly. 'He'll drive you to the finish.'

An hour later, I was cowering in the back seat of *Le Grand Fusil's* Peugeot saloon as we barrelled down the Col de la République, just ahead of the peloton. Gem, one hand on the wheel, one hand gesturing and his head turned away from the hairpins ahead, launched into another of his epic monologues. 'Breetessh Petroleeeum!' he said every 30 seconds, shaking his head, and adding an amused chortle for dramatic effect.

'*Ah oui – ha ha! – bien sûr!*' I responded in a circular conversation that lasted through the Rhône valley and on into the afternoon, until Pascal Richard climbed to victory in the Alps, at the little-known ski station at Vaujany.

When I climbed out of Gem's car at the finish, sweaty-handed, nauseous and in desperate need of a pee, I thanked him for the 'experience'. 'Now you're part of cycling's big family!' he called grandly, as I limped cross-legged towards the nearest Portaloo.

Later that week, when we stopped at a mid-stage press buffet somewhere near Aix-en-Provence, I watched as he launched into a 'bah, kids today!' style rant, and gave a group of French journalists an extended blast from the Géminiani hairdryer. Yet in his more reflective moments, Gem revealed surprising insight. Once he described how, in post-war France, the sight of the climbers of the Tour reaching for the sky would gladden hearts downtrodden by years of Nazi occupation and fear.

'The fans always had a weakness for climbers,' Gem said. 'Robic, Bartali, Coppi, Kübler, Koblet. They all won the public over because they were such great climbers.'

Thus the Ventoux, which like Alpe d'Huez was first used in the early 1950s, became a theatre of post-war dreams, an impossibly intimidating arena where the great climbers fought against a fearsome obstacle, and, like France itself, were eventually liberated from their shackles.

As the fans, riders, teams and media discovered just how spectacular the Ventoux could be, it became a regular haunt both for the Tour de France and the Dauphiné Libéré, the week-long early-June stage race that traced a tortuous route through the French Alps.

The Dauphiné, first held in 1947, was – like the Tour – created to fuel newspaper sales, in this case the Grenoble-based Alpine paper, the *Dauphiné Libéré*. The race first took the peloton over the Ventoux in 1949, via the banks of snow lining the route up from Malaucène, in a 246-kilometre stage from Gap to Avignon. It returned frequently throughout the 1950s, including in 1951, the summer of the Tour's first visit. It was also included in 1950, 1953, 1955 and 1957, en route to a regular stage finish in Avignon.

As a final test for the Tour, the Dauphiné became almost essential and for many recent Tour champions – from Miguel Indurain to Lance Armstrong to Chris Froome – that preference continues.

Géminiani was among the favourites prior to the 1952 Tour. He'd demonstrated his resilience in 1951, and now felt he could challenge for victory. But by the time the race reached the south of France, Coppi had already won the first time trial to Nancy and the summit finishes at Alpe d'Huez and Sestrières. He led the peloton by almost 25 minutes and the race was effectively decided.

As Coppi stole the show, the Tour organisers, fearful of a loss of interest, doubled the prize money for second place in Paris, hoping to stimulate exciting racing from his closest rivals. Drama had become even more important as, for the first time, the Tour was televised. That, in itself, was a race against time. Two cameramen shot footage of the race from BMW motor-bikes, and, after the stage finish, it was rushed to Paris. There, in the Rue Cognacq-Jay, legendary broadcaster, playwright and polar explorer, Georges de Caunes – father of Antoine of *Eurotrash* renown – added his commentary over a highlights package.

TVs were not widespread in France in 1952, with only around 50,000 households, mainly in Paris, actually having a set. But already, the power and reach of television was firing the race organisation's imagination. These days the needs of live television take precedence over all other considerations, includ-ing, often, those of the riders.

On the morning of 10 July 1952, the convoy gathered in Aix-en-Provence. If the riders knew that the Tour's outcome was already decided, French everyman and winner of the 1947 Tour de France, Jean Robic – or 'Biquet' – was on a mission to take victory on the Giant. Robic's ungainly style of climbing saw him expend almost as much energy rocking sideways as he did moving forward. This was married to a constant gurning, matched only during intervening years by Thomas Voeckler, a winner of the Tour de Yorkshire, who also led the Tour itself for nine days in 2011.

Like Biquet, Tommy's have-a-go-hero face-pulling has endeared him to French fans. He instinctively seems to know when the TV cameras are on and the live broadcast begins. I can't confirm, however, if his face resumes normal status during the ad breaks.

There is a great YouTube clip from the 2014 Tour of Voeckler climbing wearily to the ski station at Chamrousse. Far behind the peloton-fixated prowling TV motorbikes, there is no gurning; instead, just a mantle of exhaustion as he slowly plods to the finish. The clip, shot on a spectator's phone, captures him pedalling through a bend as a bunch of sun-struck, inebriated fans jeer mockingly at him. In the tradition more perhaps of Géminiani than Biquet, the outraged Voeckler slams on the brakes and starts shouting back.

'Oi! You ever ridden a bike?!' he rants.

Stunned, the shamefaced fans quickly apologise – 'Sorry! Sorry!' they mumble. Head shaking in disgust, Voeckler rides on.

Up on the Ventoux in 1952, Robic's own facial rictus was in overdrive as he mauled his machine and fought his way towards the summit. Biquet's decisive attack would probably cause uproar today. After French team-mate Géminiani had made a tentative move at the St Estève bend, the slight, gurning Robic followed suit – just as Coppi punctured.

The continuing tradition of the Tour being raced on the basis of national rather than sponsored teams consistently threw up odd bedfellows and tactical conundrums. Géminiani and Coppi, for example, had raced as trade team-mates during the 1952 Tour of Italy, which Coppi had won. Now, only a few weeks later, they were rivals and Géminiani was one of a team stabbing him in the back.

Given the commercial interests, national teams would be unthinkable now. Imagine if, for example, a British team set out to win the Tour with a line-up including all the stars – Wiggins, Froome, the Yates twins, Geraint Thomas and Mark Cavendish. That might be a chimp too many, even for Dave Brailsford to manage.

In 2012, some of those riders raced together for Team Sky. But it's well known that those alliances were fraught, that Cavendish was miserable and that relations between Wiggins and Froome were particularly tense. Little, however, compares to the Biquet-and-Gem hotel bathroom fracas in 1952. After a stage through Belgium during the Tour's first week, in which Géminiani had chased a dangerous breakaway while Robic sat in his slipstream before himself attacking, the Breton was holding court as he sat in his hotel room's bathtub. Gem overheard his team-mate bragging to journalists, saying he had 'played dead' and had effectively used Géminiani for his own ends. Enraged, Gem burst in and pushed Robic's head underwater. Only after a team manager and a soigneur had wrestled with him did he let go.

Géminiani found Robic irritating and pretentious. Even though he was born in the Ardennes, Robic saw himself as a French everyman and insisted on playing the part of the definitive stubborn, arrogant Breton. 'I was born in the Ardennes by mistake,' he maintained defiantly.

The 1952 Tour wore on with an uneasy truce between the pair. Géminiani won the stage to Mulhouse and was working his way back up the race classification, when a puncture halted his climb of the Galibier. Neither Robic nor a French team car stopped to help him as he stood stranded at the roadside.

Nor did Robic hesitate to attack when Coppi, wearing the *maillot jaune*, punctured on the way up the Ventoux. The Italian, with his 25-minute cushion to fall back on, didn't panic and rode his way steadily back to the leading group. Up ahead, at Chalet Reynard, where a huge crowd had accessed the mountain via the new road climbing up from Sault, Robic dropped his final companion, Gilbert Bauvin, and headed on towards the summit. Behind him, Géminiani played the part of the perfect team-mate, sitting menacingly on the rear wheel of any pursuer as his bathroom betrayer built a two-minute lead.

In spite of his diminutive stature, Robic had a reputation for being a fearless descender, helped perhaps by the canny use of a lead-filled water bottle for the longest drops. Whether 'Leatherhead' – he had a penchant for a leather hairnet helmet – put some extra lead in his pencil as he swooshed down towards Malaucène is unknown. With his new team boss Marcel Bidot – Gem's 'donkey' – yelling encouragement from the team car as he exited Malaucène, Robic forged on into the Rhône valley, winning in Avignon by over a minute and a half from Bartali, Géminiani and Coppi.

And Coppi? He went on to win the 1952 Tour by over 28 minutes, with Biquet, for all his gurning, finishing fifth overall, more than 35 minutes behind him.

By the mid-1950s the Dauphiné and the Tour, for any pretenders to success in July, went hand in hand, particularly if both races included the Ventoux, as was the case in 1955. Bobet, once so vulnerable to criticism of his climbing ability, was the dominant force on the Giant that summer. Wearing the world road race champion's jersey, Bobet had already proved irresistible in that year's Dauphiné, winning three stages, including a time trial, and finishing second on the stage that climbed the Ventoux.

But a month later the Giant took him, and others, to the brink, in a traumatic stage that revealed the dangers the extreme conditions on the mountain sometimes posed. The drama of the 1955 Tour's ascent of Ventoux was a prelude to what was to come a little over a decade later.

'Zonzon' had won the Tours of 1953 and 1954, and with Coppi and Koblet absent, he was the clear favourite for final victory in Paris. But Bobet was fighting illness while fending off the irrepressible Luxembourger Charly Gaul, among the greatest climbers of his generation. Gaul had already staked his claim, flamboyantly winning the 253-kilometre stage to Briançon, and putting a 14-minute gap into Bobet in doing so.

While the French national team's Antonin Rolland held the lead as the race arrived in Marseille, the Ventoux stage was to be pivotal for both Bobet and Gaul. The methodical Bobet, after two successive Tour wins, knew he was in danger of being outshone by Gaul, who personified the romance of the mercurial lone climber against the fearsome mountains. The French public, despite his success in the Tour, didn't see Bobet the way they saw Robic, as one of their own.

Boos and whistles had mingled with the cheers that greeted Bobet the previous evening when the Tour arrived in Marseille. As he listened, stoically, he realised that the Ventoux offered him a chance to suffer for his public, with the panache that the French had come to expect of him. He and team manager Bidot hatched the plan for a major attack on the Ventoux, but it was a bigger gamble than his rivals knew at the time. The already anxious Bobet was fighting the agony of a chronic saddle sore so severe that he rode for long periods out of the saddle in an attempt to relieve the pain.

Radio and newspaper reports of that day's 198-kilometre stage over the Ventoux describe it as 'torrid'. A succession of attacks came and went and by the time the peloton reached Cavaillon, on the banks of the Durance, the field was already fragmented.

Steadily, the temperature rose until, by early afternoon, it was nudging 40 degrees. In the villages en route to Bédoin and the foot of the Ventoux, the riders reached into the crowd, grabbing bottles of cold water wherever they could. Some fans even brought hosepipes to the roadside, showering the baking bunch as they pedalled past. But the heat didn't deter Ferdi Kübler, of

Switzerland, from attacking. After his double victories in the Ardennes, the Flèche Wallonne and Liège–Bastogne–Liège, and his 1950 Tour win, Kübler had thought he was special, at least until the afternoon in July 1955 when the Ventoux taught him a harsh lesson.

Accounts of what exactly was said vary, particularly between the key protagonists who later contradicted each other. The spoken words may have been different but there's no doubt that, as Kübler launched himself at the gradient, Géminiani, sitting on the Swiss rider's wheel on behalf of Bobet, gave him a word of warning.

'Easy tiger' – or words to that effect – said Gem, as he watched the Swiss rider enthusiastically churn the pedals. 'The Ventoux's not like any other climb, you know ...'

Kübler scoffed at Gem's advice. 'Well, Ferdi's not like any other rider,' he said with a swagger as he stormed off up the mountain, Géminiani cursing in his wake ...

Or did he?

Interviewed years later, in *Vélo* magazine, Kübler denied the story. 'It's not true,' he said. 'I never said that. Géminiani is a great storyteller. In the peloton his nickname was "Telephone". We're good friends but this story, it isn't true.'

It is certain, however, that it was Kübler's first time racing on Ventoux. He was 36 years old and it was excruciatingly hot. Even before he got close to the summit he was in a state of delirium, frothing at the mouth, his hook nose drooping low over the handlebars as he weaved back and forth.

He wasn't the only one swooning in the heatwave. Some spectators had already fainted and Belgian climber Richard Van Genechten, third in the 1954 Tour's King of the Mountains classification, fell exhausted at the roadside and had to be given oxygen. Further down the mountain, French rider Jean Malléjac collapsed unconscious on the verge, 'his face the colour of a corpse' according to one witness, with race doctor Pierre Dumas fighting to revive him. After 15 desperate minutes lying unconscious at the roadside, eyes wide open and lifeless, the Breton was given oxygen, loaded into an ambulance and finally came around.

Kübler pressed on, steadily losing both his speed and his marbles as he did so. Zigzagging his way through the final kilometres, he was caught and left behind by Bobet. Now riding at a snail's pace, Kübler was followed – at one point on foot – by his team director, Alex Burtin, who ran alongside, yelling encouragement. By the time Kübler hauled himself over the summit, and began the descent, Bobet was already in Malaucène.

This, then, was where the Kübler story really took off. En route to the finish, he crashed, twice apparently, then sat in a ditch, swore unintelligibly in German, and frenziedly downed beers in a bar, before setting off again – in the wrong direction. He finally got to the finish in Avignon 26 minutes behind Bobet, whom he'd been hoping to overcome. Bemused by his collapse, he announced his retirement, citing his age and the pain of cycling. 'Ferdi has killed himself on the Ventoux,' he said in his valedictory speech.

Kübler was a font of great stories, some no doubt exaggerated over the years. One related the tale of a frantic tyre change, mid-race, by one of the domestiques. 'We had to change our own tyres when we punctured,' he recalled. 'Once, my domestique, Emilio Croci Torti, helped me. I saw him, when it was cold, tearing a tubular off the rim with his teeth. Word of honour. It was unbelievable.

'And we had to ride with a spare tyre wrapped round our shoulders. I put them round my shoulders just so, with the valve just where it ought to go. You had to, because if you crashed, the valve could cut into your back.'

Racing during those Fabulous Fifties, long before marginal gains, Twitter accounts and the talk of air-conditioned, luxury mobile homes, was tough. 'Every morning at the start,' Kübler said, 'we got a card with the name of the hotel we'd be staying at that night. We had to get there on our bikes after the finish, which often wasn't easy.

'On the Tour, you'd often get to a hotel where there'd be just one room set up as a bathroom for everybody, with a single bath. It was full of water but it was never emptied. You had to share it with your team-mates, so you can imagine the colour at the end of it.'

How much of all that yarning is actually true? Probably only some of it, but it doesn't really matter. These memories are not digital: there's no video evidence to refer back to. Instead, they are based on memory and eyewitness accounts. As such they are mythical and fluid, shifting with time. What is clear, however, is that Kübler should have listened to what Géminiani said to him at the foot of the Ventoux.

Ferdi was the last of the Coppi, Bobet and Koblet generation of Tour winners to survive. He finally let go, four days after Christmas 2016, aged 97. In one of his last interviews, his memories captured exactly why that post-war period had been so compelling for so many. 'I became a champion because I was poor,' Kübler had told L'Équipe in 2003. 'I fought to eat and to make a better life. I won the Tour because I dreamt of it and because I knew that after I'd won, I'd never again be poor.'

Bobet's performance in July 1955, which due to his saddle sore was no less painful, was at the opposite end of the spectrum. After passing and dropping Kübler and Géminiani, he crossed the summit of the Ventoux almost five and a half minutes ahead of a struggling Gaul, and, despite a puncture as he closed on Avignon, he held on to win the stage. But the victory almost broke him and after the stage, he took to his bed telling his brother Jean that he couldn't carry on.

Rolland clung on to yellow until the Pyrenees, when he finally ceded the *maillot jaune* to Bobet, who sealed his third consecutive overall victory. But Bobet paid for it and after that third win, only finished one more Tour, that of 1958. The chronically infected saddle sore ultimately required surgery and there were rumours of a more serious illness. Precise details remained unclear, partly because Bobet was always discreet and perhaps also because such areas of the male anatomy remained something of a taboo subject in the mid-fifties. Those rumours of something more than a mere saddle sore, of cancer, haunted him after he retired, as did speculation over his amphetamine abuse.

Bobet died in March 1983, of cancer, the day after his 58th birthday. Yet it was the sight of Malléjac, comatose and in a deranged state, collapsed halfway up Ventoux that baking afternoon, which resonated most – and which shone a light on the growing excesses of unsupervised doping. Malléjac, unsurprisingly, always insisted he had been 'given something' – doped effectively – that day, against his will. There was an inquiry, of sorts, and some sabre-rattling against 'prescriptions' by the Tour organisation. But it had been a wake-up call and one that had only intensified Pierre Dumas's anxieties.

In an interview on 11 July 1967 – two days before Simpson died in that year's Tour – Malléjac claimed not to have appreciated that his life may have been in danger at the time. 'It was only afterwards, when people explained what had happened,' he said.

The circumstances of his collapse were eerily similar to those of Simpson's. 'It was really hot, really hard,' he said. 'I'd had stomach problems for a couple of days and was suffering at the start. We started tackling the climb and, well, I had some problems.

'I remember passing a spectator, who gave me some water, and then, a few metres later, falling. I don't remember anything more than that, only that I was there for 15 or 20 minutes, unconscious.'

In an interview that only alluded to doping, Malléjac said that he'd drunk from a bidon – a bottle – given to him by a soigneur, half an hour or so earlier. 'It was still in my jersey pocket in the ambulance, but then when they wanted to analyse it, it was empty,' he said, in an answer that suggested either skulduggery or a heightened state of denial. 'That astonished me. It seemed strange.

'It's possible it was doped, maybe. I don't want to accuse anyone but I'd like to know what was in the bidon,' he said, before adding: 'I put my trust in the people around me on the Tour de France . . .'

If that remark smacked of naivety, his final comments were almost unbearably prescient. 'The riders are going faster and faster,' he said. 'The faster the races, the bigger the gears and obviously the body becomes more fatigued. That's when the body needs more support than before.

'It's very dangerous for a rider, continually intoxicated, continually needing doping. They risk becoming addicted.'

Within 48 hours, Tom Simpson had died on the same mountain where Malléjac had collapsed, 12 years earlier.

Charly Gaul always liked forests and mountains. When he retired from racing he became a hermit for a while, living in a woodman's hut in the Ardennes forest, hunting most days and living without running water or electricity. 'I spent my days planting vegetables,' the Luxembourger recalled after he came out of the forest and rejoined the world. 'Roe deer would come and graze at the bottom of my garden. There was nothing but trees and water.'

Gaul, who had worked in an abattoir before turning professional, was at home at altitude too. 'It's beautiful up high in the mountains and the views are fantastic,' he said. 'I feel happy up there.'

The south side of the Ventoux, cloaked in deep, dark forest populated by deer and wild boar, leads ever upward until it emerges into the white light to offer panoramic views of the south of France, far below. Such a place might have been created with Gaul in mind.

There are two maverick climbers who embody the existential ideal of the haunted loner, exorcising his demons in splendid isolation as he races towards the glowering peaks. One was Charly Gaul and the other, Marco Pantani. Both were angst-ridden and tormented, both were isolated and both feuded with the other stars of their era. Both men also won Tour de France stages on the Ventoux.

Géminiani described Gaul as 'a murderous climber, always the same sustained rhythm, a little machine with a slightly higher gear than the rest, turning his legs at a speed that would break your heart, tick tock, tick tock, tick tock . . .'

Gaul's win, as those Fabulous Fifties ended, came on 13 July 1958, in the Tour's first ever mountain time trial. He came to that year's race brimming with resentment, particularly towards Bobet, who he blamed for instigating an unsporting attack in the 1957 Giro d'Italia, as Gaul urinated at the roadside.

On the eve of Bastille Day 1958, the 21.6 kilometres from Bédoin to the summit of the Ventoux were lined by 100,000 people. While Gaul had set his heart on a stage win, intrigue surrounded relations between the three French stars, Géminiani, Bobet and Jacques Anquetil. Long before the Tour had started, the infighting within the French national team was making headlines. Team boss Marcel Bidot found himself caught in the middle, as he realised that Géminiani's loyalty to Bobet might derail Anquetil's hopes of a second Tour success. Anquetil hammered the point home, arguing that he would never be able to rely on Géminiani, whose devotion to Bobet was obvious. Either Bobet or Géminiani had to be dropped from the team, the defending champion told Bidot.

In the end, Bidot dropped Géminiani, which is why, when he was gifted a donkey as a mascot by a loyal fan, Gem made great play of calling the beast 'Marcel'. But the falling-out didn't prevent Anquetil and Gem later forging a new bond as rider and manager, once Géminiani had retired from racing.

As he lined up in Bédoin, Gaul, even though he'd always disliked racing in intense heat, had every reason to be confident. Géminiani, ostracised by the national team he had served so well for so long, was riding for a French regional squad and was keen to undermine 'les Judas' – Bobet and Anquetil. Gaul, meanwhile, had already shocked Anquetil by winning the first time trial in Châteaulin, and the absence of rest days seemed to suit a rider whose stature was growing as the Tour went on.

The riders left the Bédoin start line every two minutes, with Federico Bahamontes, the great Spanish climber, already on the mountain as Gaul set off. Bahamontes was quick enough, but he was no match for Gaul. As he rounded the bend at St Estève, keeping a wide line to avoid the rough road surface on the inside of the bend, Gaul, in stark contrast to Bahamontes and Anquetil, who had already been forced to stand on the pedals to maintain their speed, stayed in the saddle. He began tackling the Ventoux's toughest section and quickly closed on Bobet, who had started immediately before him. Gaul rode through the airless forest, fixated on revenge, closing relentlessly on Bobet's rear wheel until he drew level.

He stared straight ahead as he passed Bobet and was soon well beyond him. In fact, he was past the rider who had started eight minutes ahead of him, Louis Bergaud, before he even reached Chalet Reynard. Alone with the summit in sight, Gaul rode on across the bleached scree, before he reached the final bend and launched himself over the finish line, 31 seconds faster than Bahamontes, but more than four minutes quicker than Anquetil. Gaul's time for the climb, on a bike that weighed 13 kilos, of 1 hour, two minutes and nine seconds, stood as a record until Jonathan Vaughters, racing for US Postal in the 1999 Dauphiné Libéré on a cocktail of doping products, beat it 31 years later.

Géminiani crossed the line five minutes behind Gaul, yet after all the years of working for others was compensated by the *maillot jaune*. But his joy was short-lived and he soon realised that Gaul was now overall favourite. Three days later, Gaul's legendary attack to Aix-les-Bains broke him. Géminiani, who ended the stage in tears, lost more than 12 minutes to the Luxembourger, the eventual winner of that July's race.

Yet Gaul, like Koblet in 1951, never attained such heights again. There were, as with his peers, tales of amphetamine abuse, with one account of Gaul's growing disenchantment with the demands of racing making its way into *L'Équipe*. One evening in St Gaudens during the 1962 Tour de France, Gaul spoke to his team-mate Marcel Enzer.

'You know, Marcel, I'm scared now,' Gaul said.

'Scared of what?' Enzer replied.

'There are too many guys blundering around because they're on stimulants,' Gaul said. 'They can't react properly.'

Gaul was thinking of Roger Rivière, who had plunged into a ravine on the Col de Perjuret in 1960, his reactions blurred by an over-reliance on doping. Rivière's injuries confined him to a wheelchair for the rest of his life.

The warning signs were everywhere. Gaul knew it and so did Pierre Dumas, scarred by his frantic quarter of an hour crouching over the stricken Malléjac on the Ventoux in 1955. But nobody, it seemed, was willing to act on them. And the Ventoux, more exhausting and asphyxiating than perhaps any other climb, revealed the truth with frightening regularity.

III

You never forget your first Tour de France. I went through it in mine, I can tell you. I finished the 1960 Tour a bloody wreck, two stone lighter than when I started, my face cut and sore, and totally exhausted.

It had all started so well. I got into a breakaway on the first day, and was the best-placed British rider. I even became leader 'on the road' at one point, but didn't hang on to that lead to the finish of the stage. I was still second overall, though.

But it was a real eye-opener. It was a hell of a fast race, very intense, and for some of the other British lads it was almost too much. It wasn't their fault but the racing in Britain hadn't hardened them up for a race as quick as the Tour. I didn't feel I was carrying them, or anything like that, but I knew I'd never get the support that I needed if they stuck to national teams. And when we got to the mountains, the cracks really started to show.

I'd been looking forward to the Pyrenees. I thought maybe I could move up the general classification a bit, climb into a better position. I did just that on the first mountain stage, even though I took a tumble coming down the Aubisque, but I don't think I'll ever know why things went so wrong after that.

The second mountain stage included the climb up the Peyresourde. I'd attacked, with Gastone Nencini and Roger Rivière, but suddenly my head was swimming and I felt as though I would burst. The climb seemed to go on for ever. I couldn't breathe. I felt like I was being asphyxiated. I slowed to a crawl to save myself and had to watch as the whole bunch rode past me and on up to the top of the pass. It was bloody humiliating. I thought I might recover going back down the other side, get down fast, catch up, but I didn't.

When I got to the hotel, I couldn't stomach any food and went straight to bed. I slept right through, but that still didn't fix it. The next day, I had to get through the stage to Toulouse. I managed it all right, but after Harry Reynolds crashed out, we were down to four riders. We were all pretty down in the mouth that night.

After that every day was agony. Brian Robinson tried to chivvy me along, but I'd gone into my own little world. Fighting for survival I was, just counting the kilometres until we got to Paris. But it would have taken wild horses to drag me off the bike. I was determined to make it because I knew Helen was coming. And I knew that if I got to Paris, I'd still earn well at the crits – the exhibition races – after the Tour. I had a few lined up. It meant a lot of driving, mind, and I knew I'd be tired, but I'd pick up a few bob, so it was well worth it.

By the time I got to the Parc des Princes, I never wanted to ride the Tour again. Helen's face was a picture when she saw me, all skinny, dark-eyed, banged-up and blistered. We didn't have long together, though. I had my round of exhibition races – the criteriums – and she had to get back to her job in Germany.

In the week after the Tour, I rode in Évreux, Milan, Turin, Sallanches and Lyon, before a few rides in Belgium. It certainly racked up a few kilometres, but it was worth a fair bit of cash too. After that it was down south, to Nice. I borrowed a car and floored it to get there in time, driving the thousand miles on my own in 24 hours.

But I was done in. I had one last crit to race in, in central France. I was so tired that I crashed and came down with a bit of a bang. In some ways, that was a blessing because I packed it in, exhausted.

Now, at least, I could rest.

PART 2

'I felt shocked and then saddened. Life does this to you sometimes: leads you up a path and then drops you in the shit.'

— WILLIAM BOYD, *Any Human Heart*

Summer

Early on an August morning, I slide wearily out of bed, walk across a cold, uneven tiled floor and make my way downstairs. The Provençal sun is already filtering through the unopened shutters, dust rising in the shafts of sunlight in the lounge. At this time of the year, the sun appears around six in the morning, rising first over the distant Alps and then the Montagne de Lure and the Plateau de Sault, where the morning air carries the scent of lavender, before it climbs above the eastern flanks of the Ventoux.

I unlock the doors to the terrace, step into the sunlight and open the parasol. The outside wall is already warm to the touch. A startled lizard scampers down the wall into a crevice. It is too hot to sit anywhere but in the shade.

In the kitchen, I grind some coffee beans – 'Carpe Diem' from TOMS Roasting Co., on South Congress Avenue in Austin, Texas. I'd developed a taste for Carpe Diem during my four-day sojourn to see Lance Armstrong. I flew home with a rucksack stuffed with the beans.

I've always liked the little homilies, the unintended double entendres that permeated the lexicon of the Armstrong myth. 'Go hard or go home' or 'Ride like ya stole something' and, of course, 'Carpe diem'.

'Man, that fuckin' mountain. Carpe diem, dude . . .'

Somehow, when I got back to the Ventoux, Carpe Diem felt

like the right bean to be drinking. Now, however, I was halfway down the last packet and feeling anxious. But at the end of the ride I was planning that day, it was unlikely that my brand of coffee would make much difference.

A decade or two earlier, the knot in my stomach might have been caused by the prospect of attempting the Ventoux twice in one day, as in the Tom Simpson *randonnée*. But today it was caused by the thought of a Tour of Ventoux – a long, lone ride of over 120 kilometres around the base of the mountain, through gorges and over low passes, down lonely valleys, past deserted villages and then back, through Malaucène and into Bédoin, hub of 'Ventoux country', before the final climb home to a hot shower and a welcome beer.

Even after all the years spent on the road, travelling and covering bike races, I struggle to think of a more scenic route: through the Gorges de la Nesque, on beyond Sault and into the Toulourenc valley and up the Cols des Aires and Fontaube – corniche climbs familiar from Paris–Nice and the Dauphiné, with striking views of the Ventoux's stark north side – before heading over the Madeleine climb and, finally, back up the hill to Blauvac.

These are beautiful roads, and perhaps my favourite roads in all the world. It is a route with a little of everything: steady, big-gear roads, some long descents and some well-graded climbs. But I'd never completed the circuit on one day. I knew it would never be harder than when it's 27 degrees at eight in the morning. That's because you know it will be reaching the high thirties by mid-afternoon, when the blue sky bleaches to off-white, as if the furnace is too much even for the heavens to bear.

Simpson died on such an afternoon, in what became the defining moment in the history of a mountain so daunting that it killed a man in the toughest endurance event in sport. That day though, it was even hotter and said to be nudging 42 degrees.

For once, I've put in the miles. Nothing scientific has been done, there's been no lab testing, power meters or wind tunnels; instead I've trained *à la* Pantani – on feel alone. I've lost a little weight in the spring, done some hill repeats and ridden decent distances. I'm far from quick, but I am steady. I know I can handle the distance: it's the heat that worries me.

After I've changed, I open up the freezer compartment in the fridge and pull out two bidons. I drop them into the bottle cages on the bike. They're both frozen solid, but I know they will be tepid after the first hour or so of riding. I cram two fruit bars, a banana and some caffeine gels into my back pocket. I pull on a gilet and zip it up halfway. I'll keep it on all day, despite the temperatures, zip undone for the climbs, pulled up for the descents.

I hate the aftertaste of the gels – 'spunk bags', as a friend calls them – but they're a necessary evil sometimes and they seem to work, albeit briefly. Over in the Toulourenc, the long, remote valley road in the shadow of the Ventoux's north side, there are few villages or cafés and it's unlikely any will be open on a Sunday. There, or in the rolling valley roads through the Baronnies hills – that's when I am sure I will need the gels.

Lastly, I pull on a plain white racing cap, just like I would have done back in the day, back in the alpha-male 1980s, when wearing a helmet marked you out as a 'soft-cock tosser' – as the same friend once said – rather than a responsible and intelligent adult. I need the cap to shield me from the blinding sun moving across the cloudless sky. The helmet sits on top. There's a few minutes of perfunctory stretching before I pull on my shoes and I finally leave the house at just after eight.

My legs are tight and the first pedal revs climbing up through Blauvac village sting a little but once past La Calade, the restaurant by the church, where a couple sits drinking coffee in the shade, I am warmed up. To my right, the Monts de Vaucluse give way to the irrigated flatlands stretching beyond Isle-sur-la-Sorgue, towards the Bouches-du-Rhône, while on my left the humpback of Ventoux dominates the skyline.

I ride through the avenue of plane trees on the approach to Villes-sur-Auzon, their root systems buckling the verge of the road, passing the wine cooperative run by Éric Caritoux's brother-in-law, Bruno. There's a smell of baking and coffee in the still, hot air as I ride through the village. I turn right, leaving Villes, and pedal towards the Gorges.

The climb begins steadily and my heart rate adjusts. After a few minutes I hear voices over my shoulder. A chiselled group of six, in VC Monieux jerseys and white arm warmers, spin past with a single muted '*Bonjour*'. I think about accelerating and tagging onto their back wheel but I know it would be too much, too soon. By the time I have thought it through, they have gone and are exiting the next bend. I glance up and see them, synchronised, a few metres higher on the road ahead. For a while after that, I am alone with my breathing, as the hedgerows give way to the rocky walls and high cliffs of the Gorges themselves. The gilet, now fully unzipped, flaps open.

The long climb to the top of the Gorges becomes a false flat, a barely perceptible gradient. Sunday, though, is hunting day, and every now and then white vans, dog cages in the rear, come into view, parked up on the verge. Somewhere ahead, I can hear shouting, dogs barking, above the road. As the shouts of hunters and barking of gundogs grow louder and echo around me, I find an easy tempo.

Up ahead, there is a rustling in the thick scrub. A Pastis-fuelled hunter, stumbling around, I think, as a few rocks drop onto the verge. Then almost nonchalantly, a *sanglier,* the size of a calf, emerges and trots across the road, just in front of me. The giant boar quickly disappears into the bushes clinging to the steep drop on the right-hand side of the road. The shouting and barking recede behind me. I slow a little and look down into the thicket below the road. Already the beast is hidden from view.

The road winds upwards, following the cliff, and passes through dank unlit tunnels until it levels out at the top of the Gorges. I wheel to a stop at the viewing point to eat and drink. Opposite is the Rocher du Cire, a towering 200-metre-high cliff, supposedly home to hundreds of bees' nests. A century or so ago, in a test of courage, young men – including the poet Frédéric Mistral, who came here in 1866 – would abseil down to gather honey, as part of their rites of passage. Not any more, however. A few may still have the old skills, but most of them stack shelves and drive low-loaders in the retail park at Le Pontet, in the sprawling suburbs of Avignon. Maybe their dads still come up here sometimes, pootling their way up the Gorges on their off-the-peg bikes from Decathlon or the Leclerc hyper-marché in Carpentras.

Overlooking the Rocher du Cire is the Ferme St Hubert. Hidden in the forest behind that, is the Mur de la Peste, a plague wall, built in 1721 in a bid to keep out the pestilence coming north from Marseille. The wall, which stretched between the Durance river and the Ventoux, was guarded day and night, but proved ineffective. There were 126,000 deaths in the region from the plague between 1720 and 1722.

The remote and lonely road past the Ferme St Hubert was also the scene of fighting in August 1944, when a German convoy, raiding the farm for supplies, tangled with the local 'Maquis', the Provençal name for the French Resistance. As the Germans headed on towards St Jean-de-Sault, the Maquis opened fire with a machine gun. The Germans fought back, forcing the Maquis to retreat. Local boy Robert Giraud, 19 years old at the time, was a casualty, shot in the head as he covered his comrades.

The Maquis were hugely active across the slopes, foothills and gorges around the Ventoux, defending the lonely roads that climbed and descended through the wooded hills of the Drôme and Vaucluse. They had some notable recruits, including Irish poet, writer and Resistance sympathiser Samuel Beckett, who fled to the Vaucluse region in 1942 as the Gestapo began a purge of the Resistance and other subversives in Paris. Beckett, who travelled to Germany during the 1930s, hated the Nazis and despised their racism. 'You couldn't stand by with your arms folded,' he said.

Much later in his life, asked why he had joined the Resistance, he said: 'I was fighting against the Germans, who were making life hell for my friends, and not for the French nation.'

His flight from Paris, south to the 'free zone' of the Vaucluse, took six weeks, much of it spent hiding from German patrols. 'I can remember waiting in a barn until it got dark,' Beckett told his biographer, James Knowlson. 'We could see a German sentinel in the moonlight. The Germans were on the road so we went across fields.'

With his partner, Suzanne Déchevaux-Dumesnil, Beckett made most of the 700-kilometre journey south on foot. They holed up in Roussillon, a village perched on red ochre rock in the valley between the rough scrub of the Monts de Vaucluse and the more manicured Luberon range. But they were constantly uneasy. The Maquis were active in nearby Gordes, just a few kilometres away, and even though he spoke fluent French, Beckett was the odd foreigner, with Irish accent and Jewish first name, living on his nerves and dodging German patrols.

He found work picking grapes on the Bonnelly farm and also finished *Watt*, his second novel, during the evenings. He didn't neglect supporting the Resistance either, storing weapons in his yard and helping the Maquis carry out acts of sabotage against the Germans as they patrolled the hills of the Vaucluse.

Beckett certainly rode a bike when he lived in the Luberon valley. I don't know if he ever tackled the Ventoux – how would he have found the time, given that he was busy fighting Fascism, dodging Nazis and being a literary genius every evening? – but he loved bicycles and had the gaunt, hook-nosed, hollow-cheeked appearance of a post-war climber. Riding alongside Bobet, Coppi, Koblet or Kübler, Beckett, haunted eyes and ruffled, stand-up shock of hair, would have been a stylish addition to any post-war peloton. He would have relished the sense of liberation that drew the crowds to the roadside and, surely too, his post-race existentialist analysis would have been the stuff of legend.

Beckett's interest in cycling is widely believed to have fuelled the title, at least, of *Waiting for Godot*, his best-known play, completed at the start of the 1950s and premiered in 1953. He shared a fascination for two-wheeled endeavour with Ernest Hemingway, and once apparently described the mythical Godot as 'a veteran racing cyclist, bald, a "stayer", recurrent placeman in town-to-town and national championships, Christian name elusive, surname Godeau, pronounced, of course, no differently from Godot'.

And there was in fact, a real 'Godot' – Roger Godeau, a relatively undistinguished road rider, but an accomplished track rider, most at home on the boards of the Vélodrome d'Hiver in Paris – the infamous 'Vel d'Hiv', used as a base by the Nazis to stockade Jews before transportation – where he held the Derny Hour Record. A contemporary of Rik Van Steenbergen, Stan Ockers and Jean Dotto – the first Frenchman to win the Vuelta a España – Godeau's stocky build earned him the nickname 'Popeye', something he learned to play on. He appeared in six-day races in Frankfurt, Berlin and even travelled to New York, but never truly shone on the road.

Yet legend persists, rather shakily, that Godeau was always slow, always at the back of the peloton, although his track speed might suggest otherwise. So there are two vague stories, often repeated, of how Beckett summoned up the title of his renowned play. In the first, he is strolling the boulevards, possibly in Paris, when he comes upon a small knot of spectators, gathered at the roadside.

'What's going on?' the Irishman asks them.

'We're waiting for Godeau,' they reply.

In the second version, Beckett has made a trip to the impoverished and chilly north-east of France to see cobbled Classic race, Paris–Roubaix. He spends the day waiting endlessly at the roadside to see 'Popeye' Godeau ride wearily by. That experience may also have inspired the play's title.

I don't believe either of them.

Numerous local members of the Maquis were in hiding during the German occupation of the Vaucluse. Most roads were subject to German military checkpoints, although the many remote tracks and minor roads climbing through the wooded foothills of the Ventoux at least offered some protection. But in the communities below the mountain suspicion pervaded everyday village life, as many were believed – sometimes wrongly – to be collaborating with the Germans or the Vichy government.

One of the most infamous incidents in the villages around Ventoux came on 1 August 1944, in Sarrians, a few kilometres to the north-west of Carpentras. It explains why the name Albin Durand is so evident on many street names, squares and monuments across the Vaucluse.

Albin Durand was a farmer and a *Maquisard* in Sarrians. On a summer's night of violence and horror, the SS Charlemagne, stationed at the nearby Château de Taureau, and a group of French fascists, arrived at the Café du Casino. Their ruthless enquiries led to Durand's farm, where they began to torture him and farm worker Antoine Diouf. Durand was brutally beaten but would not give away any information. The torture became more horrific. He was given injections by a doctor, ostensibly 'to keep him alive'. Then the Germans cut off his legs above the knee with his own electric saw. Still Durand, remembered as particularly courageous, would not talk, so they took him into the farmyard, set his farm on fire and shot him and Diouf.

In 2005, Jean-Marie Le Pen, then the leader of the Front National, told a right-wing magazine: 'the German occupation was not particularly inhumane, even if there were a number of excesses . . .' Le Pen was rounded on, even by his own daughter, Marine, and subsequently fined and subjected to a suspended prison sentence.

The liberation of the Vaucluse was bloody and poisoned by recriminations. Suspected collaborators – seen as traitors – were beaten and abused, spat at and sometimes shot as 'tribunals of the people' sprang up across the region. 'Justice' under the tribunals was rough. One village doctor and his wife were accused of fraternising with the Germans and implicating Durand, while the doctor was also claimed to have performed abortions on French women who'd slept with the German occupiers. Both were shot by firing squad.

The cruelty and brutality of the occupation remains both unforgotten and, even now, in some places unforgiven. In the aftermath of the terrorist attacks of 2015 and 2016, that flame of patriotic pride flickered more brightly than ever, particularly in the south of France. In late 2015, in Beaumes-de-Venise, at the foot of the jagged Dentelles de Montmirail, there was a performance of 'Maquis Ventoux'. The evening celebrated the spirit of the French Resistance, conjuring up the secret routes on and around the Ventoux, remembering the suffering of

Durand and Diouf, as well as the viciousness of the firefights on the mountain roads, just above the Rocher du Cire.

I rode on, descending away from the top of the Gorges into the Pays de Sault. The lavender had already been harvested, but the sickly sweet aroma still hung in the air. The few switchbacks leading up to Sault pass another monument to the Maquis, before the road arrives in the small town, widely known as the lavender capital of Provence. In July 1987, my boys of summer had stopped here, wet and exhausted after riding through a thunderstorm, seeking refuge from the deluge and lunching on red wine and tripe. All of us, that is, except Peter, the vegetarian with vertigo. We had no rain capes for the long and sodden haul back to the gite in Murs, so instead bought a roll of bin bags, tearing holes in them for arms and head.

Sault has since become a regular coffee stop, both before and after climbing or descending the Ventoux, but also en route to nearby climbs such as the Col de la Croix de l'Homme Mort and my favourite, the wild and deserted Col du Négron, in the hills above Revest-du-Bion.

At the heart of Sault are the convent gardens, with views over the lavender fields and across towards the Ventoux's white summit. I stopped at the Promenade café for a *grand crème* to wash down the warm banana I'd pulled out of my jersey pocket. On market days, Sault has a cheery feel to it, but on quieter days it can be bleak. That may be due to the proximity of the eerily beautiful Plateau d'Albion, where France stationed an arsenal of nuclear warheads until the late 1990s.

Now the missile sites lie abandoned, with some given over to solar power. There are few villages, and only a semi-deserted Foreign Legion post betrays much sign of life. One former missile silo, high on the hills south of the Plateau d'Albion, is now the acclaimed Bistrot de Lagarde d'Apt. But the Plateau, ringed by hills and with few cars or cafés, makes for spectacular riding on rolling, wide roads, built specifically to take the large military vehicles and missile transporters that have long since gone.

There is one great café stop, at a quiet crossroads on the edge of the plateau. Just below Simiane-la-Rotonde's circular fortress, you can sit outside the Chapeau Rouge bakery, tearing into fresh almond croissants and sipping sweet coffee, the Ventoux far behind you and the Lure mountain, its slighter, distant twin, over your left shoulder.

This crossroads reminds me of the deserted bus stop in Hitchcock's *North by Northwest*. I sit there sometimes, drinking a *grand crème*, scanning the landscape and the long straight roads, not for low-flying crop dusters, but for signs of life. For a long time, nothing happens, nothing at all. But every now and then, a lone two-wheeled silhouette emerges from the shimmering heat haze. I watch them approach, until they whirr past, head down, making their way on across the vast landscape framed by mountains, before they are out of sight once again.

Bottles refilled and crammed with ice, I left Sault and set off towards Aurel and the long descent through warm, lavender-scented air, across the border into the Drôme *département*, and then on into the Toulourenc valley. The north side of the Ventoux is completely different in character to the south side, more Alpine and dominated by an intimidating near-vertical cliff, rising out of the Toulourenc to the summit of the mountain. There is little reason to stop between Sault and Malaucène.

The roads to the north are far more remote, with few settlements, a handful of cars and a slight atmosphere of foreboding. There are a handful of *villages perchés*, but most of them – Savoillan, Brantes and St Léger du Ventoux – are not particularly welcoming. I haven't stopped for a coffee in any of them since persons unknown badly scored my saddle outside a café in Brantes, years ago.

After a few kilometres, I swung off to the right and onto the steady climb to the Col des Aires, away from the Toulourenc, following the slopes of the Baronnies hills and along to the Col de Fontaube, where the view of the Ventoux's north face, the immense scree and the strange observatory is at its most dramatic. And there, as I rolled through the hairpins coming down the Fontaube's north side, bottles empty, skin reddening, legs weary, a mere 80 kilometres into my ride, was where it started to get to me.

It was on the way towards the Ouvèze valley that, even at the hottest part of the day, I realised I was cold. It's a strange sensation to get goose bumps in 35 degrees, but despite my best efforts to manage the conditions, I was cooking, slowly.

I carried on, zipping up the gilet, tearing open a gel, gulping it down, now desperate, not for more iced water, but for hot coffee and sugar. I knew from past experience that I was now 'bonking', hitting the wall. I kept riding, past the raised chapel of Notre Dame de Consolation at Pierrelongue, feeling suitably inconsolable. I slowed hopefully in Mollans-sur-Ouvèze, circling the sleepy main street for a café, but mid-afternoon in August was siesta time.

Annoyed with myself for this stupid error, I ploughed on, following the Ouvèze valley and crossing back into the Vaucluse *département*. In high summer the Ouvèze river is reduced to a trickle, but it remains notorious for one of the most devastating flash floods in the history of the brooding and violent storms that sometimes envelop the Ventoux. In late September 1992, a huge *tempête* – described at the time as a 'giant rain-making machine' – broke over the region, shrouding the Ventoux's north face, which effectively became a giant sluiceway, emptying itself into both the Toulourenc and Ouvèze rivers.

During the storm, the temperature in Sault dropped by almost ten degrees in 30 minutes. Three hundred millimetres of rain fell in nearby Entrechaux in six hours. 'The effect could not have been worse if a dam had broken,' one rescue worker said afterwards.

The Toulourenc and Ouvèze converge at the foot of the Ventoux. In the path of the torrent flowing off the mountain was sleepy Vaison-la-Romaine and a busy riverside campsite, the Moulin de César, just south of the town's old Roman bridge. The flood waters peaked during the afternoon. At least 11 people, of all those who drowned in and around Vaison, were swept away at the campsite. Video footage shows a deluge of filthy water rushing towards the bridge, caravans and camper-vans – some still occupied – bobbing like corks until they smash into the bridge's stonework and shatter like glass.

The water rose higher than any previous known flood level, tearing through houses built high above the riverbank. The frantic rescue operation wore on into the evening, with heli-copters plucking soaked and frozen locals off rooftops. Vaison was devastated by the tale of one victim, a baby lost to the waters, after her exhausted mother, awaiting rescue from the torrent, could no longer cling on to her.

More than 80 houses were destroyed and almost 50 people killed by the floodwaters of the Ouvèze and its tributaries. The catastrophic flooding of Vaison, caused in part by the angry storms that broke over the Ventoux, became one of the most infamous episodes in the region's history.

By the time I finally reached Malaucène, my neck and back were aching. Thankfully, the bakery at the foot of the road lead-ing back up the mountain was open. I bought a thick wedge of *tarte au pommes* and click-clacked across the road to the shady Terrasses du Ventoux café where, with shaking hands, I devoured it and drained two *grands crèmes* in quick succession.

I sat for a while, then filled the bidons again, mixing apple juice with ice cubes. The climb out of Malaucène and over the wooded Madeleine and down into Bédoin is no great obstacle, but my legs were like wood. I hauled myself across the Ventoux's southern foothills, the air thick with heat as the late afternoon *canicule* reached its zenith. I knew that another pause could lead to a phone call asking to be picked up, so I rode on through Bédoin – ignoring the temptation to join the Lycra-clad loungers enjoying an ice-cold beer at the pavement tables – and downhill away from the mountain, towards Mormoiron, picking up pace as the final haul uphill to Blauvac – and journey's end – loomed on the horizon.

The days on a bike that end at snail's pace, hunched over the handlebars, after you have ridden beyond your limits, are always the most painful. Sometimes, however, they can also be the best. I hadn't spent so many hours riding for years. Now, as well as an aching back, I also had ridiculous tan lines to show for it.

Not for the first time, riding in the shadow of the great mountain had reconnected me. For the rest of that year, I rode regularly, for hours at a time, until, eventually, just before Christmas, the dark and chill of the British winter finally overwhelmed me.

IV

I was bowled over when Helen told me she was pregnant. After that, our lives changed for ever. But 1961 was a funny year, what with all the success I had early on, in the spring, and then the disappointments that came later.

Winning the Tour of Flanders was quite something. It meant I was respected as a Classics champion and boosted my popularity in Belgium, even if I hadn't proved myself in the Tour. After that things went downhill. I picked up a nasty bout of food poisoning that really left me in a right state.

But then I thought, wrongly, that I was over it, so, like an idiot, I rode the Tour de France. That was a disaster – I only managed three stages, but that was three too many. And it hardly helped my bad knee either. I got that sorted out eventually with some injections from a doctor in Paris.

Things were getting tough financially and I started to feel the pressure. I hadn't won many races and, because I'd not finished the Tour, I only picked up seven criterium rides all year. We needed to move out of the apartment in Paris, if we were having a family, but, because I was foreign, I was struggling to get a loan from a French bank.

I reckoned Ken Dockray, who owned a garage in Ghent, might be able to help us find somewhere to move into. I knew Ken had a lot of contacts and, as it turned out, one of his customers had a small house available. Money was still an issue, but luckily we were hardly charged any rent. That saved us, really, because we'd spent a bit moving into the house and all my savings had gone.

The few contracts I'd been up for had fallen through, but I managed to get some track rides in Belgium. Otherwise, well – goodness knows.

But we were very happy in Ghent. Helen always loved it. It became home. I picked up a 1910 Peugeot and there was even a Tom Simpson Fan Club. In December 1963, Ken got them all to come along to the t' Kapelleke Sporting Club's annual do. Helen and I had been invited along as guests of honour. Even though it was a bitterly cold, foggy night, there was still a good turnout.

I stood up, told a few racing tales from that season, cracked a few jokes and signed some autographs. They even toasted my future success and wished me well.

It was after midnight when we finally slipped away.

~

Eddy

Late on the afternoon of 10 July 1970, low sunshine bathes the southern slopes of Mont Ventoux, turning the vast expanse of white rock yellow, as evening settles on the Vaucluse. As the shadows lengthen, the colours morph to red and gold and then, at twilight, a blueish purple, until darkness envelops the mountain and all that is visible is the lonely red light winking at the top of the observatory.

A little earlier that afternoon, his high-cheekboned face set in a rictus of determination, Eddy Merckx hunched over his handlebars and hammered power relentlessly into the pedals as he rode past the spot where, three summers earlier, his team-mate and friend, Tom Simpson, had died. When he reached the point where Simpson collapsed, Merckx faltered briefly, seeming distracted. There's a striking image of that moment, at first glance disarming and baffling, but almost unbearably elegiac and poignant.

In the photograph, Merckx has one hand on the handlebars, the other hand off the bars clutching a Faema racing cap. A shirtless man in a straw hat leans towards him, shouting encouragement, a half-timbered radio clamped to his ear. Behind him, another man has turned towards the Ventoux's bleak ridge and the Simpson memorial, as he watches the director of the Tour, Jacques Goddet, stoop to lay a wreath. As Goddet bends down to place the flowers, Merckx doffs his cap in acknowledgement. In the background, a gendarme salutes.

Merckx knows more about winning than almost any other athlete you can think of. He remains, for most, the greatest-ever cyclist. Only months before he died, Simpson, even though he was his team-mate, had become his rival. In March 1967, an ambitious Merckx bristled with frustration when Simpson stood in his way at the Peugeot team, yet he was reduced to tears by the death of his older team-mate four months later.

Ironically, given that the pair had come close to a bitter feud during that Paris–Nice, Merckx was the only high-profile rider to attend Simpson's funeral on 18 July 1967. That was partly because the rest of the British rider's peers were on that day racing to Bordeaux in stage 18. Merckx, however, was absent from that year's Tour.

He once described his tangle with Simpson in the spring of 1967 as being 'put in my place'. Merckx had taken over the lead in Paris–Nice with a solo win in Château-Chinon, although at that time he was not yet the insatiable 'Cannibal' that he later became, even if few, including Simpson, could doubt he was the coming man. Simpson, eight years older, was smart enough to see the writing on the wall. Yet he was one of the few riders ever to fend off Merckx's terrifying ambition and then hold on to win.

Their duelling during that Paris–Nice came to a head in the climbs overlooking Toulon when Peugeot team manager Gaston Plaud told Merckx to sacrifice his own chances in support of Simpson. 'I broke away on Mont Faron,' Merckx remembered, 'and Plaud came to me and said, "Tommy's arriving – can you wait for him?"' Merckx agreed to do so, and then rode in support of his team-mate. 'I made the descent, full gas, and then at the finish, Tom said, "You can win the stage." But he won Paris–Nice.'

Merckx later said that the decision to wait for Simpson on the Faron had been 'totally' against his wishes. Now, some 50 years on, sitting in a hotel bar in Ghent, Merckx can afford to look back wistfully.

'He flicked me!' he says, deadpan, of Simpson's racing in that year's Paris–Nice, before a big smile creases his face. 'Tom had a lot of character, he was very British,' Merckx says.

'But Tommy was also one of my best friends.'

He pauses and shifts in his seat.

'You see, Tom's problem was that he had too many business interests. He bought a lot of land in Corsica and, because of that, he didn't train enough to go to the Tour – and he wanted to win the Tour.

'He was too busy with Corsica,' Merckx says bluntly. 'That's the reason that he died.'

V

Eddy's a great rider. In fact, he's got the makings of a brilliant rider, but by God, he's stubborn. He's been sulking for two days now, bloody ignoring me. I'm here to lead too, though, I'm here to race – I can't say to him, 'After you – on you go ...'

I've got to take my chances – God knows he wins enough already. Plus he's a lot younger than me – he's got plenty of years ahead of him to show what he can do. 'Course, he doesn't see it like that – he just thinks I flicked him. Getting into the break on the République was just good racing – it was not an attack on him. He wasn't there – what am I supposed to do? I'd warned him what might happen. I can't hang around for him if he's not up there.

Trouble is, there's three of us here now – me, Roger and Eddy. We can't all be top dog, we can't all be leaders. But Plaud's not bothered about what Eddy wants, maybe not as much as he should be. Sometimes I think he cares more about the wine list at the hotel each night!

Maybe the atmosphere will be better at dinner tonight. We came down off the Faron into Hyères together, and I let Eddy win. I had to really – he put in a decent ride for me. I know I can win overall in Nice and he's been like a bear with a sore head since he lost the jersey in Bollène.

I don't know if he'll stay at Peugeot after this, though. He wants new riders here, more Belgians, but the French like doing things their way. You need to fit in, to be one of the lads, if it's going to work out for you. I've learned that over the years.

If I win in Nice, it will only make it harder for him to stay here. But I know that it will make things better for me and I need to win. What with the plan for Corsica and everything, I need the money. If I want a better contract, whoever I race for, I need to do well this year. And not just in Nice. I really need to do well in the Tour.

~

I shine my shoes and put on a tie to meet Eddy Merckx, just as I would to meet Ali, Pelé, Nicklaus, Charlton. Something tells me they'd all expect it. Merckx, Ali, Pelé, Sir Bobby – they are the names that typify a golden era of sport, an age of relative innocence, before live TV, corporate marketing, image rights and merchandising – and corporate doping – took over.

Merckx and I meet in Ghent, Tommy's old stomping ground, the day after David Bowie died. Ziggy Stardust and the Cannibal may seem odd bedfellows but they are cultural contemporaries. Bowie announced himself with 'Space Oddity' in July 1969, the same month in which Merckx won his first Tour de France. But this is 2016. Ziggy is dead and the Cannibal is on crutches. Merckx greets me, struggling for mobility after an operation on his troublesome hip.

Bowie was 69 when he died and Merckx is only recently 70. On this day he looks his age. Wearing a suit – he is meeting later that day with the Quick-Step board which sponsors the World Tour team – he moves uneasily through the café of the Sandton Grand Hotel on one crutch. After we shake hands, I fuss over him a little as he settles into his chair. It's quickly clear that he doesn't want any help. 'You know, I was on the trainer this morning,' he says defiantly.

As well as his relationship with Quick-Step, Merckx has other business interests. In conjunction with ASO, the parent organisation of the Tour de France, he has been the promoter of the Tours of Qatar and Oman, both new races in new territories.

And even on one leg, the Cannibal keeps going. 'I can ride,' Merckx reiterates. 'This morning I did a few minutes on the home trainers. Now they say I have to spend two or three days doing nothing. I listen to the doctor these days. Now I only ride for fun.'

Even when he retired from racing after a gruelling career punctuated by multiple injuries, as much as by success, he didn't really hang up his wheels. 'I love sports – all sports. Football, tennis – and cycling. I had a bit of a break when I retired but then I started riding again. Cycling is still the best, even though it was also my job.

'I ride with my friends, but sometimes I also ride by myself. I've just been in Monaco for a week and I rode alone. But people see me and want to take a picture, or ride along for a while.'

By the time Merckx reached the Ventoux stage in the 1970 Tour de France, he had already acquired an aura of invincibility. His victory on the Ventoux was both demonic in its doggedness and, in that late afternoon sunshine, three years after the death of his British team-mate, hugely poignant.

Merckx's mood at the start that day was doubly mournful. He had left the stage start in Gap wearing a black ribbon to mark the death only 24 hours earlier of Vincenzo Giacotto, his mentor and manager of the Faema team. 'I was good friends with Giacotto, because he took me to the Faema team.' But in terms of paying tribute to Simpson, Merckx had nothing planned. 'You can't know how the race will pan out,' he shrugged.

Unusually for a mountain stage, that day's start time had been pushed back, ensuring an even more funereal atmosphere as the peloton arrived at the foot of the Ventoux late in the afternoon. 'It was the first time on Ventoux since Tom had died and the organisation was very worried about the heat,' Merckx said.

The route took the peloton south, away from the Alps, through Séderon, Montbrun-les-Bains and Sault and then over the Abeilles climb. The bunch descended into Villes-sur-Auzon, speeding towards the intermediate sprint at Mormoiron. There, as Cyrille Guimard led a breakaway, the riders glanced up towards the Giant and took in the scale of the challenge.

'Ventoux's a very special mountain, because you can see it from so far away – the great bald mountain,' Merckx says with a theatrical flourish. 'And in the peloton, once you see it, everybody goes quiet.

'They're all scared. Everybody's afraid. It gets so quiet you can hear a fly buzzing through the peloton. That's how I always remember it.'

With Merckx himself reeling the break in, there was now little any of them could do to prevent the inevitable. So it was, that, 13 kilometres from the summit and in lengthening shadows, the Belgian accelerated so strongly that, by Chalet Reynard, there was only one possible outcome. 'I was alone on the mountain for a long time because I attacked in the trees,' he remembered. 'The last rider with me was Joaquim Agostinho, but before the Chalet, I broke away from him.'

It's hard to imagine any rider of the modern era attacking the Ventoux as aggressively as Eddy Merckx did on that afternoon. The powerful Agostinho, whom Merckx had been wary of since the previous summer, was no pushover, but Merckx simply powered away from the Portuguese. His aggression towards the gradient was almost animalistic. As the sun dropped into the Rhône valley, Merckx's supremacy proved overwhelming to his rivals.

'It was a long time on my own, yes, but if you want to win the stage, well . . .' he says. 'Sometimes if you wait too long you can't make the difference. You have to attack earlier to tire them out.

'You're never sure, though. You hope to make the difference, to win the stage, but Chalet Reynard is still six or seven kilometres from the top.'

This was not graceful or elegant riding, but a demonstration of strength and ambition. Footage shows Merckx overpowering his bike, crushing the pedals, mouth agape, frowning in concentration as he contains the pain.

Now though, surely, riders would think that such an attack, so low down the Ventoux, was too big a risk?

'Bah,' Merckx says with a roll of his eyes. 'But it's also a risk to wait to the last moment. These days, the tactics are different. They're afraid – they're afraid of each other.'

As he rode through the desert of bleached rock, his characteristic hunching over the handlebars became more pronounced, and the pain in his back, caused by a crash a year earlier, visibly more intense. In an effort to manage the pain, Merckx reached into his jersey pocket for an Allen key and lowered his saddle slightly, even as he rode up the mountain. 'I was adjusting my saddle because of the crash in 1969,' he said, of the notorious stack-up on the velodrome in Blois, which, he has said, could have killed him. 'After Blois I suffered a lot because my hips were turned.

'I think my leg was broken in the crash, but after six weeks, I started riding again and my hips were out of alignment. Back then, there was no osteopath or physio. I often needed to make the saddle higher or lower, so I became a specialist at adjusting the saddle while I was riding. It wasn't the first time. I had to do it in other races too, once or twice.'

Only with three kilometres to go – within sight almost of the Simpson memorial – did he falter, as the commentators watching on TV screens at the summit exclaimed: '*Merckx en difficulté!*'

Even then, he didn't forget his obligation to Simpson. 'I still remembered,' Merckx said of the moment he removed his cap. 'It was for Tommy – he was a very good friend. I liked him very much. He was a mentor to me when I was young.'

He won the stage easily from Martin Van Den Bossche, who reached the summit well over a minute later. Lacking the energy even for a victory salute, Merckx crossed the line in a state of near-collapse. He pushed and shoved his way through the mêlée that greeted him, saying he had 'fire in his belly'.

'Listen, it's a fact that after the finish you have the TV, radio and press and really I did feel a bit dizzy,' he said. 'I told them: "Enough, I'm not good."'

'I already had too much oxygen in my lungs. Then the doctor gave me oxygen, which was ridiculous because it was the worst thing they could do.'

Suddenly, three years after Simpson, some immediately feared the worst, even though the stage had been timed to avoid the scorching heat of the Ventoux in mid-afternoon.

The prospect of another collapsed star spread panic. Breathless and seemingly close to passing out, Merckx and Van Den Bossche took refuge in an ambulance.

'Merckx came in the ambulance and we were in there for an age,' Van Den Bossche told journalist Daniel Friebe for his acclaimed book on Merckx. But others still insist that Merckx, while undoubtedly exhausted, was cunningly ensuring a quick exit. In the event, he and Van Den Bossche were sped down the mountain with a police escort.

'It wasn't a tactic,' Merckx insisted. 'But after an effort like I made on the Ventoux, and then you have to do Belgian TV, French TV, radio ... It was a good thing because we got to the hotel early.'

Van Den Bossche always found the whole tale amusing. 'We arrived at the hotel an hour ahead of our team-mates who had been blocked on the mountain,' he said.

Cunning and astute it may have been, but the growing resentment towards Merckx's dominance soon became open. During that Tour, he and his team rejected the race organisation's official hotel allocations. That, his past rejection of partisan French values at the Peugeot team and his blunt criticism of other French-isms, hardly endeared him to host press or public. Forty-three years later, Chris Froome would experience the same frosty reception after his own dominant win on the Ventoux. Like Merckx, he and his team then obsessed over negative media coverage, forgetting perhaps that the biggest gain of all might be simply to be liked.

~

I'd had a lot of disappointments in 1965. That's cycling I suppose. But it's not always easy to bounce back, even though I know that you have to keep plugging away. There's been times this year, when I've thought the devil was against me, when everything seemed to go wrong, no matter how hard I tried or how hard I rode. I had psyched myself up for the Tour de France. Because Anquetil wasn't there, I felt I had a pretty good chance. I knew it would be tough of course, but winning the Tour is the biggest goal for me – it has to be.

Once we got to the Pyrenees, things picked up and I climbed up to seventh place, but I had a tumble when I was coming down the Aubisque. It was pretty standard – I ripped my jersey and shorts and picked up some cuts and bruises, but I also cut my hand. A few days later, after we'd crossed into Spain for a finish in Barcelona, it started bothering me more, and by the time we left Montpellier for the stage over the Ventoux, it was giving me grief.

I'm not very keen on the Ventoux. It's like another world up there. The dust clings to you, it's always baking hot and there's all the insects buzzing the whole time. I told Vin Denson once: 'I hate those little bastards!' But despite all that, and the fact that it was so hot, I felt I rode well. I was suffering, but I could see that everyone else was suffering too, and I got ninth on the stage and stayed in the top ten.

It was a couple of days later that the roof fell in. After we finished in Gap, I got the doctors to take a look at my hand. They sorted out an abscess and put a dressing on it, but I didn't sleep well and the next day we had a nasty stage, going into Briançon over the Vars and Izoard. I was left behind on the Vars and by the end was just happy to get to the finish.

My hand was now a real problem because I couldn't even hold the bars tight and to top it off, they also found that I had a kidney infection! Somehow I still thought I could get through to Paris and I stuck at it, but after we left the Alps, I knew the game was up. I was weak as a kitten and couldn't carry on. Once I got to the hospital, all hell let loose. My hand was in a real state and then they told me my blood was poisoned. In fact, the doctor there wanted to operate on my hand there and then – he said otherwise I might lose it! After all that, I rested for almost two weeks. It took a while to get over another disappointing Tour, though.

So I put it behind me and started thinking about the rest of the season. There were still plenty of big races to come, including the World Championships in Spain. I had a good feeling about it. I felt I had a good shout there, that the circuit in Lasarte would suit me.

One of the reasons was that, in contrast with the Tour, the Worlds is just one day's racing. The British team had a far greater chance of running the show on a single day than over three weeks. I knew if I could get them to believe in my chances, that we could have a really good go at it.

It probably suited me that on the day itself it was raining. That was better than too much heat, at any rate. Barry Hoban worked like a maniac for me and I made it up to the big break. The riders were mainly Spaniards, which of course sent the locals crazy but which suited me too, because I could sit in, bide my time, wait for the right moment.

That moment came about two laps from the end. I went, hard,

giving it as much stick as I could and only Rudi Altig could follow. I knew Rudi well. He was a good man to be with, because he doesn't shirk the effort – he does his bit and I respect him for that. We got the gap and worked well together. But I knew it would be touch and go in a sprint. To be fair, I bluffed him a bit, made out I was tired and couldn't do that much to help. I think he looked at me and thought he had it in the bag.

But in the end, I was too quick for him. I kept thinking he was coming past me, but he never did and, to be honest, at the line, it wasn't even that close. As soon as I'd crossed the line, I was mobbed. 'Unbelievable!' they all said afterwards and we had a great party than night, lots of champagne and lots of fireworks, but really, I'd always believed I could do it.

Being World Champion was big news at home. I'd never been so popular and I did enjoy getting greater recognition. I got a lot of offers to make public appearances and I reckoned that was all worth a few bob. It all put me on the map and I even ended up writing for the *Sunday People*, although that was nothing, really – not compared to being on *Desert Island Discs* and winning the BBC Sports Personality of the Year!

～

The Franco-Belgian film, *Roi du Mont Ventoux*, produced in 2013, puts five stage winners – all of whom won at the summit of Ventoux – up against each other in virtual 'real time', based on archive footage. Merckx's 1970 stage victory is the oldest of the chosen five.

Why these five? Because when the film was made, they had climbed to victory at the summit via the identical 21-kilometre ascent from Bédoin, during Tours of the 'modern' era, perhaps better defined as the era of live television coverage. Using footage from 1970, 1987, 2000, 2002 and 2009, the film pits Merckx against the tragic Marco Pantani, Generation EPO's Richard

Virenque, Jean-François Bernard, the French Tour champion that never quite was, and, finally, against 2009 stage winner Juan Manuel Gárate.

However spurious a thesis it may be – they all started from different stage towns in stages of differing length and difficulty, while Merckx's win came nearly 40 years prior to Gárate's – the aim is to establish who is the king of Mont Ventoux.

'Some pretty good riders have won up there,' says Bernard, on one of his rare non-hunting days, before adding a caveat. 'Gárate won on the Ventoux, but you can win some races in the right circumstances.' He shrugs, a little dismissively. 'And he had a lot of circumstances.'

One infamous victory, Chris Froome's in July 2013, is missing of course. Analysing Merckx's performance, all steel frame and muscular woollen-jerseyed flogging of huge gears, against Froome's skeletal marginal gains and high-throttle cadence, some 43 years later, would have been intriguing. Froome's victory is still the subject of endless speculation, fuelling a million tweets, his explosive accelerations endlessly pored over for 'tells' of pharmaceutical enhancement or motorised doping, all of which he utterly refutes. But the film was made before his victory happened and is therefore not included.

It's clear within a few minutes of the film starting – judging from the smirk on his now fuller face – that the tanned, boyish, but slightly louche Virenque, stage winner in 2002, is confident that he will, inevitably, be crowned king on what he calls 'his' mountain. Even though he is from the Var, Virenque claims the Ventoux as home ground. 'I have home advantage there,' he says. 'It's my climb, my fans are there.'

Virenque's cockiness contrasts with the melancholic 'Jeff' Bernard, forever depicted as the prodigal who never came home, staring wistfully out, baggy-eyed, at the Parisian autumn, as he rides a train to the TV studios. Virenque sits in the back of a Mercedes taxi as he is chauffeured to a studio in Luxembourg, while Davide Boifava – Pantani's former sports director – strolls into a Milan studio and stands in for the late Italian. Gárate, a respected climber but hardly a household name until his Ventoux stage win in 2009, watches – a little oddly – in kit, from a studio in Spain.

And Merckx? Well, he was busy of course. Or perhaps he thought the whole thing a little ridiculous.

What was it he'd said to me in Ghent that lunchtime, waving his hand dismissively? 'Bah, you can't compare generations . . .'

'Why not?' I asked him.

'The bike was heavier and the gear changers were on the bike frame. We had to sit down to change gear. We had to take one hand off the handlebars to change gear. Now you can stand on the pedals and change gear and that makes a big difference.

'If you sit down to change gear you lose a lot of time. Maybe in the last two kilometres in 1970, I didn't change gear much . . . plus it's different racing up Ventoux after 200 kilometres to racing up it in a time trial.

'The equipment is now completely different. The most important thing is to be the best of your generation. I was the best in my generation.'

Merckx's 1970 victory came at the end of a 170-kilometre stage in a Tour that included 29 stages and had no rest days. Already that year, he had won Paris–Nice, Paris–Roubaix, the Giro d'Italia, and several other major races. Such a programme of racing would be unthinkable for a modern-day Tour contender. 'Cycling today has changed,' he said. 'When I didn't ride a Classic I felt bad, I felt sick. It's not like that any more.'

For Ventoux obsessives such as myself, the film is oddly compelling. There are little details – the black-and-white shots of an elegant Merckx riding through Bédoin and on towards the forest, prior to that display of irresistible force – that linger in the memory. The footage of Merckx, grainy, monochrome and of poor quality, is almost unbearably elegiac. It compares with George Best skipping past the keeper against Benfica in 1968, Bobby Moore and Pelé embracing in Mexico in 1970, or the otherworldly images of Neil Armstrong stepping onto the moon in 1969.

The climax of the Merckx win, played out against a melancholic backdrop of fast-lengthening shadows, is watched by knots of spectators in Ray-Ban aviators, shielding their eyes against the setting sun, as the Belgian produces one of the most famous exploits of his career. Those pictures contrast with the weary resignation of Jeff Bernard, hiding his disappointment behind blunt pragmatism, clearly unable to forget that he came within a hair's breadth of winning the 1987 Tour. His brutal assessments, the bitterness of the coiffed Virenque towards Lance Armstrong and the ambivalence of all towards Pantani's deranged stage win, not to mention his whole career, all spice up a 72-minute opus that only once or twice drags.

Asked to predict the outcome of the virtual race as the film starts, Bernard plumps for Merckx. 'He was always so strong, he always gave it his all,' the 1987 time trial winner says. Virenque rates himself as second fastest, behind Merckx, but ahead of Pantani.

Bernard's 1987 time trial win, which started under the shade of the trees in the Allée des Platanes in Carpentras, was an early example of marginal gains, or at least the philosophy behind the concept. Proof also that looking for an edge, beyond being fitter, skinnier or smarter, is nothing new. To the horror of some, the Frenchman rode a low-profile time-trial frame in the earlier flatter section of the stage, switched to a lightweight climbing bike on the approach to the Ventoux, and then rode that to the summit.

'The day before the time trial, I'd decided to pull out all the stops. *Ça passe ou ça casse* ... It was make or break,' Bernard explains. But he knew that a bike change, from low-pro time-trial bike to carbon-fibre climbing frame, soon after the 20 kilometres-to-go point, seemed radical at the time.

'Everyone said: "You're mad. Don't do that – you'll blow up." But I had the second bike, a climbing bike, for when we hit the real climb. It was a wild gamble, but it paid off.'

Not everyone thought him mad. 'Bernard got his strategy spot on that day,' said Stephen Roche in his book, *Born To Ride*. 'He may have lost 15 seconds or so making the switch but it was a smart thing to do. He was in a class of his own.' Bernard's stage win, two years after his mentor Bernard Hinault's final Tour win, set French pulses racing. Jeff was immediately seen as Hinault's successor.

But after taking the yellow jersey on Ventoux, his high hopes fell apart the very next afternoon after a combine of star riders – many of whom were also French – isolated him. Part of that, at least according to Roche, was due to a rash TV interview Bernard gave after his stage win on the Ventoux.

'We heard him on the TV saying: "I've just shown everybody I'm the strongest guy in the race,"' Roche recalled. 'It wasn't a good time to knock our pride by saying he had all but won the race ... it was clear that all Bernard's rivals came to the same conclusion as they sat in their rooms that night.'

In the hotels ranged around the foot of the Ventoux, Roche, Fignon, Charly Mottet and Pedro Delgado opened the Tour's road book and studied the next day's profile in even greater detail.

Bernard's puncture, the next afternoon, before the summit of the Col de Tourniol, and the flurry of attacks in a chaotic feed zone soon afterwards, ended his hopes. It was also a pivotal moment in French cycling. Since that day, no French rider has looked capable of taking the yellow jersey all the way to Paris.

'It's every pro's dream to race in the Tour,' Bernard says. 'Naturally, my biggest disappointment is not to have won it.'

'I came very close,' he says defiantly during the film. 'But that's the thing – when you're not in the running you're not bothered, but, when you get that close . . .'

Perhaps unsurprisingly, the 2000 Tour's peloton, racing at the very zenith of EPO use, leads the virtual race into the pivotal bend at St Estève, where the gradient ramps up. Bernard is just behind, with Merckx, despite the gap in years, third. Yet Merckx's bike alone, added to his componentry and clothing, was significantly heavier than those of his more recent rivals. 'His bike weighed over ten kilos,' Bernard says. That compares with much more lightweight contemporary weights.

By the time the rival groups have climbed far into the forest, Merckx, riding 30 years earlier on a heavier bike, in lower-quality kit and using lower-quality componentry, has caught the Pantani–Armstrong train of July 2000. Nevertheless, Merckx was right that day in Ghent. There is no comparison to be made, due to the huge advances that have happened in sports science and in equipment since the Belgian climbed the Ventoux on a steel frame, wearing a sweat-soaked woollen jersey.

His riding too, however impressive, is old school. Even if you choose to ignore the spiralling vortex of white noise in the power-output debate, Merckx's tactics were, at their most understated, instinctive, high risk and gung-ho. No sports director would sanction such an attack in the modern Tour.

Lastly, in the aftermath of the Festina scandal of 1998, in which Virenque was the central character, two rest days were introduced as standard in Grand Tours. A 29-stage Grand Tour with no rest days would not be possible in modern cycling.

With 13.6 kilometres to the summit, Merckx, riding the Ventoux in the Tour for the first time, and with the bullish but suffering Agostinho on his wheel, is easing clear of Pantani by a few seconds. The footage may be poor quality, but it does not disguise the irresistible force of Merckx's pedalling. 'Merckx was a cut above everyone,' Gárate says.

'He's untouchable,' states Virenque. What would he do to them these days, same bike, same kit, you ponder, as Merckx crushes the road beneath him.

Agostinho's team car draws alongside the Portuguese and a mechanic squirts cold water from a bidon down his team leader's back. Another rider empties the remnants of a bucket of water over his head. As he watches, Bernard's features crease into a 'them were the days' wry smile.

The virtual climb wears on, Merckx and Pantani yo-yoing at the front, but Gárate already two minutes behind the Belgian, as he races in front of far bigger crowds, an estimated half a million, in 2009. 'There wouldn't be as many spectators there if the Tour was in September,' observes Bernard, a little obviously, as he edges ahead of Pantani and Merkcx.

But, as Bernard points out, he is time-trialling, not reacting to the ebb and flow of those around him, or seeking to save his strength for the explosive attacks still to come. Bernard is racing the mountain, make or break as he put it, not the riders alongside him.

Virenque, meanwhile, is getting slower: with 12 kilometres to go in the virtual showdown, he's almost three minutes behind Merckx. By the time the leaders – Bernard, Pantani and Merkcx – get to the Maison Forestière Jamet, just short of the Virage du Bois, with 10.3 kilometres to the summit, Gárate and Virenque are out of contention. Virenque, watching his demise, squirms a little in his seat. 'Lots of fans wrote my name on the road,' he points out, clutching at straws. As he grudgingly admits, he's a lost cause, even before Chalet Reynard. Meanwhile, Bernard's lead increases.

But why is Virenque's 2002 time so slow, even against

Merckx's from 1970? Yes, his was the longest stage of the five – 221 kilometres, the second longest in that year's Tour, against Bernard's 36.5 kilometres, the second shortest in 1987 – and he had been in a long break through the stage, but, as Gárate points out, the timing of the Ventoux stage during the Tour's three weeks is also significant. 'It makes a difference if it's in the first ten days or the final week,' the Spaniard says. 'That's more important than the length of the stage.'

With nine kilometres to go, the Cannibal is alone on the Giant, crushing the cranks, pummelling the pedals, as his final companion, Agostinho, definitively cracks. It's a reality check for the Portuguese who, after matching the Belgian until midway up the mountain, struggles so badly that he fails even to finish in the top ten.

As he falls out of the virtual running, Virenque talks through his confession to doping, which came in 1999, a year after the Festina Affair. 'I didn't want to become some kind of ambassador or whistleblower,' he claims. 'So I saved my confession until later.

'It was commonplace in every team,' he says, by way of explanation. 'I did the same as any other rider.'

Back from his ban in 2002, Virenque sought revenge on the Ventoux. Of his winning attack, a little over eight kilometres from the summit, Virenque said: 'My brother was at the roadside and screamed encouragement at me. It gave me a new lease of life.'

Virenque, the highest-profile name in what was then the biggest drugs scandal ever to hit cycling, was vilified for his part in the Festina Affair. Judging by his relative rehabilitation as a TV pundit and the number of autographs he signs each day, he has, in some corners at least, been forgiven. 'Richard had a bad time after Festina,' Bernard says. 'We thought that affair would be a big wake-up call. But things actually got worse in the following years.' Even Boifava, Pantani's manager, admitted that cycling had yet to heal itself. 'It's become increasingly difficult to make cycling credible,' the Italian says.

'There's a lot of hypocrisy,' Virenque maintains. 'The managers in cycling, the federations, the journalists – everyone knew what was going on.'

'Doping is about making money. In July, it's Dallas,' says Bernard, perhaps meaning Vegas. 'Whether or not the riders are taking drugs, people want to watch the Tour and they want action.'

A kilometre and a half from Chalet Reynard, Bernard leads Pantani by 30 seconds and Merckx is still just 40 seconds slower. Merckx, his shoulders and head bobbing, remains seated, legs churning. In stark contrast, Pantani's speed ebbs and flows as he stands on the pedals, hands on the drops, his short accelerations keeping pace with the rear of the Armstrong-led group just ahead.

Bernard watches on, and recalls seeing Merckx on the Ventoux as a kid at home. 'I remember the black-and-white TV and I remember watching these pictures,' he says. 'I don't see who can compare to Merckx.'

A handful of mute fans watch the Cannibal's lone escapade as, to a chorus of buzzing cicadas, Merckx continues his relentless progress, followed by a flotilla of official vehicles and TV motorbikes. By Chalet Reynard, the Belgian has bridged the decades, overtaking Pantani and riding only five seconds slower than Bernard. With five kilometres to go, Merckx is now riding through the arid upper slopes, a little slower than Bernard, but almost half a minute faster than Pantani.

But the hierarchy begins to shift in the virtual race when Pantani rejoins the Armstrong group. And then the Italian attacks. 'He was so full of surprises,' Boifava says, a little indulgently. Pantani's acceleration takes him into the lead, edging clear of Bernard and distancing Merckx.

'I knew he was using certain substances,' Virenque says of the Italian, who was kicked off the 1999 Giro d'Italia on the threshold of victory for failing a hematocrit test. 'But there comes a moment when you overdo it and you get reined in.' Virenque, after all, should know.

Boifava, meanwhile, remains loyal, describing Pantani as a 'born champion'. 'He didn't need doping. When he raced as a junior, he was already a great champion.'

Veteran cycling writer Gianni Mura, the bear-like correspondent to Italian newspaper *la Repubblica*, famed for reading his copy down the line, even after the advent of email, once asked Pantani why he accelerated so hard on the climbs. 'To cut my agony short,' Pantani replied.

Of Pantani's death in 2004, attributed after a series of investigations to a mix of cocaine and antidepressants, Boifava says only 'everyone blamed cycling'. 'It's difficult to know what really happened. In the end, we all failed – because none of us managed to save him. I felt guilty because we couldn't save him.'

Three kilometres from the summit, Merckx has fallen a minute behind the Italian, but as Pantani's accelerations fluctuate, in a bluffing lead group whittled down to Armstrong, Jan Ullrich, Joseba Beloki, Roberto Heras and Santiago Botero, Bernard is once again virtual race leader. That's until Pantani attacks again, this time with Armstrong hot on his heels. It's a moment of footage, so tainted, so brimming with bitter memories, that everyone else – even confessed doper Virenque – watches with disdain.

'I remember Armstrong in 2002,' Virenque says, 'and he was – I think – "carried" by the authorities, and by the Tour organisers.

'*I* – a French cyclist – finished first at the top of Ventoux,' the Frenchman rants. '*I* spoke to the media, *I* did the anti-doping tests, but there, for Monsieur Lance Armstrong, the Tour organisers had put a helicopter at his disposal, to take him from Mont Ventoux to his hotel.

Ignoring that a helicopter evacuation from summit finishes has now become standard practice for the race leader, Virenque continues. 'And *me*, the little French cyclist, was left there, in the road, no escort and with all the traffic jams. It took me three hours to get back to the hotel that day. You can't help but feel bitter about things like that, about that sort of set-up.'

'I think he was protected,' Bernard says of Armstrong's years of cheating. 'I don't see how it's possible otherwise.'

On screen, Armstrong speeds to Pantani's back wheel and, with absurd ease, takes the lead. It's his best performance on the climb, the doped alpha at the peak of his powers, a blur as he passes the Simpson memorial, Pantani sprinting in his wake to hang on.

'... All the symbolism of those toxic years is present here, in this image,' says the voiceover, although some may argue that there is just as much symbolism in the showreels of Virenque, Landis, Rasmussen, Hamilton and all the others, raising their arms, fists pumping, pointing to the sky, during those 'toxic years'.

Cut back to Merckx, at the same spot, now pedalling like a weary cyclotourist, reaching for a non-existent lower gear on his downtube, all his earlier *puissance* drained, his face as haggard as the most unwashed Tour-weary hack on the final road transfer to Paris.

A little over a kilometre from the summit, wearing the now defunct and late lamented combine jersey for the best-performing rider across all classifications, Bernard, the spittle swaying from his chin, emerges through the crowds. The Frenchman leads the Pantani–Armstrong EPO train by just over 30 seconds. With 700 metres to go, he is still the quickest, but by just 20 seconds. Watching his own performance 26 years later, in a studio in Paris, Bernard's eyes widen.

Armstrong accelerates again and Pantani loses ground, but then, oddly, at the moment when he should make the kill, the Texan relents a little.

Bernard's flushed face is a picture of pain as he mauls his bike against the gradient and closes on that loathsome final right-hand bend. 'I never collapsed,' he insists as he watches his younger self impassively. 'I climbed at my own pace. Between Chalet Reynard and the summit, I never lost time.'

As Armstrong continues to monitor Pantani, the gap to Bernard stretches to 50 seconds – and stays there. The Frenchman crosses the line, having climbed from Bédoin to the summit in a time of 58 minutes and three seconds. He is the quickest of the five, spanning a 40-year timescale.

'*Écoute* ... I've won the Ventoux twice!' he says, beaming. 'I've just beaten Pantani, Merckx, Virenque.'

'Bernard's performance over the last kilometre is incredible,' says Gárate. Perhaps, too, that shortest stage distance is a decisive factor, but set against that is his 1987 equipment, second oldest after Merckx in 1970.

Further down the mountain, and now beyond the Simpson monument, Merckx pedals on. The Belgian finishes in third place, taking 61 minutes and 42 seconds for the ascent. Gárate, riding 39 years later, is eight seconds slower. Beyond the finish line, Merckx pulls on a rain cape and appears close to passing out. For all the fireworks from Armstrong and Pantani, it is Merckx's performance, in that 29-stage Tour with no rest days and on equipment little changed since the 1950s, that is the most resonant.

Virenque, at the climax of the longest stage of the five, a stage some 200 kilometres further than Bernard's time trial, finishes almost six minutes behind Bernard, in 63 and 50 seconds. He is the slowest of the five. Predictably, though, he is still eager to put a positive spin on that outcome. 'That day I beat Lance

Armstrong, who wanted to win at all costs. It's my favourite climb and I pulled off a special ride ... *Et voilà* ...'

And Armstrong, who crosses the line just behind Pantani, after sacrificing victory by making a misplaced peace offering that even now, nearly two decades on, still rankles? Well, even in virtual cycling, Lance still can't conquer the Giant ...

Of the five, there's little doubt that, set in context, Merckx is the 'king' of the Giant. Stage winner in 1970, second in the 1972 stage of the Tour to the summit, more than any other rider he consistently managed the Ventoux's capriciousnesss. His first experience of the Ventoux came in Paris–Nice, climbing up from Sault. 'But in 1970, I also recced the Tour route for a Belgian radio station, so that every day, before the stage, they would play my comments on the stage. The first time was hard, that's for sure, but people had warned me about it.'

On a stifling July afternoon in 1972, he also climbed the Ventoux, but this time from Malaucène, on a 207-kilometre stage from Carnon-Plage to the mountain's summit. 'There's a big difference between the two climbs,' he says. 'Malaucène is not easy either, but it is more like other climbs, more Alpine. The main difference is that from Bédoin, once you get to Chalet Reynard there is no protection.'

After the dramas of July 1971, Merckx's great rivalry with Luis Ocaña of Spain was expected to be the 1972 Tour's focal point, but the Spanish climber had failed to dent Merckx's aura of confidence as effectively as in the past. The Belgian, riled by the suggestion that he had only won the 1971 Tour after Ocaña crashed in the Pyrenees – a suggestion which had more than a grain of truth to it given that Ocaña's lead over Merckx had eclipsed eight minutes – was out to prove a point.

The Ventoux's north face offered Ocaña a fresh opportunity to attack. As the leaders arrived at the foot of the 21-kilometre climb, Merckx's team, riding at 50 kilometres an hour, took up the pace. But it didn't deter the Spaniard, who accelerated four times. Yet Merckx contained every attack. Instead, it was Bernard Thévenet who profited. 'Bernard took the opportunity because Luis and I were watching each other,' Merckx remembered. 'I got away from Ocaña but it was too late.'

Thévenet's win on the Ventoux was all the more remarkable given the severity of his earlier crash on the seventh stage as he descended the Aubisque in the Pyrenees. That bang caused a temporary bout of amnesia, although he still managed to make it to the end of the stage. After a check-up in hospital, Thévenet raced on.

The opening kilometres on the Ventoux climb, ridden yet again in a mid-afternoon *canicule*, had left Thévenet breathless. 'Merckx and Ocaña set a crazy pace at the bottom,' he said. 'It was either let go or explode following them. I sat up a little and then, further up, got back in contact.'

In the final kilometres, Raymond Poulidor also tried his hand, but it was Thévenet, dropped earlier on the climb, who took advantage of a lull to accelerate clear. He rounded the last bend of melting tarmac, overlooking the Ventoux's steep north face, the hills of the Drôme spread out far below, to announce himself as a contender.

French journalist Antoine Blondin, writing in *L'Équipe*, described Thévenet as 'the revenant'. Merckx came in 34 seconds behind him to take second on the stage, with both Ocaña and Poulidor cut adrift in the final kilometre. 'Thévenet went, but he went too late,' Merckx said. 'I came back on Thévenet's wheel – okay, I didn't win the stage because I was riding to win the Tour – and Luis and I were watching each other too much.'

Nonetheless, it's a performance only two summers after his lone win, on the Ventoux's south side, that Merckx remains fiercely proud of. 'Luis never beat me on the Ventoux,' he says in Ghent. 'OK, Thévenet was good, but he was not better than me on the Ventoux.'

Eddy Merckx prefers to avoid the subject of doping. His attitude is no different when the subject is broached in Ghent. Perhaps he's keeping a pact with the dead when he blames Tom Simpson's demise on business interests and a lack of training, rather than showing any willingness to discuss amphetamine abuse. Perhaps also it's too close to home and this man, now in his seventies, doesn't want to desecrate the golden memories of his youth.

Doping controls were instigated for the first time in the 1966 Tour de France. The following morning, as the race left Bordeaux, there was a rider protest, with much of the anger being directed at race doctor, Pierre Dumas, even though then Tour director, Félix Lévitan, had described the inaugural tests as 'an honour'. There were three positive tests during Merckx's career, in 1969, 1973 and 1977. He has always maintained he was a clean rider and that anything found in his system was not there through his own volition.

His positive test for amphetamines in the 1969 Giro, when victory seemed assured, mirrored Pantani's experience. Amid accusations and recriminations, he was kicked off the race in tears, his expulsion triggering questions in both the Belgian and Italian parliaments. With a one-month suspension mooted, it also threatened his participation in the 1969 Tour de France. But Merckx, the biggest star in the sport, was semi-exonerated after the UCI decreed that he had not knowingly doped. The positive test was upheld but the ban lifted, enabling him to start that year's Tour.

In the aftermath, Merckx did nothing to defuse the explosive conspiracies, the allegations against rival teams, dope testers, the Giro organisers and even the public. 'The Italians can't be trusted,' he said at the time. 'I should never have come here. I've won too many times here.' He maintained that he had been wronged but by 1977, when he tested positive for the third time, on home turf in Flèche Wallonne, the excuses were wearing thin.

Like Armstrong, there is defiance when the subject of doping is raised. Who are we to judge what it was like back then, with little or no anti-doping legislation or culture, no tests or sanctions? That attitude was echoed by Armstrong, when I interviewed him, almost 50 years after Simpson died. *'What do you know? You weren't in the war, you weren't in the trenches. You don't know anything about cycling . . .'*

One man who was not a rider but who was in the trenches was Tour doctor, Dumas. From 1952 until he became head of drug-testing in 1969, Dumas watched the unrestricted excesses of cycling first-hand. He tended to Malléjac when he collapsed on the Ventoux in 1955 and, on the same mountain, fought to save Simpson, 12 summers later.

During most of his time on the race, either on a motorbike or in the doctor's car, doping, although generally frowned upon, was not banned. During those years, Dumas claimed to have witnessed it all. Pill-popping, hysteria, riders openly injecting mid-race, riders blaming illness on bad fish, and an almost voodoo-esque belief in the soigneurs and their magic suitcases.

After the scare on the Ventoux with Malléjac, Dumas became increasingly aware of just how pervasive amphetamine abuse had become. 'The cyclists took everything they were offered. It didn't matter what they took, as long as they believed in it,' he said. 'If someone won a stage using a certain product, they all wanted it.

'They had no idea what they were doing. I was horrified. It all scared me shitless.'

VI

I love Corsica. The beaches are beautiful, it's always sunny and the kids love it. I've bought some land and I'm planning on building there – it's a big commitment but I see it as a long-term investment.

I've always fancied a place in the sun. Somewhere calm, warm, by the sea, where the kids can swim and Helen can relax and enjoy a sunbathe in the afternoons. It's not much to ask for, really, is it? A nice house and a nice car. Not after all those years making sacrifices, grafting on the bike.

It will all cost money. I'm not stupid – I know I have to get the most out of my racing career. And to do that, I need to show them all what I can do – then they'll realise what I'm worth.

Who knows how long I'll be a professional anyway? I'm not getting any younger and I need to make my money now, while I'm racing. I know that I have to do better in the Tour. It's all very well winning smaller races, but I've had my fill of being a nearly man. I've had too many disappointments. If I didn't have to ride it, I wouldn't, but it's the Tour that makes you a star.

The Tour is the race that earns the big money. The Tour is the race that ensures you're never forgotten, even when your racing days are over. The Tour is the race that makes a cyclist immortal. So I've got to prove I can do it in the Tour. I've got no more excuses. I can't keep saying, 'Next year I'll be better.' I'd only be kidding myself.

I mean, I can see what's going on at home, with the Beatles, Carnaby Street and miniskirts and all that. There's money to be made if you're famous. I don't just want to be famous in France or Belgium. I want to be famous at home as well. Like in '62, when they made a fuss after I'd got the yellow jersey in the Tour. There was a big shindig at the Albert Hall that winter, dancing girls from the Moulin Rouge, plenty of free drink and me up on stage, riding the rollers. It nearly brought the house down! Now, that was fun.

If you want to be competitive, you have to play the game. We're all professionals – it may look like it's fun sometimes, riding along on a sunny day, having a chat and a laugh, but it's our job too. We're paid to get results. That's how they value you.

So I have a scientific way of doing things. I look after my kit and keep it clean, because if you don't then you can easily pick something up, like a saddle sore from dirty shorts. I like a proper massage each night. Some of the lads just have 20 minutes or half an hour, but that's not enough for me. I need a lot more work on my legs than that. I'm sure it makes a big difference.

Every now and then you need a pick-me-up, a tonic or some medicine. You can't last the pace without tonics. There's a lot of twaddle talked about druggies in cycling too, but I don't worry about that.

Pills, when you need them, are necessary. A couple of Mickey Finns every now and then aren't going to hurt. And tell me where you draw the line between dope and tonics. Even the experts can't agree on that one!

But I've never taken dope. I take medical aid. There is a big difference between tonics and dope. Besides, there's not much drug-taking in cycling, not as far as I can see – certainly not as much as the TV and newspapers make out.

~

By July 1967, Tom Simpson was almost as desperate to hang on to what he'd got as Eddy Merckx was to break through. Simpson wanted to consolidate his value, to be considered a potential Tour de France winner and to ensure that he maintained the level of profile that he had already achieved. Winning the 'Course au Soleil' – the 'Race to the Sun' – in March and holding off Merckx as he did so, had shored up his standing among the best teams.

But when it came to the Tour, he knew, too, that time was running out, that his weakness in the heat and in the biggest climbs held him back. The decision to run the 1967 Tour de France on national lines, rather than as trade teams, also weakened his hand. Tour director Jacques Goddet's move separated Simpson from both of his Peugeot team-mates, Roger Pingeon and Merckx. The Frenchman became a rival, while Merckx, then just 22, watched the Tour from his home, after making his debut in that year's Giro d'Italia.

At a stroke Simpson's ambitions of a strong result in the Tour were dealt a devastating blow. He knew that a British national team had no hopes of rivalling the strength in depth of the French, Spanish, Belgian or Italian teams. Great Britain's best cyclists, willing though they were, were not equipped to deal with the rigours of the Tour.

And then there was the Ventoux, looming large on the horizon, expected to be a pivotal moment in the 1967 Tour and the ultimate immovable obstacle for a rider who suffered in the heat and at high altitude. As spring on the Côte d'Azur turned to summer, Simpson and the Ventoux, the mountain that had already driven a series of riders to a state of collapse, were on a collision course.

Long after Simpson's death, Merckx made it clear that he'd never seen the British rider as a Tour winner. 'He probably made a stupid mistake on the day,' Merckx said of his team-mate's death in Rik Vanwalleghem's biography. 'He continued to kid himself he could win the Tour. His ambition knew no bounds and he ended up paying the price for it.'

Golden Years

If the 1986 and 1989 Tours de France were notable for their intense rivalries – Bernard Hinault and Greg LeMond in 1986 and LeMond and Laurent Fignon in 1989 – the 1987 Tour was characterised by cliff-hanging uncertainty, and by the importance of time-trialling. There were 209 kilometres of time-trialling in that year's race, run over 25 stages and with five summit finishes, including the mountain time trial to the summit of the Ventoux. It was a Tour for rouleurs who could hold their own on the major climbs.

Jean-François Bernard was such a rider. He won two time trials that July, including that gut-wrenching ride on Ventoux. But 'Jeff' is remembered as a French nearly man and the first in a long line of home hopefuls – including Virenque – who flattered to deceive.

The previous year's winner, LeMond, was absent in July 1987 because he was recovering from a hunting accident, while his and Bernard's mentor, Bernard Hinault, had retired. That turn of events had opened a path for third-year pro, Bernard. Riding for the Toshiba team, Jeff had been prematurely anointed as Hinault's successor, both by the outgoing French superstar and by the extraordinary Bernard Tapie, the entrepreneur whose attitude to rider wages smashed cycling's old-fashioned salary structure.

Bernard had announced his talent by winning one of the

longest stages of the 1986 Tour, a 246-kilometre trawl across the Gard, Vaucluse and Drôme, circumnavigating the Ventoux en route from Nîmes to Gap, the 'gateway to the Alps'. He won that near eight-hour stage by three minutes after breaking clear on his own. His success was a brief distraction from the internal battle being waged within the La Vie Claire team, between its two leaders, LeMond and Hinault, as documented in Richard Moore's book, *Slaying the Badger*.

Before then, he'd been detailed to ride for his leaders, whatever the circumstances. The trouble was that nobody in the team could agree which leader to ride for. At least, Bernard says, that Tour was never boring. 'The night of the time trial in Nantes, LeMond ate a Mexican meal with his wife, instead of staying in the hotel with the team,' he recalled. 'The next morning he had dreadful diarrhoea. The doctor gave him something to stop it, but it didn't work, he couldn't keep anything in.

'There was no question of him abandoning, because he was supposed to be there to win. So for the whole of that stage, I was detailed to stay with him.'

LeMond's glass stomach was well known in the peloton. He was also stricken with the same malaise during the 1989 Giro d'Italia. 'It was running down his legs and he had to stop four times to go, and every time we had to chase back to catch the peloton.'

LeMond, already on edge due to his broken relationship with Hinault, somehow made it to the finish, but it didn't end there. 'It stank,' Bernard said. 'Luckily, nobody shared a room with him. He was frightened of sabotage so he kept his bike in his room.

'That's how bad things were. Hinault died laughing at the whole thing, but kept it quiet.'

Tapie, meanwhile, was luxuriating in the soap opera and relishing the publicity.

Described as a 'French Donald Trump', although his lustrous

head of dark hair had no need of hairspray or a comb-over, the extraordinary Tapie was part Alain Delon, part Terry Venables — an olive-skinned, chameleon fixer, once a singer, once a soccer magnate, once a convict, once an actor, once a clothing manufacturer, once a politician. Tapie didn't have much time for cycling's old-school niceties. He wanted to make money, grab airtime and, most of all, win.

His blind ambition was encapsulated by LeMond as he described the time, after a Tour stage in 1984, that he was summoned to the Frenchman's hotel. 'I saw this beautiful girl, like a Bond girl, arrive on a motorbike at our hotel in Alpe d'Huez,' LeMond remembered. 'She said: "Greg LeMond? Come with me — Monsieur Tapie wants to meet you." It was like something out of a spy film.

'She took me to the La Vie Claire hotel on back roads, so nobody would see us. Tapie was waiting for me with Hinault. He showed me a prototype Look pedal and said: "You're going to earn more than you can dream of . . ."'

LeMond signed with Tapie's La Vie Claire team soon afterwards.

Tapie didn't renege on the outlandish promises he made to his riders. When Jeff Bernard took his solo stage win in Gap — a mere sideshow to the drama unfolding between his team leaders, LeMond and Hinault — the entrepreneur offered to buy him a gift. 'As a laugh, I said, "I'll have a Porsche!" He moaned a bit but then he said, "Ah, OK." In November, the Porsche I'd asked for turned up . . .

'Tapie made cycling more media-friendly,' Bernard said. 'At the 1986 team presentation, we had spotlights, dancing girls . . . Usually it was just a bunch of suits and Daniel Mangeas [French cycling's answer to Phil Liggett] reading out your results.'

In a sport dip-dyed in old-school chauvinism, Tapie was also an unlikely feminist. Told by his team *directeur sportif* Maurice

'Momo' Le Guilloux that any attempt to put Madame Tapie in the team car would be blocked by the Tour's organisers, Tapie responded: 'Oh yeah? We'll see about that ... I promise you that if she isn't in the car, we're quitting the race and going to Club Med.' Dominique Tapie spent the day alongside Le Guilloux, untroubled, in the passenger seat.

Tapie was an innovator. He was a globalist, happy to sign up little-known Americans and Canadians and to borrow influences from contemporary culture. Look-style pedals soon became standard and the La Vie Claire jersey, based on the systems art of Piet Mondrian, was distinctive, funky and remains, even now, much loved. But by the 1987 Tour, there had been a change of scene, and not just because Hinault had retired and Toshiba had moved in as title sponsor.

Bernard's first stage win in his debut Tour, as a 24-year-old, deluded many into thinking that a successor to Hinault had already been found. The French media bought into the notion of seamless continuity, of Hinault passing the torch to another Frenchman. That left others, equally ambitious, on the sidelines. One was La Vie Claire's brilliant young American climber, Andy Hampsten, who watched the Bernard bandwagon gather momentum. 'I thought, "I'm not sticking around for the Jean-François Bernard show,"' Hampsten said later. He went on to win the 1988 Giro d'Italia, memorably leaving his rivals behind in a freezing blizzard on the climb of the Gavia.

Others saw Bernard as cannon fodder, doomed to fail, a sheep in wolf's clothing, David Moyes after Alex Ferguson. The mercurial Tapie, missing the drama and tension of the Hinault–LeMond years, was readying to move on too. 'He didn't want to hang around and didn't understand why we weren't winning any more,' said Yves Hézard, sports director at Toshiba, of Tapie's limited faith in Bernard. 'He never came to a race with me after that.'

Poor Jeff. It could have been so different for him. If he had been more discreet and a little less cocky, if he'd kept his wits about him on the road to Villard-de-Lans, he could have been a Tour de France champion, famed for a dazzling win on the Ventoux; he could have ushered in a new generation of young French talent. Instead, the line of French Tour winners ended in 1985. There hasn't been one since, just a long line of pretenders and nearly men.

So Jeff is remembered for what might have been, for one tantalising glimpse of an imagined future, high on the Giant, face creased in pain, sweatband across his forehead, drool spooling from his chin, in July 1987.

The Accidental Grand Tourist

OJ Borg, never one to sit still, wants more, more of the Ventoux. In fact, OJ can't get enough of the bloody thing. We've ridden up and down the climb numerous times, shot a sunrise and a sunset, and we've met the deputy mayor. My legs feel like pipe cleaners after climbing repeatedly through the bend at St Estève.

But there must be more, surely? So we sit in Bédoin, pondering what other content we still need for the short film he is making for the BBC on the myths and legends of Mont Ventoux. 'I'll try Caritoux again,' I say. So I call Éric Caritoux, local hero and the most famous cyclist in the Vaucluse, and this time he picks up.

'Why don't you come over now?' he says in his balletic Provençal twang, in which 'demain matin' becomes 'domanga matanga'.

'Great, and thanks Éric,' I say. 'Where exactly . . .?'

He gives me precise directions. 'You know where the road from Flassan drops down towards Villes-sur-Auzon and there are some vines running uphill on your right with a small *chemin* leading to a *borie*?' he says, as if this is as well known a spot as the Place de la Concorde.

'*Ah! Oui* . . . yeah – I know . . .' I say a little uncertainly.

'*Ça marche?*' says Éric. '*C'est OK . . .?*'

It turns out, in fact, to be perfect. After we head south across the vineyards and olive groves running below the dreaded virage at St Estève and quickly arrive in Flassan, we find Éric among the vines, and film him chatting as the sun goes down on the mountain – his mountain.

Caritoux, the surprise winner of the 1984 Vuelta a España, is as much a part of village life in Flassan as the flurries of snow in early January, the tar-melting heat of August, or the wafting woodsmoke of November. Tucked into the southerly slopes of the Ventoux, with expansive views across the Monts de Vaucluse and on towards the Rhône valley and the distant Luberon, Flassan defines the ubiquitous 'sleepy French village' of tourist guides. The only café and restaurant, Chez Camille, is now closed, after chef Camille Stabholz ended a short tenure and moved across the Ventoux foothills to L'Entre-Pôtes in Le Barroux.

Before that the restaurant had been run by the Reynard family for 55 years and had become a local legend, famed for extremely hearty *cuisine de terroir*, such as *sanglier* stew, as well as a groaning cheese board of fetid fromage, wheeled tableside, by the rotund and red-faced maitre d'. The Reynard wine list relied almost exclusively on local cooperative-produced reds, with Château Pesquié as a top-end choice. They had no time for newer, less traditional, producers such as Château Unang or Les Amidyves, considered far too *arriviste* to be endorsed.

Since the restaurant and bar closed, Flassan has become, if it's possible, a lot quieter. But there are a few holiday homes, a primary school and, on the outskirts, a new development, which should breathe some life into the village.

As well as being home to Caritoux, the nearly forgotten French Grand Tour winner, Flassan is notable for having played a pivotal role in the development of New Labour. In a holiday home, in the summer of 1994, Alastair Campbell and Tony Blair thrashed out their grand plan for the media rebrand of the Labour Party. It was in Flassan that Campbell, against the advice of Neil Kinnock, finally succumbed to Blair's winning charm and agreed to become his press secretary.

The main road, the D217, snakes through the village, past the closed-up restaurant, and then begins a long, rough-surfaced climb, of long ramps and broad hairpins, winding up through the maquis and then deep into more mature woods, before joining the road over the Col Notre Dame des Abeilles, and eventually dropping down to Sault. It was here, on this cracked old road, on the flanks of the Giant, that Caritoux first learned to climb. He knows the back roads around the Ventoux, and on through the Vaucluse, almost as well as the lines on his face.

Éric sits among the vines, talking Ventoux, childhood memories of cycling through the Vaucluse, the never-resolved spats with Laurent Fignon, and his lifelong love for this bucolic landscape, its cherry orchards, vineyards and olive groves sheltering in the lee of the mountain. After a few minutes, his brother-in-law Bruno arrives, with a bottle of Côtes du Ventoux, cuvée Caritoux. They open the bottle and Éric turns the wine gently in the bowl of his glass, dipping his hook nose towards it and breathing deeply.

Behind him, the white rocks at the summit slowly turn auburn in the setting sun.

Éric Caritoux's a middle-aged man now, but you can still sense the wiry build of the professional racer who won the Tour of Spain, and many other races, beneath the jeans and the fleece jacket. His résumé, of 30 race wins during a long career, is impressive. It includes the Vuelta in 1984, and twice the championship of France, in '88 and '89. In fact, the first race he ever won was on the Ventoux, when, famously, he beat Fignon.

Caritoux should have been a bigger star than he was, but he raced in the shadow of Hinault, Fignon, Bernard, Madiot and the others, even though on the Ventoux, at least, he often had the better of them all. He first tackled the Ventoux, riding as far as Chalet Reynard, in 1971, when he was 11. 'I was a schoolboy from Flassan, riding an eight speed,' he remembers. 'My mum and dad drove behind me, and I only had to put my foot down once.'

His 1982 Tour de Vaucluse win, on the roads he'd ridden as a boy, was snatched from under the nose of future Tour de France champion Fignon, in the decisive time-trial stage from Bédoin to Chalet Reynard. It was a startling performance. Also relegated by almost two minutes in the time trial was Swiss climber Urs Zimmermann, who went on to finish third overall in the 1986 Tour de France.

Fignon, beaten by a little-known French amateur from the CC Carpentras club, was enraged. 'He accused me of being paced by a motorbike – we barely spoke to each other again,' Caritoux remembers. As it turned out Caritoux had the last laugh. A year later, having turned professional, he rubbed the Parisian's nose in it once again, beating him on the Ventoux by an almost identical margin.

Now, Caritoux lives a simple life. Since he retired from racing, he has done some corporate work – driving guest cars for Tour promoters ASO and telecoms sponsor Orange, or guiding tourists over the Ventoux – but he's happiest tending to his vines, producing table grapes. He was working in the vineyard in the spring of 1984, a second-year professional on a break between races, when a phone call came that should have changed his life. 'It was May, and I didn't have any races lined up. I was working in the vines, at the foot of Ventoux, when my grandmother called me in. "It's Monsieur de Gribaldy!" she said.'

'De Gri' – or 'le Vicomte' – was the boss of Caritoux's Skil team. Jean de Gribaldy had an instinctive eye for talent. He'd already signed a rough-and-ready Sean Kelly, after turning up, unannounced, at his parents' farm in Ireland with a contract in his hand. Kelly was *le Vicomte*'s star rider, Caritoux a useful young apprentice.

'De Gri told me to get to Geneva and fly to Málaga because I was racing in the Vuelta – the Tour of Spain,' says Caritoux. But Caritoux was bemused. 'I thought we weren't racing?' he said to de Gribaldy.

'I've changed my mind,' his boss told him brusquely. In fact, the race organisers had threatened de Gribaldy with a hefty fine if he and his Skil team, even without Kelly, didn't show up.

Caritoux's last-minute dash to Spain came after the usually indefatigable Kelly, weary after a gruelling spring that had included wins in Paris–Nice, Paris–Roubaix and Liège–Bastogne–Liège, cited fatigue and withdrew. Having already shown what he was capable of by winning the Ventoux finish at Chalet Reynard in that March's 'Race to the Sun', Caritoux might have expected more support. But 'de Gri', whose relationship with Kelly was intense, merely saw the Vuelta as an obligation to be fulfilled.

Caritoux was worthy of more respect. He had become a renowned climber. When it came to the Ventoux, he was acknowledged among French riders in the peloton as peerless, particularly after an amateur career in which he had always shone when racing over the Giant.

The fifth day of the 1984 Paris–Nice was a split-stage day, something almost unheard of in modern stage racing. A short and intense morning stage, from Orange in the Rhône valley climbing to a finish at Chalet Reynard, was followed by an afternoon stage from Sault to Miramas, in the Bouches-du-Rhône. Only 64 kilometres long, the morning stage to Chalet Reynard drew the Caritoux fan club to the snow-covered verges of the Ventoux's lower slopes, expecting springtime fireworks. Their local hero didn't disappoint.

Almost within sight of his home in Flassan, the 23-year-old

forced the pace through the forest on the steepest ramps above St Estève, pulling away with Kelly, Robert Millar, Hinault, Fignon, Phil Anderson, Steven Rooks and Stephen Roche on his back wheel. When, in the closing moments, he realised that team leader Kelly's overall position was secure, Caritoux took his chance, clawing back Millar's lone attack and outsprinting the Scot to claim the stage.

In a '*Course au Soleil*' controlled by Kelly, but best remembered for Hinault's swinging right hook to a protesting naval-yard worker's grizzled jaw on the stage to La Seyne, Caritoux had proved his worth on the Ventoux's most fearsome section – from St Estève to Chalet Reynard. Despite that, he was still seen as a poor substitute for Kelly by both de Gribaldy and the Vuelta organisers. But the last thing cash-strapped de Gribaldy wanted was to be penalised by one of the organisers of the three Grand Tours. So Caritoux became *de facto* leader.

'He was on his uppers,' Caritoux recalls of 'de Gri'. 'So he had to get us to the start. And he didn't even show up – it was his assistant, Christian Rumeau, who was sports director.

'They told us: "The result's not important." We just had to be there.'

With that motivational masterclass ringing in their ears, it's no wonder perhaps that Skil lost four riders almost as soon as the Vuelta began. But Caritoux, the unsung climber from the foot of the Ventoux, chose to bide his time. 'Pedro Delgado came into form in the second week,' he says, of the Spanish climber, 'and I followed him all the time.'

The seventh stage of the 1984 Vuelta included four climbs and climaxed on the Alto de Rasos de Peguera. It was there that Caritoux played his hand, attacking against expectations, to win the stage as Delgado took the race lead. Yet still Caritoux remained under the radar. Stage 12 climbed to the Lagos de Covadonga summit finish. Race favourite Alberto Fernández, now expected by Spain to make his move, went on the attack, working hard in an effort to drop both Delgado and Caritoux.

But the boy from Flassan counterattacked with Reimund Dietzen to take more time in the final moments of the stage. It was enough to put Caritoux in the race lead, ahead of Fernández and a faltering Delgado. After that, things got nasty. Caritoux's race leadership, at the expense of two Spanish favourites, bred resentment. With a top-three finish in the 1983 Vuelta and Giro d'Italia already under his belt, Fernández was relying on over-hauling Caritoux in the remaining kilometres of time-trialling.

But the Spaniard was wrong to be so complacent. 'He thought he'd be able to get rid of me easily in the time trials, so he'd got his team to neutralise the racing. But that suited me – by that time I had hardly any team-mates left to help me,' recalls Caritoux.

The Frenchman, in those pre-Google days, made the most of being an unknown quantity. His form in time trials remained unheralded, at least in Spain. 'When the Spanish journalists asked me what I was like in time trials, I told them I was pretty rubbish and that I had no chance.' Caritoux's bluff was swallowed whole. When it came to the first 'race of truth', on stage 14, he kept the overall lead.

Again there were consequences. During the time trial, Caritoux was punched and shoved by spectators and then pelted with rotten fruit. Some even tried to shove umbrellas into his front wheel. At the finish, he needed a police escort to and from the presentation podium. Even then he refused to be intimidated. 'I was 23 – I didn't have any real sense of how dangerous it was,' he says.

When the threats failed, other tactics were wheeled out. In the final days of that year's Vuelta, Caritoux says that his team was offered 100,000 francs to throw the race. 'The Vuelta champion in those days won just 40,000 francs,' he says. 'We got together and decided, as a team, to turn it down. I thought that winning the Vuelta was priceless.'

Delgado hadn't become as defeatist as Fernández, though, and attacked in the final real mountain stage, to Segovia, launching a last-ditch attempt to overhaul Caritoux's overall lead. Controversially, Italian star Francesco Moser joined the chase with Caritoux, helping to reel in the attack, and the Frenchman's lead remained intact.

He started the Vuelta's final 33-kilometre time trial with a 37-second lead over Fernández. Caritoux kept his nerve and held on to win overall, by a mere six seconds after 3,593 kilometres of racing. It remains the slimmest winning margin in Grand Tour history.

Back home, Caritoux's victory was greeted with muted celebrations. He remained in the shadow of both Fignon – who took his second Tour de France later that year as Caritoux, riding for Kelly's interests, finished 14th – and Hinault, at that time a curmudgeonly sleeping giant. Despite his Vuelta win, Caritoux was not hailed as a star.

Nor was he as media-friendly as either of his better-known compatriots, who, it has to be said, loved the attention. Caritoux was a man out of time. His bashful peasant demeanour, his thick accent, his love of his vines, didn't play well with metropolitan France in the mid-1980s. Instead, it was Fignon, the urbane Parisian, twice beaten on the Ventoux by Caritoux, who was the man to watch. He came within a hair's breadth of winning the 1984 Giro, but through a combination of gamesmanship and bias – which included a TV helicopter hovering ahead of him in the final time trial – lost out to the same Moser who had lent Caritoux a helping hand in Spain.

Hinault, meanwhile, was desperate to be top dog in France again and had yet to learn to bite his tongue. 'I race to win, not to please people,' he said, unaware that the occasional show of panache, which came in his final Tour in 1986, would endear him to the public just as much as a major win.

The mid-1980s remains the last dominant period of French cycling, exemplified by the bitter rivalry between Hinault and Fignon and the rise of protégés such as Jeff Bernard, whose career was defined one afternoon on Mont Ventoux.

Caritoux played his part in that tradition, even if he was largely overlooked. It's still a little tragic that so few remember Éric Caritoux, the peasant lad called to the phone from the vineyards of the Ventoux by his gran, a champion by accident, just to save his boss's face.

Near the end of Éric Caritoux's career, there was – predictably – an amphetamine-related doping scandal, dating back to his time track racing, after a police raid at the Six Day race in Paris–Bercy in 1986. Yet according to Willy Voet, later to become soigneur to the infamous Festina team led by Virenque, when Caritoux – who looked after Voet's children following the Belgian's arrest during the Festina Affair in July 1998 – won the Vuelta in 1984, he was not 'using anything'.

In modern cycling, mention of natural talent is often greeted with a roll of the eyes, but if any rider can properly claim that his ability was shaped by his environment, it's Caritoux, born and raised on the slopes of the Giant. Even so, his Vuelta win was almost considered a fluke. Yet he was sixth overall the following year, and went on to ride 12 Tours de France during his career.

Now he is back at the foot of the Ventoux, looking after his vines and orchards and running holiday homes hidden away on the slopes south of Flassan. Helped by his brother, Jean–Claude, he took on his family's land as soon as he retired, in 1994. Now the emphasis is on table grapes and cherries. 'Our wine grapes lost 50 per cent of their value in ten years,' he says. 'It was better to adapt.'

The Caritoux cycling tradition has continued. Éric's daughter, Kim, already a cycling prodigy before her teens, raced for the local Christophe Vélo Club in Montfavet, named after former Tour legend, Eugène Christophe. By the time she was 14, Kim was good enough to ride in the French National Championships, but given her father's pedigree, and that of her mother Nathalie, also an accomplished rider, that was hardly a surprise.

Meanwhile, Kim's father still rides his bike, still climbs the mountain that he first rode up as an 11-year-old. The Ventoux is still 'his' mountain, still a climb apart. His analysis of the Ventoux's enduring appeal is pragmatic. 'Compared to other climbs,' he says, 'you have 15 or 16 kilometres of climbing, without any let-up. Apart from Chalet Reynard, where there are 300 metres of flat road, it climbs all the way from St Estève.

'Depending on how fit you are, you put it in a 21, or 23, and don't really change gear until you get to the top. On many other climbs, you get a couple of kilometres of flat road, or some false flat, or even a little descending. On the Ventoux there's no chance to recover.'

Perhaps unsurprisingly for a native of Flassan, Caritoux rates the southern ascent ahead of the north side.

'Coming up from Bédoin is harder. But there's not much between them – it's almost as bad from Malaucène. You start at 300 metres above sea level and, in 21 kilometres, you climb to 1,909 metres altitude.

'From Malaucène, there are some harder sections and others where you can really move up through the gears. But there's nowhere to recuperate on the south side, and that's the big difference.'

And the road up from Sault? Caritoux is dismissive. 'That's

on the big ring, at least up to Chalet Reynard. But coming up from Sault? That's just so you can say: "I climbed the Ventoux."'

By the mid 1990s, the language of the Tour de France had become as theatrically overblown and grandiose as its ethical malaise had become ingrained. Unnerved by the lack of champions, French media coverage inflated histrionically the vain hopes of Virenque, Laurent Jalabert, Luc Leblanc, Christophe Moreau and many others.

There was little public talk of doping, at least not in print. There may have been no certainty of who was using what, but there was plenty of speculation. Yet winning performances were mythologised, and riders were glibly described as heroes or legends, not just in the French press, which had a tendency to romanticisation – a particular citation here for Virenque's tear ducts – but elsewhere too.

The period was characterised by some of the most tedious Tours, when the robotic and dead-eyed Miguel Indurain time-trialled his rivals into the ground. These races were almost wholly devoid of suspense. It speaks volumes that, ten years after LeMond had become the first English-speaking winner, it was a bald Dane, Bjarne Riis, previously best known as one of Fignon's domestiques and using EPO as freely as Coppi used amphetamines, who ended the Indurain years.

There was a Ventoux stage in the 1994 Tour, although the finish was not at the summit of the mountain, but in Carpentras. The winner was an Italian lead-out man, known for his abject climbing, whose imposing physique made him the least likely winner in a stage over the Giant.

On a searing afternoon, Eros Poli, at six-foot-four the tallest man in the Tour peloton, rode alone across the Rhône valley until, eventually, as the villages of the Vaucluse fell away behind him, he turned left at St Estève and began climbing towards the summit of the Ventoux. The pain wracked the Italian's chest and he closed his eyes in an effort to contain it. Poli was riding so slowly that he could hardly bear to look down at the computer on his handlebars. When he did, and saw his speed drop to single figures, he was gripped by a crippling panic. 'I thought I was dying,' he says now as he remembers the day that changed his career. 'I'd never ridden so slowly before.'

But this was not a funeral, this was a rebirth. Poli, lead-out man to sprinting superstar Mario Cipollini, and a mere *passista*, as he puts it, was reinventing himself. Against all odds, Eros won on the Ventoux proving romance wasn't dead.

Poli was the unlikeliest of mountain goats. Instead, all eyes were on his compatriot Marco Pantani, who had burst to prominence only a few weeks earlier, exploding the race in the mountains during the Giro d'Italia. Poli's breakaway to the foot of the Ventoux was the latest in a series of attacking efforts that ultimately won him the *Prix de la Combativité* – the combativity prize – for that Tour.

'It was between me and Pantani,' he remembered. 'I think I beat him by one point.

'I was in a breakaway three times, first on the stage from Rennes to Futuroscope, about 18 minutes ahead at one point, and then with Thierry Marie, on the stage in the Pyrenees over the Peyresourde, Aspin, Tourmalet and to Luz Ardiden.'

Perhaps, then, Poli attacking in the mountains wasn't quite so unusual after all. Yet nobody would ever have expected that the break that would finally stick, right to the finish line, would be his solo ride over Mont Ventoux. As he admits, Poli was 'very good' at leading out star team-mate Mario Cipollini in the sprints, but he also acknowledges that he'd be the first one 'crying in the mountains'.

It was a good day for an Italian to pull off a surprise win.

Only hours earlier Roberto Baggio had ballooned his penalty kick over the crossbar, costing Italy any lingering hopes of victory in the 1994 World Cup final. I was watching the match on a giant screen outside a bar in Montpellier's Place de la Comédie. As Baggio's penalty sailed into the sky, tables and chairs flew through the air, hurled in rage by a handful of holidaying Italians.

The morning after that disappointment, Poli said that his largely Italian team was, understandably, down in the mouth. 'Everyone was in a bad mood. It was too hot in our hotel and some guys had even taken to sleeping on the terrace. It was a brutal Tour that year.'

Poli's lone breakaway, over the summit of the Giant, to Carpentras was 170 kilometres long – a rare feat, particularly on such feared terrain. Would such an attack be possible in the modern era?

'It's hard to repeat that, but it's possible when it's very hot – and that day it was 42 degrees,' he said. 'In heat like that, the peloton doesn't want to race fast. They prefer to take it easy for as long a time as possible. Maybe they made a mistake in their calculations, though, that day.'

Yet this was still the most prestigious race in the world, and one of its most coveted mountain stages. Even so, Poli's solo attack was almost a mistake. 'It was a counterattack and I got the gap in a few seconds. They tried to catch me for about ten kilometres, but it was so hot that they needed to sit up and drink. And they let me go.'

Once he'd broken clear, Poli, unworried by his isolation, settled into his effort and found his tempo. 'I rode a 100-kilometre time trial,' he laughs. 'I didn't wait for anybody; I didn't need another rider. When it's flat, I don't need company.'

Poli says that he 'loves' riding in hot weather. 'The first part of the stage was flat, rolling road, so it was fine for me. I'd calculated that I needed 25 minutes at the bottom of the climb. I knew I'd lose about one minute a kilometre.'

Nonetheless, when he got to Bédoin and began climbing, Poli started to worry. 'It was very bad. I was too slow.' Worse was to come at St Estève, when any lingering optimism quickly evaporated. 'For the first time in my life, I saw my speed drop to single figures. That was the worst moment. I was thinking: "I'm going to die; I can't climb the Ventoux like this. This is impossible." But I tried to keep calm.'

Another limitation was his weight combined with the archaic gearing ratios. 'The cassette on my gears was a big problem. The maximum gear was 24 sprockets – now they come with 27, or 28, but at the time everybody was riding 39 at the front, 24 at the back.'

For a couple of kilometres, Poli recalled, his speed was eight or nine kilometres an hour – 'a very low speed. Then I found a rhythm. They kept reminding me how big the gap was and telling me that it would get better further up. But I was very tired and the change of rhythm was so hard. I needed time to recover, but on Ventoux there is no place to recover.

'I knew I had a lot of power, though. Every time I watch it again I think: "OK, I'm suffering but I'm looking good. For a guy my size, it's not so bad."'

For the biggest rider in that year's peloton it wasn't bad at all, but the clock was ticking. Poli, riding at half the speed of the pursuing group, knew he had to keep going. 'The flatter part just before Chalet Reynard gave me a little confidence because it was easier. Then when I got to that last bend, the switchback before the top, well, it was uh-ma-zing!'

As he rounded that final bend, Poli almost stalled, but, hunched over the bike, he ground his way to the summit and, protecting a four-and-a-half-minute lead, headed back down the other side towards Malaucène. From the top to the finish line in Carpentras, in the usual location, the Allée des Platanes, was about 42 kilometres.

'It was a great feeling to get over the top. I knew I needed more than two minutes to make sure that, in case I had a puncture, or if they were able to see me in the distance, they wouldn't catch me.'

Far behind Poli, the gruppetto, or the bus – the group of domestiques and sprinters who band together and pool resources during each mountain stage – was making its way up the lower slopes. Phil Anderson, Max Sciandri and Raul Alcala of the Motorola team, exhausted after an afternoon working for their Colombian leader Alvaro Meija, were riding in the gruppetto when a dispute broke out between Alcala and Australian rider Neil Stephens.

According to Anderson, his compatriot was so anxious about the time cut – the point at which the prospect of elimination loomed large – that he went to the front of the gruppetto and upped the pace. 'Stephens lifted the tempo and you could see the group start to splinter,' Anderson recalled. Alcala was less than pleased and rebuked Stephens, but he and the Australian ended up standing in the road, halfway up the Ventoux, fists flying in the baking heat. Luckily for them, no race commissaires or TV motorbikes spotted the brawl and they went unpunished.

Poli meanwhile, with the Alps on the horizon and the Drôme laid out far below, had launched himself into the descent. 'It was very fast. And, with me, plus the bike, I was heavy – well over 100 kilos . . . I think I was doing nearly 100 kilometres an hour, maybe about 95, 97 was my top speed.'

Not for a minute did he think to take it easy. 'No, no – I had no fear. I didn't need a helmet! I was racing my bike – doing my job.' Winning in Carpentras was, he says, 'the best'.

'I was usually the last one over the line on a mountain stage.

So it was great to be first, to have the fans there for me, waiting for the winner.' As he crossed the line, Eros had time for one last grand gesture, spreading his arms theatrically and bowing to the crowd.

'It was a spontaneous thing – like I was on the stage at La Scala in Milano.'

Eros Poli is in his early fifties now, and divides his time between his home in Verona and acting as a guide for upmarket holiday brand, InGamba, in locations such as California, Arizona and Vancouver. Cycling remains at the heart of his existence. 'I ride a bike every day,' he says, 'even when it's below freezing. I ride for fun and to keep healthy, because I love to eat and drink.'

There are no 170-kilometre lone breaks involved, though. 'No,' he laughs. 'My maximum is two or three hours, no more.'

He rode the Ventoux twice in 2015, on both occasions with guests from InGamba. 'Both times it was from Bédoin, but once I came up from Sault. But Bédoin is the one – for me, the climb of Mont Ventoux is from Bédoin. I'm not bothered about climbing up from Malaucène.'

These days he's planning other spectacular sorties, including three days riding from San Francisco to Santa Barbara on the Pacific Coast Highway. 'I spend some time in Arizona working for InGamba, and sometimes we go to Santa Monica. I design the trips and guide with the guests.'

There are two critical dates in Poli's career, a decade apart. He cherishes his gold medal from the team time trial in the 1984 Olympic Games and his victory ten years later, on Ventoux. 'They're the two biggest days in my career.'

Poli and his team-mates had just one glass of champagne that night. 'We still had to get through the Alps. The next stage was over 200 kilometres, to Alpe d'Huez,' he smiles.

'My legs felt like a piece of wood the next morning. They

gave me a team-mate to look after me for that stage but I was still the last rider to arrive at Alpe d'Huez. But all the fans had waited for me, to clap and cheer. That was really nice.'

After his win on Ventoux, Poli – the Giant's giant-killer – became something of a people's favourite. 'Every day after the Ventoux, I had a TV motorbike following me over each mountain. *'Eros Poli has passed the top of the Galibier, Eros Poli has crossed the top of the Glandon . . .'*

Until America came calling, Poli had been thinking about moving to the Vaucluse, maybe to set up a small bed and breakfast in Malaucène, and ride the Ventoux with his guests. 'Now I'm too busy with InGamba, but maybe I'll go back one day,' he says, a faraway look in his eyes. 'Maybe when I retire.'

While always keen to remind people of his Olympic success, Poli says he enjoys talking about the most famous moment in his road racing career. But he might not have had his chance had it not been for the absence of Mario Cipollini, the flamboyant leader of his Mercatone Uno team, not that he of the hundred nicknames and smutty jokes would have had any interest at all in the Ventoux. Cipollini played up to his playboy image throughout his career. There were the endless boorish boasts of mid-race sexual conquests – don't come a-knockin' when this team bus is a-rockin'! – and an arrogance that was more suited to a prize fighter. 'Super Mario' was cycling's Tyson Fury.

'An orgasm lasts a few seconds, a victory lasts for ever,' he once said, a motif which is perhaps the lothario's response to Lance Armstrong's 'pain is temporary – quitting lasts for ever'.

Cipollini's total disdain for mountain stages also ensured that he never finished the Tour de France, much to the irritation of the race organisers, although he did manage to complete the Giro d'Italia. It also guaranteed that, unlike Poli, he managed to spend a significant amount of July, oiled up and ready for action, on the beaches of Tuscany.

The Americans

It's autumn 2015. Jet-lagged, I'm wide awake in a Texas hotel room, long before dawn. I shave, take a shower and surf the TV stations, pausing at the Weather Channel. It may be cold in the hill country, the rooftops outside flecked with dew, but it's already snowing up north, in Utah, icing up the canyons and the buttes. I peer out at downtown Austin through the curtains, and lean against the window frame, staring red-eyed at stop signs towering over empty streets.

Across South Congress Avenue, a shapeless figure shuffles slowly up the sidewalk, pushing his possessions in a shopping trolley. Slowly, the world turns, until the familiar pale light emerges, the rays hit the mirrored glass and the cityscape comes into relief. By the time I get out, heading downtown, the Texan sun is up and firing.

I walk a few blocks. There's a vast shop selling boots and only boots. 'God Bless Our Drones', says a sticker in the window. Further on, there are hip slacker cafés, with Talk Talk playing, where I sit and drink flat whites and kill time. Just like 20 years earlier, when I first went to Austin to interview Lance Armstrong, there's a lot of waiting around. I keep on walking until I cross the Colorado river and arrive in the streets near the Texan Capitol, where they held a ticker-tape parade when Armstrong won his first Tour de France. That, however, was a lifetime ago, in a different reality.

Since his prime-time confession to doping, Armstrong and I have been back in contact. For a long time there was a wall between us. A lot had been said, most of it uncomplimentary. I was a Judas, who had once, as he endured chemo, been a trusted confidant, but who later became the snake with arms, blacklisted, mocked, reviled.

My sense of betrayal was no less acute. I'd believed in his comeback for the first Tour win, but lost faith absolutely during the second. I grew to loathe the dumb myth and the grating denials, the sight of him and his entourage inducing a churning frustration in my guts.

His confession broke the dam. I no longer saw a duplicitous, bullying fake. I had witnessed that for long enough to have wearied of it. Instead, I saw him lost in self-justification, scrambling, desperate and damaged. Lance had been the king of a sham world; his new one, however, was all too real.

I carry on walking, a little aimlessly, before heading over to West 4th Street, to Mellow Johnny's — *maillot jaune*, you see? — the Armstrong-owned high-end bike shop. This is where they still sell you the dream — and where it doesn't matter whose version they're peddling. It's a ground-floor warehouse building wrapped around the street corner. There, hanging on the wall, are seven yellow jerseys. There, in the racks of clothing, bikes and accessories, are all the key brands.

In Lance's shop, you can buy products from Trek, Nike and Oakley — all of whom washed their hands of him after his confession — and Rapha, sponsors of Team Sky, those champions of zero tolerance. These are uneasy bedfellows at the best of times, but their presence, and a poster of a jubilant yellow-clad Lance, ten foot high, looking down on them all from a nearby wall, perfectly sums up cycling's dysfunctional history.

Downstairs, his former US Postal team-mate Kevin Livingston runs a training and fitness practice. On display are a lot of the famous bikes – the World Championship-winning bike, the Flèche Wallonne bike, the first Tour win bike, the Alpe d'Huez-winning bike and so on. But there is no Mont Ventoux bike. That's because Lance never won there. For all his determination, for all his firepower and for all his doping, he never really 'got' the Ventoux.

Ironically – and the more you think about this the odder it becomes – the one time he could have conquered the Giant, sentiment got in the way and he 'let' somebody else – Marco Pantani – win.

Lance Armstrong – the bully, the win-at-all-costs alpha male, the über-competitive, Mister Stop-at-Nothing Lance – decided to let another rider win. How the hell did that happen?

The cab driver who picks me up from South Congress, to drive me across Austin to Lance Armstrong's house, hates cyclists. 'Look at this guy,' he says in disgust as a crusty teenager on a BMX weaves around in front of us. 'Do you get this in England?'

We cross the Colorado river and make a left. 'There's a lot of mansions where you're going,' he says. 'Better make sure we get the right one.'

Ten minutes later, I'm standing in front of a grand house, set back from a leafy avenue, three, maybe four cars, SUVs, jeeps, parked in front. If these are reduced circumstances, it doesn't look that painful.

This, then, is Lance's house. I have a realisation that, given our shared history, knocking on this particular front door seems a very odd idea. But then life is short and people can change – surely you have to believe that? And I have come a long way to do this. Still, I hesitate for a moment, mulling over the past.

There is a rush of memories that makes my head spin – of everything and everyone from Willy Voet to that duel with

Pantani on the windswept Giant; from every dope-addled rider and protestation of innocence to Floyd Landis and Riccardo Riccò, and every circular conversation and think-piece and libel meeting and dinner table argument.

I steady myself and then knock. Seconds later, grinning as if nothing ever happened between us, Lance Armstrong snatches open his front door.

'Hey – where'd you get all that grey hair from?' he drawls, his own salt-and-pepper crop clear to see.

'Writing about you,' I say as we shake hands.

He's trim, even gaunt, in baseball cap, body warmer, track pants and trainers. Just like in 1996, only back then his cap hid the baldness from chemotherapy and the scars on his head from surgery. We walk through to an open-plan lounge and kitchen, kids' shoes scattered around, an NFL game on a big screen in the background. There's some art on the walls, maybe not as much as there once might have been, but he's clearly still a collector.

'Peace offering,' I say, as I hand him a coffee table book on links golf. He's just back from playing in the desert near Phoenix. Lance Armstrong, golf nut.

We sit and he leafs through the book. His hair is flecked with grey, his eyes lined and tired. He seems diminished. Later, though, when we talk in depth, the jaw still juts defensively and he bristles with the same defiance. I prattle on, edgily, about playing backwards out of pot bunkers, and tackling blind tee shots on the wild, impossible courses on the west coast of Ireland.

'Let's go get a drink,' he says and then we're out the door on foot, heading to a local bar, no minder, no agents, no bodyguards, no entourage. So we walk and we talk, but I am struggling to match the Lance Armstrong I knew from Tour de France finish lines, tense press conferences and angry exchanges in confrontational interviews, with the grey-haired, laid-back, middle-aged man walking beside me.

It's a ten-minute stroll, past grand houses, some grander, even, than his. He can walk here, untroubled. Nobody accosts him, no passing cars screech to a halt. There is no lynch mob.

'Look at these hipsters,' he whispers slyly, as some typical Austinites, head to toe in seventies vintage, smiling beatifically, walk towards us.

'Hey, how ya doin'?' they say as they pass.

Do they recognise him? Does everybody recognise him, but just not flag up the obvious?

'People are really nice, you know,' he says a little later, as if surprised. 'I've learned that.'

Since The Fall he says he's seen the best and worst of human nature. Some people who he thought would always be his friends ostracised him, while others, some of whom he didn't expect much of, hung around.

'People lean in or lean out,' he shrugs.

I tell him I went to Mellow Johnny's, and ask why his shop is selling the brands – Oakley, Trek and Nike – that championed him but then dropped him.

'I don't have any choice,' he says.

We reach a restaurant, with an upmarket bar attached. They know him here. 'Hi's' are exchanged, hands shaken, as he walks in. He's reserved two seats at the bar. While he does the rounds, I slip onto the furthest of the pair of bar stools, set aside in the darkest corner. After a couple of minutes he joins me.

'C'mon – don't do that to me, Jeremy,' he says and moves me aside. We swap places and he settles down, hidden in the shadows. The baseball cap stays on.

We order margaritas and, in my jet-lagged state, they slide down easily and hit my head pretty quickly.

There are times when Lance Armstrong's whole history reads

like that of a character from a James Ellroy novel of modern Americana, a great sweeping romance of dysfunction, washed-up dreams, battered beauty, and lost last chances. Lance is now a mythical figure, a two-wheeled Icarus. But he's also a survivor. He hates any philosophising, any metaphysics or semantics, any intellectualisation of his downfall.

'Sanctimonious bullshit,' he will say if you veer into this territory. He has time for defiance but little for self-pity.

Ultimately, it is his fault, nobody else's – he did it, he fucked up. Shoulder the blame, be a man. Don't get cute. There are winners and losers in life. This time he lost. He knew the stakes; he knew the form. *They all did.*

Apologise yes, but, for fuck's sake, get up. Have some self-respect. Don't mope. Don't be a pussy. Don't crawl around crying, begging forgiveness.

And after all the hand-wringing self-justification I have had to listen to from dopers over the years, I respect him for that.

So we catch up, ending a 15-year sulk, free of any animosity, talking about having kids, the state of the US bike industry compared to the boom time in Britain, rising rents killing the art scene on Austin's East Side. We talk about the meetings he's had – with former soigneur Emma O'Reilly, whistle-blower Christophe Bassons, and ex-professional Filippo Simeoni – 'Simeoni said that every day somebody came into his café and mentioned my name to him – *every day!* I feel so bad about that.

'But at some point I have to stop saying sorry,' he shrugs. 'How many times is enough?'

It will never be enough, I think.

We order more margaritas.

He has many pet gripes: those in the press who've profited from his downfall, the ongoing negotiations with USADA over his lifetime ban, and the 2009 Tour, in which he insists his third place was clean and that retrospective tests will prove it, but, he says, 'Nobody wants that proven ...'

His phone flashes and, suddenly, it's time to go: the family's calling. We head out to the street. Out of nowhere a car appears, to drive him home and then take me back to my hotel. After Armstrong is dropped off, the car heads across town and the driver, a young guy, starts chatting. 'I'm still a real fan,' he says. 'I just didn't want to say anything.

'Everything is so slanted against him, all the coverage in the media – I mean, I saw those films – they're so biased, just raking over the bad stuff. When I think of all the money he raised, all the good he's done for Austin ...'

Quickly, we're past the State Capitol, through the stop signs, across the mighty river and back in South Congress, outside the door of the hotel. I climb out of the car and then realise I should have tipped, but when I turn around, he's already gone.

It's the small hours back home. I'm half-asleep before I reach the door of my room. My head hits the pillow and I'm gone.

Yes, I know.

I know what you probably think of him, and I can guess what you think of me, for even talking to him. After the way he behaved, after the way he treated people. How can I let him off the hook so easy?

The one certainty about doping scandals is that the athletes always pay, while the 'system' – the collective of bureaucrats and administrators, promoters and sponsors, coaches and managers – survives to live, work and sell another day. That's why Nike, Oakley and Trek are still cashing in on the Armstrong name, from sales of their products in Mellow Johnny's, just a few blocks from the site of those ticker-tape receptions, in downtown Austin.

The UCI has never accepted culpability for any doping scandal. Even though it runs cycling, the governing body would have you believe it is powerless and blameless when scandals occur, just as they were with Simpson in 1967 and with Merckx in Savona in 1969, with Festina and 1998 and Puerto in 2006.

Name all the scandals, list all the corruption and cover-ups – from Armstrong and the UCI, through to Blatter and FIFA, the Russians and the IAAF – and it's clear that the business of sport is so conflicted, so compromised as to be seemingly incapable of self-regulation.

To me, the truth is pretty banal: Lance Armstrong was not the devil in Lycra, just as he was never Jesus on a bike. He was an opportunist, embittered by serial rejection during his youth, who grew to embody the ethics of the landscape he inhabited. He learned that cycling was a lawless sport and that there were no boundaries: so he exploited that, just as others exploited him. He fought like a dog to get into a position of power and then fought like a dog to defend all that came with it.

I don't think he needs to apologise to any promoters, to any journalists, to any sponsors. They were all part of that 'system'. His remorse should be directed at those he gave false hope to and those whose careers were damaged or ended by the culture he embodied. His paranoia and cynicism damaged his peers, many of whom were less well-equipped to protect themselves.

But he was as abused as he was abusive. Ultimately, when the moment came to exile him, he proved as disposable as any rider caught in that culture. 'Lance Armstrong has no place in cycling,' Pat McQuaid said, as if the UCI, after all the years of sitting on its hands, was fit to pass judgement.

The backlash – the ongoing 'crucifixion' of Armstrong – has been as absurd, overblown and self-serving as the canonisation ever was. In fact, the continuing obsession with him plays perfectly into the hands of those who still want their own true histories obscured.

How can ASO excise him from the record books, when

Bjarne Riis, Marco Pantani, Erik Zabel and all the others remain enshrined, cited as champions? How can the great and good in athletics – Steve Cram and Seb Coe – sit back and mock cycling's traumatic history, while they have failed to clean up the chronic corruption within their own sport? How can Trek, Oakley, Nike ditch Armstrong but then profit from sales of their merch in his bike shop? How can the UCI wash their hands of responsibility, when all the evidence they needed to investigate him was always on their doorstep?

At the heart of all this, at the heart of the broken Legend of Lance, at the heart of the doping that blighted the careers of Malléjac, Simpson, Pantani and so many others, is corrupt governance. To my mind, this long-standing dysfunction – allowing hypocritical, cynical administrators to grow fat and wealthy from the exploitations of others – is far worse than individual cheating. It is far worse than anything Lance Armstrong ever did.

Two days later, we meet again. Once again, we walk from his house down the same leafy avenues to our lunch table. There, he settles into a chair on the deck and stirs the crushed ice in his 'Arnold Palmer'. 'It's an ice tea with lemonade,' he explains. 'The John Daly is an Arnold Palmer with vodka. But I've never had one. I like vodka but it doesn't sound that good.'

Once again, I'd sat in the wrong place. Once again, he insisted we swap. He wanted his back to the door. And, yes, the cap stayed on. Armstrong says he's not anxious, not paranoid, even if a Jimmy Kimmel special could be dedicated to him reading out 'mean tweets'.

'People are perfectly decent,' he maintains. 'I've never had anyone get in my face. Nobody hassles me. I mean, sometimes you get the sense that they might want to, but people are nicer than you think.' In Austin, at least, it seems that Armstrong can relax.

'I don't think that many people have read the books or seen the documentaries. I think the percentage is remarkably low. They might have read an Associated Press story, *USA Today* or the *New York Times*, but not the books.'

Even so, his televised confession to Oprah Winfrey in 2013 opened a trapdoor beneath his feet. He says now that he was unprepared for the repercussions and the ensuing free fall. 'My business manager, Bart, has a perspective on the Oprah interview that I think is pretty spot-on. He says that for the diehard cycling fan Oprah didn't say enough, didn't burn anybody or name names, but that for most people, it was way too much, because all they heard was blood bags, EPO, doping.

'It was either not enough or too much,' Armstrong shrugs. 'In the end, everybody was pissed off.'

So why do it then, why do it that soon?

'I was going to get sued by *everybody*. I was going to get deposed and they were going to ask those questions a thousand times. That's why I did it. I'd rather do that, bad as it was, or bad as it ended up, somewhat on my terms. If I'd done it in a deposition, they would have just leaked it, so you'd have had this grainy video, where they're really being dicks, just hammering me, and then that gets leaked to the world. I didn't want it to go that way either.

'The thing I'd say now, and that took me years to understand and that I didn't understand then, is that Oprah came too soon.

'I was stuck. I wanted to get it out of the way, but it was too soon, it was still too fresh, and I hadn't worked through it all in my own head. I still haven't.'

Armstrong soon learned that in professional sport, everyone's your best friend – until you're damaged goods.

He shrugs again. 'I've learned who my friends are. I knew when it was all going on that a lot of people were there for the party, there for the ride.'

And for the money, I say . . .

'Some people surprise you that they ran – you're like, "What a dick!" – but then others surprise you when they lean in. "Hey, I'm still here – what can I do to help?"

'So you see the best and worst – you get both sides of it. And there are still people I can count on . . .

'The innocent ones had a genuine sense of betrayal,' he acknowledges, 'but the people that knew, the people who now act appalled – there's a special spot in hell for those people. To turn around and act so appalled . . .

What about UCI Presidents Hein Verbruggen and Pat McQuaid? Hein always had your back, I say. I had run-ins with him about you . . .

'Yeah, but what was Hein gonna do?' he says dismissively. 'Go to 1997. What do you do? You know that everybody's using EPO . . .'

He stares at me. 'What do you do?' he demands again. For a moment I can't believe that he's standing up for the UCI.

– *But Verbruggen was so weak, I say. He was running the sport, he*—

– 'Okay, so what's strong? Tell me strong,' he interrupts.

– *I don't know exactly. I wasn't president of the UCI. More though – much more than what he did*—

– 'Okay, smart guy,' he says, a hard tone to his voice, 'what the fuck would you have done?

'So let me tell you: there was nothing to do. We now know all these guys operate the same – the UCI, the IAAF, FIFA. They're sitting on this stuff thinking, "If we nuke this, our sport is burned to the ground."

'They would have known what happened to me, they would have seen what happened to the sport – total meltdown. They'd go, "No way – you're not messing with our equity." That's what they'd say.'

*

Lance Armstrong climbed the Ventoux in the Tour de France, the Dauphiné Libéré and, although not all the way to the summit, in Paris–Nice. But as his list of victories elsewhere grew, success on the Ventoux repeatedly slipped from his grasp. Meanwhile, upstart team-mates and rivals – Jonathan Vaughters, Tyler Hamilton and Iban Mayo – blew him away. The Giant looked on, taunting him.

'I consider the Ventoux the hardest climb in France,' Armstrong says. 'I don't think anything compares. Alpe d'Huez doesn't compare, the Pyrenees don't compare.

'People ask me: "I'm going to France – what's the hardest climb?" and they expect the answer to come from the Alps or the Pyrenees, but the answer lies right in the middle.'

No matter the stage wins on other famed climbs – the Alpe, Sestrières, Pla d'Adet, Plateau de Beille, Luz Ardiden, La Mongie – the Ventoux always eluded him. 'Nothing really compares in terms of difficulty. I mean, Alpe d'Huez is steep, but every two or three minutes you get a ten-second window when it's essentially flat, when you go through a switchback. So you get a little bit of recovery, but the Ventoux is truly relentless.'

Armstrong, like almost every other rider, cites the turn at St Estève as the decisive point. 'The run up to that can be really nervous, and windy sometimes, with everybody fighting for position. St Estève is to me the real start of the climb, and then the next milestone is Chalet Reynard, where the trees end.

'After Chalet Reynard, it becomes a completely different climb,' he says.

Perhaps that's why, I suggest, the telling attacks in recent years have come before Chalet Reynard?

'Oh *really*?' he says sarcastically. 'Attacks? I didn't know there were any attacks in cycling any more. The Tour is boring. The coverage is boring, the racing is boring – there are moments that are exciting, but 90 per cent of the time they're just sitting there, riding through France.'

Like others before him, Armstrong found the Ventoux a stifling, breathless environment. 'For whatever reason – and at two thousand metres at the top it isn't that high – but it always felt like it was four thousand metres. The air even *looks* thin. I'm no scientist but there's something about the air up there …

'The other thing that's always a factor is the wind. It's so exposed. There's something going on there, but I tell you, it's my favourite climb. Plus I love that area, below the Ventoux. It's pretty special.'

Long before they scrapped their way to the summit of Ventoux in the 2000 Tour, things were not good between Armstrong and Marco Pantani. But what happened on the mountain that day only made things worse.

Tyler Hamilton was riding for the US Postal Service team defending Armstrong's overall lead, pace-setting on the Giant's lower slopes. 'My stage ended before we reached Chalet Reynard,' Hamilton said. 'Kevin Livingston and I were switching on and off, but I think Kevin had a better ride that day.'

Hamilton led into the bend at St Estève, kicking hard as the gradient increased, with Livingston on his shoulder and Armstrong just behind. Within seconds of Hamilton's acceleration, the field had disintegrated. 'Once you take that left-hand turn at St Estève and it kicks, you quickly realise where your legs are. You don't know until you get there, but you soon find out. From there it just goes, and goes, and goes, all the way up.

'You come out of that bend,' Hamilton says, 'and it's like a bomb has gone off in the peloton. It's either: "Thank you! I have good legs", or the immediate realisation: "I'm not gonna be able to hang with these guys."'

Hamilton, jersey unzipped almost to the waist, face creased in pain, led the peloton through the forest. 'We were switching that whole Tour on who'd be the last guy riding for Lance,' Hamilton recalled. 'I burned my matches before Kevin.'

So high was their tempo that US Postal had already reduced the lead group to just six riders, well before reaching Chalet Reynard. As ever, Armstrong focused on controlling Jan Ullrich's one-paced diesel. Ullrich, for all his power, he could handle, but the American never liked the jumpy, snappy climbers, their unpredictability and volatility. That afternoon, Armstrong was wary of two: Roberto Heras of Spain and, of course, Pantani.

As Armstrong's group closed on the summit, he thought Pantani had cracked. He hadn't expected the familiar shaven head to reappear at his shoulder on the upper slopes, and then to attack. There is a dark Darwinian beauty to the extreme battle, high on the Ventoux, between Armstrong and Pantani in those final kilometres as they raced diabolically to the summit, goading each other, haring blindly past the Simpson memorial, unheeding of history, in a crazed culmination of Generation EPO's excesses.

It was repellent and dysfunctional but, in many ways, it was compelling too. Both of them later paid the price: Pantani's public humiliation as his career nosedived was nothing compared to the sordid death that almost destroyed his family. Armstrong's athletic successes were dwarfed by the loathing, scorn and detestation heaped upon him and his family after his downfall. For somebody who had once enjoyed Christ-like status, it was a long-drawn-out crucifixion.

But there was a twist that day. As they neared the summit, Armstrong realised he could show some solidarity with the Italian, offer him an olive branch, somehow make amends for Pantani's own humiliation when he was thrown off the 1999 Giro d'Italia in the crucifixion at Madonna di Campiglio.

Pantani, the instinctive climber, the *artiste*, beloved Italian icon, the posturing prima donna, who would die of addiction within four years, battled against Armstrong, his nemesis, the all-powerful but unfeeling radio-controlled Robocop, cold, pragmatic, scientific. It was here, close to the summit, that Armstrong chose to offer Pantani redemption. As they sped towards the top, propelled and then buffeted by a gusting Mistral, the Texan drew alongside the Italian and called out a few words.

'I said, as best I could in Italian, "*Tu vince, tu vince*" – you win, you win – meaning that he could have the stage, but that wasn't what he heard.'

Maybe the Mistral snatched the words away and threw them into the valley below. Maybe Pantani heard them but chose to ignore them.

'I had a pretty commanding lead overall, so I felt it was OK for him to win. After everything that had happened to Pantani, I thought it would be a generous thing to do. But Eddy Merckx was right when he said it at the time – and I know now – that you never give away the Ventoux.'

Pantani, fighting to hold Armstrong's wheel as they rode on, thought the American was patronising him. 'He took it as derogatory,' Armstrong says, 'as if I was telling him he was too slow.

'But who knows what he heard – it was windy, and it's the heat of the battle in the middle of the Tour de France – it's just frenzied.

'I certainly didn't tell him to go faster – we were already going fast enough. But he took it as an insult. He wasn't the kind of guy that wanted any handouts, or any charity.'

There was little time in 2000 for sentiment or gestures, no time at those speeds and in that wind to doff a racing cap in memory of Tom Simpson, or to contemplate the past, as they climbed beyond the spot where he had died. As they rode through and beyond the brutal final right-hand bend, Armstrong hung back a little, so Pantani could move ahead and cross the line first. Even now, sitting having lunch in Austin's suburbs, the memory gets under Armstrong's skin.

'At the time it wasn't a major disappointment, but looking back now,' he says, 'we should have just fought it out and sprinted for it . . .'

Almost immediately after the stage finished, the war of words began. Armstrong was patronising, the Italian said, and he, Pantani, didn't need charity. 'Pantani does not need Armstrong to give him a victory,' he said, grandly.

Pantani was, Armstrong responded, a 'shit-stirrer'.

'No more gifts,' Lance said ominously.

When I remind him of that, Armstrong smiles, a little embarrassed by the memory. 'Look, our relationship was never very good. I think primarily we didn't get on, but there was also a lack of communication – he didn't speak English, I didn't speak Italian.

'I mean, even if you could speak his language, my sense was that he would have been a hard person to communicate with. That's not a criticism: he was just a complicated guy, but then, having said that, so am I. Put the two of us together, throw in a major language barrier, throw in a rivalry, and it's a recipe for not working out.'

Yet both of them wanted to somehow be reconciled. The next spring, brought together by Italian sportswriter Pier Bergonzi, Armstrong and Pantani met at the 2001 Tour of Valencia. 'We went out and tried to sort things out, but Marco was a volatile guy. I admired his star quality, but, in the end, I didn't really care if he liked me or not. I was on my own schedule and whether he was upset or not . . . well . . .'

Armstrong pauses. 'But when I was in France for the Day Ahead ride, in the summer of 2015, Bergonzi called me and said that Marco's mum would like to meet with me. I was pretty surprised. Not trying to be a dick or anything, I said, "Why?" I was puzzled.

'Bergonzi said, "She'd like to meet you, she cares about you, she'd just like to talk to you."'

And maybe there was a memory too of a July day on the Ventoux, when, on the mountain he most feared, Armstrong clumsily tried to forge a bond with her troubled son, only for it to be misunderstood.

'I tried to sort out some flights and tried like hell to get to Italy,' Armstrong says, 'but I couldn't make it work. But if I get back over there again, I'd like to meet with her . . .'

I eat half-heartedly, too engrossed in the conversation. We talk some more, mulling over the scandals enveloping football, athletics and tennis. 'Maybe people are at the point now where, if they follow any world sport, they realise that what they were sold is just not true,' Armstrong says.

He has little time for those who insist that he has still not apologised adequately to his peers, or to ex-colleagues and journalists who he maligned. 'The famous ones I've made amends with – every one of them. Not one of them can say, "He's not reached out to me, he's not apologised to me" – whether that's been through an apology or a settlement.

'Even David Walsh. Amends were made,' he says, citing the two-million-dollar settlement with the *Sunday Times*. 'I only bring that up because on his "victory" tour, it's the first thing Walsh comes out with – "Lance hasn't apologised to me yet."'

So, if he emailed you and said, 'Let's have lunch . . .'?

Armstrong seems flummoxed by the idea. 'Just lunch? An off-the-record lunch?' There's a long pause. 'I don't see why not – it wouldn't be my first choice of a lunch date. But why not? Jeremy, at this point, I have no fear.'

Armstrong remains dismissive of the journalist often credited with fuelling his downfall. 'It wasn't, it was Jeff Novitzky,' says the American of the federal agent who first pursued him. 'Without Novitzky, none of this happens. Everybody needs to stop taking the credit because there's one person who deserves the credit, if credit is the right word – Jeff Novitzky.

'He had the power of the badge and the gun,' he says, banging his fist on the table. 'Badge on the table, gun right here. After that, they're fucking singing. Journalists can't do that, David Walsh can't do that, Travis Tygart [CEO of USADA] can't do that. But when a federal agent says, "I wanna hear everything and if I don't like what I hear then you're looking at jail time" – then he got a lot, quickly.'

Didn't you ever worry?

'Worry?'

Yes – when it was all going on, when you were all on the programme – that somebody might slip up, that somebody might make a mistake?

'No ...'

But a lot of people knew.

'Yeah – and maybe we were too loose on that. But that's the nature of cycling. Nine riders on the team, 30 staff at the Tour – people leave and change teams, they get mad, they get upset ... You can't control all that.'

So you relied on them keeping quiet, on the power of the *omertà*?

'Honestly, it didn't cross my mind. I didn't worry about it. Maybe we should have considered that more.'

You were very loyal to a lot of people ...

'Yeah, and I still am.'

Loyalty is a big thing for you.

'Yeah, of course. It matters to me big time.'

Isn't some of that loyalty misplaced?

'I'm very loyal to Johan [Bruyneel]. I don't know if that's good or bad for me – I don't care. I love him . . .'

You *love* him?

'Like a brother. He's a great man. He's the greatest coach in the history of sports. Fact.'

I struggle not to laugh in disbelief. Lance, I say, people would fall off their chair to hear you say that . . .

'I don't care,' he replies, with that all-too-familiar fuck-you attitude, and then catches himself. 'Anna says I say "I don't care" too much.

'But,' he continues, 'they weren't in the war, they didn't race with him, they didn't race under him, they didn't race against him. What do they know? They don't know anything about cycling.'

For all his defiance, Armstrong seems finally to be aware of the impact of his confession on those who, for years, had supported him.

'All those people who had my back – they had to sit there while the others came back and said, "Hey, how do you like your boy now?" They felt like idiots. That's a heavy burden to carry and to live with. They're all I care about.'

But then he rails, too, against the perception that his success was solely attributable to doping. 'Travis put that out there. That upsets me. It's just not true. Travis had three or four key messages to pound home – most sophisticated doping programme in history, greatest fraud in the history of sport, he forced young men to put dangerous substances in their body – all of which is untrue.'

So your team-mates willingly doped? You didn't stand over them telling them to dope?

'*Me?*' he says incredulously. 'Of course not!'

And you didn't foster a culture where that went on?

'No – the sport fostered that culture. You had a substance,

EPO, that was so good,' he continues. 'And if they have an equivalent tomorrow, that was undetectable, everyone would be on it.'

None of his peers, he says, see him as a cheat. 'All these depositions – Floyd, Tyler, Andreu – they all admit, "He was the best, he was the toughest, he was the hardest-working, he was the most motivating."

'For those seven years our story was: we train harder than anybody else, we are more organised than anybody, we have better tactics, a better team, more reconnaissance, better technologies, wind tunnels, equipment . . .

'That was all true, but we just didn't mention the last part.'

But surely the last part – the doping – was the biggest?

'*No!* Of course not – the last part *wasn't* the biggest part. It would have been if nobody else had it, but everybody had it.

'So now that's been flipped. They say: "He told us it was the training, he said it was this and that, but now we know." But the idea that we just sat around and then doped and won the Tour is not true.'

You always thought that the riders weren't respected enough, that they were cannon fodder – that cycling was very amateur . . .

'It still is,' he says. 'It's getting worse. The business model is hardly a business model. The crashes are getting worse – all the road furniture – all that shit makes bike racing dangerous. It's good for traffic; it's not good for bike races.'

Does the lack of status of the riders fuel doping?

'Of course it does. The riders don't feel any sense of investment. Their only sense of investment is in their contract. When that's up in a year, or two years, they ain't got shit. So until they have proper equity in the sport, the guys are gonna be tempted – they'll look around and think, "It's every man for himself."'

'Every man for himself.'

Like Tom Simpson, I think, fending off Eddy Merckx, fighting to retain his status, doing anything to get over the Ventoux, desperate for a good result, desperate to keep his place in the firmament.

The Ventoux was Lance Armstrong's first long climb in the European peloton, his first real experience of the mountains.

'My first time on the Ventoux was Paris–Nice in 1993, when we climbed from Bédoin up to Chalet Reynard. Armand de Las Cuevas was crushing it. But I stayed in the front group, which was a big deal to me.'

But after 1993, almost every time Armstrong rode the Ventoux, it threw up questions and dilemmas. Riding the Dauphiné Libéré in June, his all-too-frequent misfires on the Ventoux only fuelled anxieties over his form for July. 'If you said, "Give me the top three regrets of your career", then not winning on the Ventoux would be one of them.'

Worse, team-mates like Jonathan Vaughters and Tyler Hamilton were climbing the mountain faster. 'Other than the day with Pantani, Lance definitely struggled on the Ventoux,' Hamilton says. 'The team and Johan tried to break down all the different reasons why Lance wasn't ever as good there. I remember once there was an idea that there was less oxygen up there, because of fewer trees – but I don't know what it was.'

Armstrong dismissed the suggestion that his serial disappointments on the Ventoux were down to abortive doping programmes. 'No – it was the hardest mountain, but there are plenty of other divisive and dynamic climbs. I mean, they're all hard,' he said. 'The Ventoux didn't require doping any more than any other climb.'

For a while, a long while, the preppy Hamilton was the alter ego to Armstrong's trailer-park street kid. Tyler came from the right side of the tracks, Lance definitely didn't. It was cycling that threw them together. As team-mates at US Postal, they lived close to each other in Nice. They trained together, pushing each other, harder and further. And they shared their 'Poe' – their cache of EPO – as they pursued doping in pursuit of excellence.

Once, in the summer of 2000, I met Hamilton at his Nice apartment, overlooking the corniche roads of Villefranche-sur-Mer, and then drove behind him as he rode over to Armstrong's apartment. I'd been to Armstrong's house before, drunk coffee on the terrace, so got out and began to follow Hamilton to the gate. 'Better wait here,' he said sharply, as he saw me step out of the car, an uneasy look in his eyes.

It took a good ten minutes for him to reappear, with Armstrong in tow. I thought little of it then, but now I wonder: were they doing 'Poe' while I sat in a hire car, waiting on the street outside?

Earlier that summer, when Hamilton won the Dauphiné stage to the summit of Ventoux and left his team captain well over a minute behind, the cracks in their relationship began to show. As Armstrong struggled further to overcome his Ventoux hex, Hamilton's apparent ease became all the more irritating. 'Lance was in yellow,' Hamilton recalled of that afternoon in June 2000. 'I had to be there on the climb and cover all the attacks. I remember that day was probably the best legs I ever had there.'

With less than a month to go until the 2000 Tour started, this was also the day when Armstrong was supposed to shine, a key test on his road to winning form. 'I kept waiting, covering attacks until we got above the tree line. I was waiting for Lance to come up, but that never happened.'

Behind him, flagging on the Giant's upper slopes, Armstrong was yet again found wanting. 'About one kilometre from the finish,' Hamilton recalled, 'Johan came on the radio and said, "You're good to go."'

Still uncertain, Hamilton used the radio to check with his team leader. 'Go – *just fucking go*,' came the blurted response.

'So I attacked,' Hamilton says. 'By the finish I was cross-eyed. It was definitely harder to breathe up there. By the time I got to the top, it felt like I was breathing through a straw.'

But within minutes of stepping down from the podium presentation, he knew that the dynamic within the team had changed. As talk of Hamilton as a future Tour contender gathered pace, Armstrong distanced himself. 'There'd been some rumblings before that. There was talk the year before, during the 1999 Tour, when I finished quite high. Winning on the Ventoux, winning the Dauphiné – now that was a big deal.'

For Armstrong, another underperformance on the Ventoux, so close to that year's Tour start, cut deep. 'Lance is a competitor,' Hamilton said. 'That day bruised his ego. It was tough because he was trying to win. It changed things between us. I could tell when he climbed on the bus that he was pretty bummed out.'

All the more extraordinary then, in the light of that disappointment, that when he had the chance, little more than a month later, to win on the Ventoux, to add the mountain he rated the hardest in France to his list of stage wins, Armstrong backed off.

Given the many and varied pan-European locations in which, over the years, I have spoken to Jonathan Vaughters, it's a little anticlimactic that when we do finally sit down to talk about the Giant of Provence, it's in the Holiday Inn, at Westfield Shopping City, in east London. But, hey, this is modern globalised cycling. Yorkshire is now as legendary as the Alps, Qatar as coveted as the Koppenberg. Not every interview is conducted on a hotel terrace in Mallorca, Liguria or the Côte d'Azur, as the sun sets over a dappled Mediterranean. Sometimes you just have to make do with sitting in a beige dining room picking at an all-you-can-eat buffet.

Vaughters, now CEO of the Cannondale-Drapac team, is one of the leading lights in the modernisation of cycling, a key figure within Velon, the collective of leading teams seeking to build a new business model for world cycling's top teams. Yet he's also resolutely quirky. His Twitter feed is a mashup of in-jokes and irony, fishing references, fart gags and wine expertise. It inhabits a corner of social media where Bart Simpson collides with Friedrich Nietzsche and Oz Clarke. Possibly.

He sits opposite me, bearded, elegantly frayed, and a little bleary from his flight to London from Denver. We had planned to meet in Whitechapel and seek out the best balti in the East End. Sadly, Jonathan's jet lag got the better of him, so here we are eating in the restaurant a few floors down from his room. He orders the Holiday Inn's finest chicken tikka masala.

'That'll get things moving,' I think to myself.

The beard and the sartorial nod towards tweedy fogeyness mark him out among the seas of corporate sportswear that dominate most major races. His eclecticism gives him the look of a professorial hipster, who's wandered into the wrong seminar. The beard also makes him seem a bigger man than he actually is, although it's true to say that he is more rounded now – in every sense – than the skinny, slightly gauche goofball with flying V sideburns who broke the climbing record for the Ventoux in 1999.

Earlier in the week, he'd dressed up as Santa for the Cycling Podcast's Christmas event. The next night he was one of a panel musing over the future of cycling at a sold-out Rapha event in Soho. He's still a little bemused by the explosion of interest in cycling in Britain. 'We'd struggle to pull off stuff like that in the States,' he says of both events.

A few years ago maybe not, but since they slayed Lance

Armstrong, well, yes, that's probably true. But it's a little ironic hearing it from Jonathan, given that he is of course a confessed doper, former team-mate to Armstrong during the glory years and a pivotal player in the infamous USADA investigation into his erstwhile team-mate which definitively debunked the Texan's iconic status.

Unlike Armstrong, Vaughters has actually won on the Giant, taking the 21-kilometre time trial from Bédoin to the summit in June 1999, during the Dauphiné Libéré. The Coloradan beat team-mate Armstrong, who could only finish fifth, to take the overall race lead. But it was a bittersweet moment and pivotal in the subsequent trajectory of both his racing career and his life.

He also won the 2001 Dauphiné time trial through the Ventoux foothills, over 43 kilometres from Beaumes-de-Venise to Valréas, beating another rider – David Millar – who was later to be a key figure in his development as a team manager. 'The day before that time trial, we'd ridden up the north side and finished in Carpentras. The north side was more difficult for me because it's a more uneven gradient. It's more punchy.'

The south side of the Ventoux, he says, always suited him better. 'It's steadier. I would think 95 per cent of riders that you speak to would rather it the other way round – they'd prefer climbing from Malaucène to climbing from Bédoin.'

Jonathan's affection for the Ventoux isn't just based on his climbing prowess. His love of Rhône wines has morphed into an obsession and, in July 2009, he was inducted into the *Echansonnerie des Papes*, a prestigious club of wine lovers centred on the Châteauneuf-du-Pape region, just the other side of the A7 autoroute, as it follows the Rhône south to the sea.

'It's not just cycling that I have a connection with,' he explains. 'They made me an *Echansonnerie*, a key holder – kinda knighted, I guess – of Châteauneuf-du-Pape.

'It's a ceremony that you get nominated for, this whole

shebang, with everyone in purple robes, but even if you get nominated you don't get the key and the robe and to be an *Echansonnerie des Papes* unless you taste and identify three wines.'

Sounds like becoming president of the UCI, I suggest. 'Hmmm, yeah, right,' he responds drily.

'One is a Côtes du Rhône, one a Côtes du Ventoux and one a Châteauneuf-du-Pape. They're all made out of the exact same grapes − slightly different soil, different temperatures − but they're very close to one another.

'And to get the key, the robe and the scroll, you have to identify the Châteauneuf-du-Pape. If you get it wrong you don't actually get a ceremonial naming as an *Echansonnerie*, it's just "*désolé, monsieur*" − sorry, bud.'

Were you nervous? I ask him.

'Shit, yeah,' he says. 'I was like, "There's no way I'm going to get this right."

'But anyways, I did and I got the robe, the scroll and the key. I like the wines from there − from that whole region. I love Châteauneuf-du-Pape and I like a good Côtes du Ventoux.'

Before the obsession with Rhône wines, though, came the obsession with climbing and the bike. And Jonathan quickly discovered that the terrain and the heat of the Vaucluse, and in particular the higher slopes of Ventoux, really suited him. 'I was always good when it was hot and dry. Higher altitude, arid − that all suited my engine better than cold and humid. It's not that you yourself go faster in the heat, it's that some of the others suffer and go slower.'

He quickly acclimatised to the Ventoux's gradients. 'I liked the dry, arid air, the lack of flat spots. It never gets incredibly steep but it never lets up. It just drags the whole time.'

And then he says something that no cyclist, professional or not, other than Betty Kals has ever said to me: 'It never intimidated me. I looked forward to the Ventoux.

'Every race I ever won at World Tour level was within 40 miles of the Ventoux. Even in 2001, when I beat Dave Millar in that flat time trial in the Dauphiné, it was around the side of the Ventoux.'

Unlike others, who tend to fall back on tried and tested clichés to describe the suffering on the Ventoux, Vaughters is more able to detail the attributes required to succeed. The specific characteristics of the climb, he says, just don't suit some riders. 'It's not for a more anaerobically explosive rider, who'd rather a climb that goes flat then steep, has hairpins, where you can really hit the steep sections hard and then recover a little on the bends. They prefer a climb where the effort level bounces around.

'On the Ventoux, you have to be dead steady with your effort. I was much better at being dead steady with my effort than I ever was at bouncing it around.

'That's why a little punchy second-category climb in the Tour of the Basque Country was much harder for me than the Ventoux. On a climb like that, I'd be suffering just to hang on to the tail end.'

Froome, he says, is also better suited to the climb than many of his rivals. 'That explosivity that Contador and Quintana have, that just doesn't suit that mountain. It's a climb for someone who can grind, grind and grind out a tempo.

'A rider like Froome can grind and grind his way up and then, in the last few kilometres, everyone hits oxygen debt and has nowhere to go. That makes it almost easy for a guy like Froome to walk away with the race.' Vaughters describes his own climbing style as closer to Froome, than Contador or Quintana.

'Ventoux was always a funny climb for me, not just the year I won on it, in '99, but whenever I competed on it. I'd always be better than I was anywhere else. I'd just be riding and I'd look around and there wouldn't be many guys left with me any more.'

Climbs like the Aubisque, Vaughters says, and specifically the Spanish Pyrenees, are a different kettle of fish. 'They're choppy climbs, the antithesis of the Ventoux. Maybe the closest thing to Ventoux would be ... well, maybe the Galibier, but not exactly.

'Other than at Chalet Reynard for about 50 metres, there's not a single flat spot on the Ventoux. It was uniquely suited to how I rode. I'd just settle into my rhythm, get to the red line and just stick it there, holding it until body parts started falling off me. Yeah, there was suffering but it was suffering where I was in the game to win.'

Vaughters held the Ventoux record, of 56:50 for the 21.6 kilometres, until Basque climber Iban Mayo shattered it by the best part of a minute in June 2004, again during the Dauphiné Libéré and, again, at the expense of a flustered Armstrong. The Coloradan's 1999 time now sits third fastest ahead of a leaderboard that includes the names Hamilton, Armstrong, Pantani and Vinokourov. Their histories of doping are now well known, which perhaps reveals more about the demands of the Giant than any verse or prose.

Vaughters, by then retired, was there in June 2004, watching Mayo take the stage win. 'I expected my record to be broken today and I expected Mayo to do it,' he said at the time. Armstrong, meanwhile, lost just under two minutes to the Spaniard.

Mayo's time was so fast that Frenchman Sylvain Calzati, dead last, finished over 25 minutes behind him, in just 22 kilometres. He and five others were outside the time limit and were evicted from the race. That performance, and particularly the whupping of Armstrong on the slopes of the Giant, made Mayo a star in Spain. Suddenly, he was a contender for the Tour. Veteran cycling writer and Spanish expert, Alasdair Fotheringham, remembers the hysteria of that summer well. 'He had the Basque cycling world eating out of the palm of his hand,' Fotheringham says. 'I still remember one Basque journalist calling me up, shouting – with no introduction – "Iban Mayo is God!" and then slamming the phone down again, without saying goodbye . . .'

Maybe Vaughters' description of his own climbing style on Ventoux also explains Armstrong's serial shortcomings on the Giant. Ventoux, so Vaughters says, is not a climb for 'bouncing around'. Steady, high-pace 'grind', as he called his own technique, was not really Armstrong's style. Armstrong liked 'bouncing around', accelerating and recovering, before accelerating again, whether it was on Alpe d'Huez, Hautacam, Luz Ardiden or Plateau de Beille. He 'got' those climbs because he knew the sweet spots; he knew where to accelerate hard and where to take a moment to recover.

Did all the doping fuel the capacity to 'bounce around', the repetition of big attacks, the high cadence, the sudden violent efforts? Almost definitely.

The only time that 'bouncing around' on the Giant worked in Lance's favour was in 2000, when he formed that unlikely tag team with Pantani. With the wind blowing over the summit and every punch and counterpunch hauling them that bit further ahead, it was no day for 'flat stick' grinders, such as Vaughters. But as Armstrong discovered, it was also a bad day to start giving out gifts.

Jonathan Vaughters' record-breaking win on the Ventoux in June 1999 set in motion a chain of events that changed his life. 'It was a weird experience in a lot of ways,' he says. 'There were a lot of things at play.

'One was that, for a very short period of time, I think Lance viewed me as an internal rival. Winning that time trial on Ventoux and beating him soundly was almost like a threat.'

Once he had taken the race lead, he says that the resentment towards him became almost comedically overt. 'Johan Bruyneel and Lance didn't really want me to win the Dauphiné and the team tactics that were played out for the next few days were subtly trying to get somebody else to win. It was an odd thing to live through.'

Vaughters, in the yellow jersey after the Ventoux time trial, held on to the race lead until the penultimate stage to Passy Plaine-Joux, when Alexander Vinokourov's attacks finally paid off. 'At that time, I was very deferent to Lance: he was Mister Alpha. I was like, "OK, if you think that's best," but years later you think, "That was the worst tactic you could possibly have employed to keep a rider like me in the leader's jersey."

'Their tactics were just nuts – and then he was still pissed off at the end of the race when I didn't win it! Like, "You let us all down . . ."'

Vaughters is quick to acknowledge the role drugs played in his success. He had experimented with doping before, in the early days in Europe, but never to the extent that he did that June. 'There had been times in my career when I had doped, but in a limited way. But that Dauphiné was the first time in my career when it had been anything and everything. It was muscled up as much as US Postal Service could do.

'I remember when I won on the Ventoux . . . If you look at the pictures, I'm sticking my tongue out and laughing. It was like, "Oh, I get it now." I'd beaten all these guys, Lance, Vinokourov, Joseba Beloki, that were almost to me untouchables.

'All of a sudden I was in the yellow jersey and I was ahead of them. I was leading the Dauphiné and I'd set the record up the Ventoux, but I was thinking, "So that's all there is to it . . .?"

'I'm not proud of that win, but at the same time, that era . . .' his voice trails off. 'From that point forward, I never spoke about that as my "best" victory in cycling. It's the best known, but I just thought it was a freak show.'

Now, after years looking up at the top table, Vaughters saw what it took to take his place. 'That day on the Ventoux I answered the question, "If I train as hard as everyone else, if I dope as hard as everyone else, am I one of the best in the world?" After that I never really felt the need to answer it a second time.

'From that point forward, I never doped as much. Yes, I did a little bit, but I never trained as hard, I was never as motivated. After I'd answered the question, if I'd continued to do it over and over again, then that's just ... greed, just gluttonous.'

Vaughters was still only 26 that summer and recalls that his disillusion with racing, stemming from that epiphany on the summit of Ventoux, took a while to take root. 'At that point I was just thinking, "I've seen the strings in the puppet show."' He pauses and then asks: 'Does that make sense?

'From that moment, it was difficult to – not to take cycling seriously – but to commit. When I left in 2002, I wanted nothing to do with cycling any more. I was done. That was three years, almost to the day, after winning on the Ventoux.

'So the disillusion was pretty quick. In fact, I still had two years on my contract with Roger Legeay's Crédit Agricole team. I basically told him, "I can't do this any more. The passion's gone. I want to go home and I don't want to come back."'

Legeay, Vaughters says, was very fair. 'He paid me until the end of the year and told me it was good that I was being honest with myself. From then on, we were better friends. I have immense respect for Roger. He's a genuine guy.'

But he hasn't forgotten the realisation that came to him as he stood on the top of the Ventoux. 'The fundamental lesson of 1999 that I have always conveyed to every athlete I've worked with since is that, despite that win, despite setting the record, I felt no pride from that win.

'I've told guys, "If you do dope you can win one of the biggest races on one of the most famous climbs and you will make a huge splash, but – unless you're a huge sociopath – you will just feel crappy about it. You might win but you will become numb to the feeling of winning. In contrast, when you win for real it's a huge release of euphoria."'

There was, he says, one final hurrah. 'When I was with Crédit Agricole and we won the team time trial in the 2001 Tour, as far as I know, everyone on that team was clean.

'That was an unbelievable feeling. We'd thought, "We're a clean team, we're going to get our butts kicked," so it was incredible. That was ten times more joyful than winning on the Ventoux.'

Vaughters says that, after retiring, he never imagined returning to the European circuit. Isolated from the scene after returning to the States, he got dragged back into cycling by accident. 'We had a junior team – 5280 – sponsored by my real estate company, kids racing around Colorado. That team started winning and we got a few more sponsors, but, I mean, I had a full-time job.'

It was technology entrepreneur, bike-racing fan and wealthy investor, Doug Ellis, who reeled Vaughters back into the European dream. 'Doug called me out of nowhere and in essence, over a couple of weeks, said we should build the next American Tour de France team.'

After meeting Vaughters in 2005, Ellis's enthusiasm for his grand plan gathered momentum. 'I kept telling him: "Dude, you're nuts – there's a lot involved and you're going to lose a lot of money and not everything is as it seems." And he said, "Well, maybe we can change that."'

So, before thinking too much about it, Vaughters found

himself heading back to the south of France. 'One of the first training camps Doug funded was at the bottom of the Ventoux.

'He gave us $100,000 and that was a great start, enough to mean we could ride the Route du Sud. So the week before the Route du Sud we had a training camp in Malaucène.'

Vaughters recalls that he loved that trip. 'We stayed at a little American-owned gite in Malaucène. We were basically camping but it was a hoot.

'I'd ride some days, motor-pace others, and then we headed to the Route du Sud. That was our first foray.'

So there's a trajectory there, I say. Of the Ventoux killing your dreams and then, a few years later, rekindling them . . .

'Yeah, in a way, that's true,' Jonathan says. 'It was beginning to bring my love of cycling back, as I had never been on a trip into that area when I wasn't just focused on my own race.

'That was the first time the Ventoux was so much more than just a profile to race up, when I saw it as a beautiful place with a beautiful landscape.'

Vaughters says that he goes to Provence whenever he can. 'In the middle of July, whenever the Tour comes through there, then I'm happy.

'Sometimes, I'll go down there with my wife and stay in a little hotel we know, close to Orange. I love that baking hundred-degree heat. There's something about it, the cicadas, the lavender fields, the scorching heat, the wine. I've done a lot of riding around there too. I'll usually ride for a couple of hours. I like the little roads, the gorges.

'For a lot of pro riders, France is the place you don't want to go to because you know you're going to really suffer, but it's the place you do have to go to to earn the decent paycheck.

'And that stay in Malaucène definitely made me think of France as a really nice place to visit, rather than this hellish place of suffering I have to go to, which is how it had been until then. When you go back and you don't have the suffering hanging over you, you think: "Wow, this place is nice ...'"

Vaughters has passed on his knowledge of the Giant to other riders: 'I have tried to give advice over the years, but the thing about the Ventoux is that it's purely physical. A lot of climbs you can say, "Well, you hit it hard here and then you back off a bit, there's a small descent," but the Ventoux's almost like an ergometer test of a mountain.

'You tell the guys: "Do everything you can – don't go into the red too early on," and that's about it.'

Vaughters acknowledges, though, that the aura of Ventoux, the intimidating scale of it dominating the Rhône valley, 'totally messes with some riders' heads', including French pros on his own team. 'A rider like Pierre Rolland, he's so ... psychological. When the French crowds are cheering for him and he's in the breakaway, all of a sudden, when you look at his power profiles, he's objectively stronger.

'When you see the Ventoux looming in the distance, you're creeping across the vineyards towards it in the peloton and then, when you hit it, it's so relentless, that totally splits his head in half ... You can see it in his SRM power outputs – his brain does not handle it. You can see little surges in power when there's cheering and applause. Then there's a little break and then another surge.'

Maybe it's a French thing for French riders, I suggest, allied to the significance of the Ventoux?

'Hmmm ... It's the opposite of how I was and how I'd ride the Ventoux. Somebody clapping for me was totally irrelevant. I was totally internally focused and he is totally externally focused.

'But you can't ride the Ventoux like Pierre, because it's so unrelenting. And that's the kind of situation when a sports psychologist might help him, you know, break it down.'

Vaughters admits that as a rider he was so focused when climbing the Ventoux that he barely registered the presence of the Simpson memorial. It's a strange admission for a man whose profile balances so delicately on the ebb and flow of the doping debate. 'I didn't even know where it was. In the races, I couldn't tell you where it was. Years later, in 2009, when Brad [Wiggins] was riding for us, I parked at the top and walked down to the memorial. That was the first time I'd seen it.'

But like so many others, Vaughters recognises the significance of Simpson. 'It's an important learning moment in the history of cycling. If you take it away, then that has a huge impact on cycling and on the attitude towards even attempting to confront doping.

'It was a moment that shaped the sport. If you're not willing to recognise what has happened, then, to use the cliché, you're condemned to repeat it.'

Vaughters' belief in second chances and in redemption – his own and those of some of his riders such as David Millar, Dave Zabriskie and Christian Vandevelde – has almost always been controversial and, as in the case of Tom Danielson's more recent misdemeanours, has also spectacularly backfired on him. In 2010, as the doping investigation that eventually led to Lance Armstrong's downfall began to gain momentum, and their Garmin team grew in profile, Ellis and Vaughters issued a statement regarding their team's willingness to assist with the investigation.

'As long as they [Garmin team personnel] express the truth about the past to the appropriate parties,' it read, 'they will continue to have a place in our organisation and we will support them . . .'

Vaughters believes that statement of intent was unprecedented. 'No team has ever said, "If you're honest, we're gonna keep you." Usually it's the reverse. I don't think Lance and Johan took that seriously, but then after some time they realised that our riders were telling the truth.'

So does Armstrong, so resentful of his team-mate's success on Ventoux in the blazing June of 1999, now blame Vaughters for his downfall?

'He does,' the Coloradan sighs. 'That's because when you had the critical mass of myself, Zabriskie, Danielson and Vandevelde' – all on Vaughters' Garmin team of former dopers and all ex-Armstrong team-mates – 'those were unimpeachable witnesses. That forced the hand of others.

'So if you take our policy away, of sticking by people even when they had told the truth, then the USADA investigation doesn't get off the ground due to the lack of federal witnesses.'

And if that happens, I say, Lance gets to keep his seven Tours de France.

'Yep, don't worry – I know that bit,' Vaughters says, more than a little wearily.

'To this day,' says Tyler Hamilton, now selling real estate in Missoula, Montana, 'I still can't believe that I won on that climb. There's the Ventoux and there's Alpe d'Huez – those two are the most prestigious.'

Hamilton says that the mountain's torrid history played its part in racking up the tension. 'You definitely feel that extra pressure, and that racing on Ventoux is a big day. There was a lot of hype about it.

'Before 2000, I'd raced it in the Dauphiné, a time trial in 1999 when Jonathan Vaughters won. I think I did a decent race – maybe top ten, top 15.' In fact, he finished ninth on the stage, more than two minutes behind Vaughters.

'I've raced it feeling good, I've raced it feeling bad, but the Ventoux is always brutal. The bottom can be pretty humid and hot, with no wind, because you're there in the trees. And the grade is just . . .'

'I always tried to hold on. You always want to stay positive, but you quickly realise, once the gradient kicks in, whether you have it or not. If you get dropped on the Ventoux, that's usually it. There's no way back.'

In July 2000 Hamilton, riding for Armstrong's bid for a second Tour win, knew what was coming. They'd prepared well – in every sense. 'We previewed the Ventoux for the 2000 Dauphiné and I'd done it before,' he remembered. And they'd doped as well, transfusing blood at the Hotel l'Esplan in St Paul-Trois-Châteaux, a 40-minute drive across the vineyards to the north of the mountain.

Armstrong and Bruyneel liked the hotel, overlooking a fountain in the Place l'Esplan. They liked the wine list too, the interconnecting rooms and the proximity to the A7, the Autoroute du Soleil, linking the Rhône valley to the Mediterranean coastline and the Spanish and Italian borders. Later, when they were dating, Sheryl Crow also joined Armstrong at the l'Esplan.

Doping, Hamilton concedes, took some of the fear of the Ventoux away. 'Because of its length and its difficulty – yes, it did. I think you felt the advantages more there. There's probably a scientist who'd say that's not the case, but it felt that way.'

US Postal's doping programme, he says, took away a lot of the fear of the Giant. 'If you're facing the Ventoux, but you know you've prepared well, on and off the bike, then you go into that stage with a lot more confidence.'

Hamilton's team-mate George Hincapie, another to confess to doping, bragged of riding with 'no chain'; Hamilton, meanwhile, recalls climbing the Ventoux and thinking, 'Where's the steep part?'

'I do remember thinking that as I was going up on the day when I won that stage. The steep parts I'd really suffered on before, I wasn't suffering that time. I was covering attacks pretty easily.

'But in that Dauphiné I also suffered a lot. So, yeah – I was "prepared" when I won on the Ventoux, but I was also on a good day.'

Hamilton, open and receptive to any questions – 'You can ask me anything,' he says more than once – seems to accept that doping taints his record. He understands people's cynicism. 'It used to bother me,' he says. 'But you could delete my whole career if you want. I wouldn't mind. I have to be OK with it, because it is the truth.

'Would I have won without doping? Absolutely not. No way. Without doping none of us would have won. *None* of us,' he states unequivocally.

'But at the same time, I took my job very seriously. I trained super-hard,' he insists. 'I'm pretty confident when I say that there weren't many guys who trained harder. We lived like monks for eight to nine months of the year. The shame is that all that gets forgotten.

'I still feel proud of my career, but I look at it differently now. It was a part of my life, when I did some things that I was not happy about. But at the time, I felt that it was the only real option.

'I could have said no and gone home. Nobody put a gun to my head. But if you didn't dope, then you weren't being professional.'

There's a sigh. 'It would have been nice to have done it all clean, to have won on the Ventoux, clean,' he says, 'but it would have been a struggle. And I'm not sure I would have survived.'

After the 2000 Tour, contrary to what he'd expected, Lance Armstrong only got one more realistic shot at victory on the

Ventoux. It came in 2002, but it was a day when tactics nullified the race and, instead, a breakaway led by reluctant repentant doper, Virenque, made it to the summit first.

Virenque, shamed in 1998 by the Festina scandal, took a celebrated victory in front of forgiving and adoring crowds. When, two and a half minutes later, Armstrong passed the crowds, the mood was different. Booed and sworn at, his experience mirrored that of Chris Froome in the 2015 Tour, when the British rider was spat at and jeered.

After the stage, Armstrong was indignant. 'If I had a dollar for every time somebody yelled "*Dopé, dopé!*" I'd be a rich man,' he said. 'It's disappointing, to be honest with you. The people are not very sportsmanlike.' As it turned out, however, the people were very perceptive.

Unsurprisingly, Armstrong didn't see it that way. 'I think it's an indication of their intelligence. But I'm not here to be friends with a bunch of people who stand on the side of the road, who've had too much to drink and want to yell "*Dopé!*" Don't come to the bike race in order to stand around and yell at cyclists. Stay at home.'

Yet again, the Ventoux had maintained its hex on him, but this time it had also demeaned him. And all the time, it was Tyler and Jonathan, equally doped, who had learned to master the mountain. Armstrong doesn't particularly recall being 'bummed' after Hamilton won the 2000 Dauphiné's Ventoux stage. 'I have good memories of the 2000 Dauphiné,' he insists, in contrast to Hamilton's recollection. 'But by 2001, the riders on the team, and the staff too, began to realise that Tyler cared about Tyler – that became the wedge between us. It's cycling, so it is every man for himself, but you can't be so selfish.'

After Hamilton left US Postal the pair became bitter rivals. Publicly, on camera, they smiled and patted each other amicably on the back. Privately, their resentments fermented. Despite that, Hamilton calls US Postal's pioneering seasons in Europe, spent learning the ropes, being the odd ones out, the underdogs, as 'the fun years'. Those were the 'thousand days' he has often referred to, the days of relative innocence before obligation overwhelmed ethics. Over the years, so many European professionals have trodden the same path.

Until he left US Postal, Hamilton could live in Armstrong's shadow. 'Once you become a team leader, it's a different kind of pressure. Once I went to CSC, I was expected to get results.' And once he went to CSC, he became Armstrong's rival.

Hamilton, for all his grit, was perhaps never likely to oust Armstrong. Both had their doping doctors in Spain and Italy, Eufemiano Fuentes and Michele Ferrari, respectively, and both had their doping *directeurs sportifs*, Bjarne Riis and Johan Bruyneel. But Tyler didn't have the cancer-avenging backstory Lance had, nor did he have the muthafucka charisma, the 'No Fucks Given' attitude that informed so much of Armstrong's dubious behaviour over the best part of a decade.

Tyler's persona, in contrast to the badass Texan, was folksy and wholesome. He remembered everybody's name and was polite, well-mannered and eloquent. He was never looking for, or needing, a fight. He travelled around Europe with his golden retriever, Tugboat, and when 'Tugs' died in July 2004, mid-Tour de France, Hamilton wrote a lachrymose blog for Velonews website. 'Tugboat was like my kid,' he said.

But it took yet another showdown on the Ventoux, a few weeks earlier, in June 2004, and once again in the Dauphiné, to reveal just how badly his relationship with Armstrong had disintegrated. This time there were no 'Americans together', no hugs and back-slaps for the camera; instead, there remained just a residue of bitterness and suspicion.

Again Armstrong struggled on the mountain, finishing almost a minute and a half behind Hamilton, fighting for air in the heat.

He was two minutes slower than Iban Mayo's record-breaking time, too. Hamilton was the only rider to finish within a minute of the Spaniard's time. Harder to take for Armstrong was that he'd ridden the Ventoux faster than he'd ever done before and that he'd been beaten by his ex-team-mate – again.

In *The Secret Race*, written with Daniel Coyle, Hamilton's unflinching account of his descent into doping, he claims that – after he finished second to Mayo on the Ventoux that June – a vengeful Armstrong called him out to the sports governing body, the UCI. 'Lance had called the UCI on June 10, the day I'd beaten him on the Ventoux, the same date they'd called me to come in [and see them], the same date of the warning letter against possible doping they'd sent to Girona. Lance called Hein, and Hein called me.'

In Hamilton's account, he confronts Armstrong and is met with furious denials. More than a decade later, I asked Armstrong again if Hamilton's version of events was true. This time, he declined to respond.

A decade and a half after Tyler Hamilton first left Lance Armstrong trailing on the Ventoux, the pair met again, as they gave evidence in the ongoing legal dispute between the Texan and the United States government. 'We deposed him, May 2015,' Armstrong says. 'Tyler's all about Tyler, and I'd say that to his face. We always had a good relationship, but then he wrote his book.'

That book, *The Secret Race*, not to mention Hamilton's confessional interview on *60 Minutes*, which, along with Floyd Landis's testimony, blew the doors off Armstrong's years of denial, still rankles. 'If I was going to write a book about a friend or a former team-mate,' Lance says, 'then I'd call up and say, "FYI – I'm gonna write this book", and just have the courtesy to tell me.'

After *The Secret Race* was published, and following an ugly confrontation with Armstrong in an Aspen restaurant, Hamilton left Colorado and moved to Montana. 'Boulder's a great place, a cycling haven, but I just needed a change of pace,' he said. 'Boulder's a bit of a bubble – it was good to take a step away.

'Colorado is so beautiful, but it's so busy now. You know – the secret's out. Missoula is still undiscovered, relatively. It's a little bit harder to get to, but it's worth it.'

Despite everything that happened, the bitter aftermath of his confession, and the wrangling with Armstrong, Hamilton has fond memories of racing on the Ventoux. 'It's always awesome,' he says. 'The fans, the signs, the people running around in chicken suits. People pulling down their pants. It's hilarious.'

Armstrong refers to the 2009 Ventoux stage, his final race on the mountain, as 'magical'. At the time, he and Bradley Wiggins, then riding for Vaughters' Garmin team, were on friendly terms. 'Our relationship was good at the time,' the American admitted. That changed, however, after Armstrong's confession to doping, when Wiggins described him as a 'lying bastard'.

These days, Armstrong is dismissive of the 2012 Tour winner. 'If you were a prominent British cyclist at the time, you had no choice but to act critical and as if you were shocked and self-righteous,' he says pointedly.

Armstrong still insists that in 2009 and 2010 he was clean. 'I did nothing. I have said that under oath. If there is a test that absolutely works and they say, "Lance, give us your samples", then one hundred per cent I'd be in favour. I'm not sure all the others would want that. But they don't want to do that because if I'm clean in 2009 and 2010 it works against their narrative.'

Despite all the bad memories, both Armstrong and Hamilton still wax lyrical when they recall their years of suffering on the

Giant. 'That was a special day,' Armstrong says of the 2009 stage. 'I've never seen that many people. It was unbelievable.'

Hamilton's affection even extends to the much-neglected north side of the mountain. 'It's beautiful,' he said. 'I never climbed it, either in a race or in training. But it looked brutal. We usually drove down that way, after the summit finishes, and I'd always count my blessings that we hadn't come up that way. The upper part looked tougher than the upper part coming from Bédoin. It's too bad they don't come up that way,' Tyler says.

'I still love Ventoux,' Armstrong says. 'I'd love to ride it again, if I was in the area.. The wine's good, the weather's good, the food's good, the people are humble and sweet. I'd love to go back there.'

After lunch, Armstrong and I walk back the way we came, past the grand houses, set back from the avenue, to his place. As we walk, I quiz him some more. He tells me he goes to therapy 'on average, about once a week'. Sometimes, he says, the whole family goes. 'People have coaches for everything, life coach, business coach, yoga coach, dietician, so I don't understand why people are afraid or embarrassed to have somebody coach that part of their life.

'I've done one session with all the kids – which was interesting.'

How did that pan out? I ask.

'I'm not going to talk to you about this – it's private.'

But it's interesting, I say – people would never have associated you, Le Boss, Mister Stop-at-Nothing, with therapy.

'I've told you, I'm not talking about it – it will all be in my book!' he says. 'At the deposition the lawyer says to me: "Are you writing a book?" I said, "Yes, but right now I'm just gathering content. This, mister lawyer, is *all* content."

'The lawyer just said, "Huh, can't wait to read that chapter . . ."'

When we get back to the house, he takes a call and directs me through the hall to the snug. The shelves are crowded with pictures of his kids. There are books too, including one on Jean-Paul Sartre, one on Willie Nelson, and another on new artists from Austin's East Side. On the table are two yellow jerseys, and on the opposite wall six, not seven, Tour de France trophies, standing in lit alcoves.

He hands me a business card: No Fucks Given, it says, in bold. He likes being provocative, the word games, the little statements, the alter egos – Juan Pelota, Mellow Johnny – none of whom, it would seem, give a fuck. But they all sound pretty angry to me.

By now I have started to think he's protesting just that little too much. Right on cue, when I ask him about hanging on to the trophies, he says defiantly, for the umpteenth time: 'I don't care.' Deep down, though, beneath all the denials and dismissiveness, the bravado and the bitterness, I am sure that he really, *really* does.

I'm about to leave when Max Armstrong bursts through the front door in his pyjamas. 'Pyjama-day at school,' Lance mutters by way of explanation.

'Hey, Max! Come and say hello,' calls his dad from the snug. 'This is my old friend Jeremy.'

'Nice to meet you, Max,' I say, offering to shake hands. Max looks bemused.

'Doesn't he talk funny?' laughs his father, always the wise guy, as we say goodbye and I head to the airport.

PART 3

'The Ventoux is a riddle, an elusive summit whose obsessive power and whiff of tragedy addle the mind.'

— PHILIPPE BRUNEL, *L'Équipe*

VII

Marseille, 13 July 1967

It's been baking hot the past few days, as we came down through the Alps, to the coast. I've struggled to cope with it, if I'm honest. My guts have been playing up again and I've had a rotten stomach. It always seems to get to me. It's even worse this morning, here in Marseille – boiling hot and bloody smelly by the old port.

I know some of the lads are worried about the heat today, up on the Ventoux. Now the press are all making it into a big thing. They keep asking me about it – 'Can you handle it, Tom? How will you cope, Tom?' – and that's not great for the morale.

They keep banging on about Malléjac in 1955. Apparently, he had a bit of a turn halfway up and got carted off in an ambulance. But I know what's coming and I'm ready. I've taken care of myself. Most of us have. The Ventoux's the last place you want to come up short, especially in this heat.

It's the same for everyone, though, isn't it? I mean, everyone's knackered and the heat just makes it worse. Nobody's looking forward to it. It's lucky Barry's here, because I know I can lean on him. We try and have a laugh, mucking about for the snappers. We've been messing about on boats this morning. That's where the bowler hat comes in! Keeps your mind off what's ahead too.

I'm still not quite right though so it'll be tough, but if I get over Ventoux, then I will have ticked off the worst of what's to come. I know I can still get higher up the classification. We've got the

Puy de Dôme, just before the final weekend. It's a steep finish, but that won't be anything like as bad as today.

Mind you, you should never take anything for granted. It was chaos this morning. We'd just got out of Marseille, through some little village, when a dog ran into the road and took half the lads down. Later on, I heard Gimondi lost Mugnaini from his team. You don't want to see a lad quit like that, of course, but that's good for my chances, even if it's bad for his.

By lunchtime, we were all burning up. There's all those scrubby little hills and narrow roads through old villages, no air and hardly any shade – Lourmarin, Roussillon and then bombing down the Col de Murs – before you get back down to the plain. That's when you can see the Ventoux, up close.

Forty-two degrees, they told us, when we got through Carpentras. The lads were all grabbing what they could to drink along the way, from bars, fountains, hosepipes. Colin picked up what he could and passed it over. But in that heat, it was never enough.

I knew Poulidor would fancy it on the Ventoux. It's a big day for him. I knew he'd have a go and then, when we got onto the climb, he took off with Jiménez. I held them for a while, but couldn't stay with them.

Now I have to stick with Pingeon and Janssen, just keep it ticking over to the top, and get down the backside of the bastard.

It's so bloody hot, though. My headache is getting worse. I must stay with the group, keep it going, but it is so dry that even at the bottom, as we started up through the forest, it was getting hard to breathe again, just like that time in the Pyrenees.

If I don't manage it, if I don't keep pushing, then that's probably it. If I lose time here then it's over, I can kiss the Tour goodbye – again.

And I can kiss a better contract goodbye as well . . .

Gone in 60 Seconds

There was always wind, always. But on 14 July 2013, there was barely a breeze when we got out of the car on the summit of Ventoux. As we drove towards the top of the mountain, through crowds brandishing banners celebrating the downfall of Lance Armstrong, we came across Dave Brailsford and *Sunday Times* journalist David Walsh, walking back from a stroll to the Simpson memorial.

We paused to say hello, Brailsford as enthused as ever. 'Better catch up with my new mate,' he said, as Walsh walked on.

Photographer and co-traveller Pete Goding hopped out and got a shot of the pair together. Given the constant sniping at Team Sky, it was soon pirated by others, touted by conspiracy theorists as evidence of Walsh's supposedly cosy relationship with Sky.

Walsh, seen as Witchfinder General after his pursuit of Armstrong, spent the 2013 Tour 'embedded' with Brailsford's team. The outcome of this was his book, *Inside Team Sky*, in which he vouched for the team's propriety. An earlier template for this was set by former professional, turned sports writer, Paul Kimmage. He had spent the 2008 Tour travelling with Jonathan Vaughters and the Garmin team.

Kimmage's 2008 articles on Garmin were deemed by many to vindicate the team's and manager Vaughters' ethical stance, despite the significant number of confessed and apparently repentant dopers among team personnel. Kimmage, deeply sceptical and seen as a very tough nut to crack, had, in effect, vouched for Garmin's good intentions.

By 2013, however, Team Sky's hesitancy over having a sports journalist on board seemed to have dissolved yet it was Walsh, not Kimmage, who began travelling with the team. In the aftermath of USADA's reasoned decision on Armstrong's doping, Walsh's stock as exposer of deceit was at a peak. That may have been the characteristic that made him most appealing to Brailsford. Post-Armstrong scandal, Walsh vouching for Team Sky had huge PR value.

My own feelings about the effectiveness of any journalist being embedded in any environment are mixed. Is it really a given that a journalist will get to see behind the façade? Added to that, it is almost inevitable that when you spend weeks travelling with a group in such a hothouse environment, you relax, you build relationships, you let down your guard. And if that happens, surely it must compromise your objectivity?

I sit watching the final 45 minutes of the 2013 Ventoux stage in a pop-up studio for a Dutch TV station, perched on the Col des Tempêtes, just below the summit of the Giant. Two steps too far out of the back door and it would be a very long fall into the Toulourenc valley, far below.

The Dutch presenters are in make-up, watching on monitors. A cameraman I've seen on almost every finish line I've ever stood on walks past and nods in recognition. 'Hi, how are you doing?' I say in acknowledgement. I have no idea what his name is.

On the studio monitors, Nairo Quintana is making his big play. His attack, 13 kilometres from the summit, however great his abilities, is either overconfident or naive. In terms of the recent history of racing on the Giant, this is a long-distance punt, with little hope for success. Maybe it's a sign of desperation in the face of Froome's apparent ease, or of a lack of knowledge of the nuances of Ventoux.

Long distance worked for Merckx, Poli, and even for Virenque – something that Armstrong now wishes he hadn't allowed – and, with the podium positions being fought out behind him, it worked for Gárate in 2009. But with the Alps still to come, it is unlikely ever to work for a rider harbouring dreams of winning the Tour. Or maybe, given Froome's current form, the Colombian is just thinking of the stage victory. He has to try something after all, because the British rider appears to be in complete control.

Quintana arrives on Mikel Nieve's shoulder just after the Virage du Bois. Behind him, Froome is speaking into his radio. Soon afterwards, with ten kilometres still to race, he moves over to the right-hand side of the road and snatches a musette from a Team Sky helper. Moments later, Pete Kennaugh, pace-setting for Froome over the past few kilometres, is gone, engine blown with nine kilometres left. Such is the decrease in his pace that – unlike Hamilton and Livingston in 2000 – he nearly grinds to a halt, coming close to a track stand before he wearily moves off again.

But this is Team Sky and there's always another rider to pick up the slack and ensure the pace remains unremitting. Now Richie Porte takes over, while Froome rides tempo in his wake, Alberto Contador already looking stressed, dancing on the pedals, baring his teeth with the effort. And then, as they near Chalet Reynard, there are just four: Porte, Froome, Contador and Roman Kreuziger, chiselling their way into Quintana's slim lead.

Back in the team cars, the directors watching on dashboard televisions can sense what is coming. They know Contador's 'tell', the continuous dancing, too much of it sideways, the bared teeth and now the sagging shoulders. Froome knows it too.

Struggling to be heard above the crowd, Froome barks into Porte's ear. Then, just before the seven-kilometre to go mark, as the gradient eases to five per cent, his legs explode – there's no other word for it – and Froome is gone. His astounding increase in cadence – here, on this mountain of all mountains, the dreaded Ventoux – comes after the draining climb from St Estève to just below Chalet Reynard. This moment, analysed and pored over for years to come, changes Froome's career, for ever.

Camera phones track him speeding through a left-hand bend, his acceleration even taking TV motorbikes by surprise. Froome's legs whirl, as he reduces the Ventoux to an overblown spin class. In the wake of this attack, will come scepticism and derision. He will be openly questioned, compared to the proven dopers of the past, and continuously asked to explain his performance. Eventually he, and his wife Michelle, patience exhausted, will become enraged by the experience.

But on this day, as he speeds through the 1,400-metre altitude point, Froome, and also Brailsford, watching at the summit, aren't thinking about any of that.

Froome flies past Mikel Nieve and on through the next bend, Contador now receding further behind him, slumping back into the saddle, yesterday's man, physically and psychologically diminished. Watching alone on the Dutch TV station's monitor, I feel an inevitable disbelief. Then comes a wave of déjà vu, of gnawing doubt and rising panic. Maybe I should feel delight in such a performance. I can't, though, because I know what will happen next.

Almost immediately the media chooses sides. Eurosport's British commentary team, not known for being critical of the sport, loves it, while Belgian TV's team is less than flattering.

'The scooter is launched! It's an out-of-body Lance! He's burning the watts! It's a Martian – on the moon!'

As Froome pulls away from Contador it gets worse.

'*What would you call that? An attack – or a spasm?*' they muse.

For a moment, as the sport takes in what it is witnessing, there is a lull. Froome races on, with Contador and Nieve now collaborating in pursuit. Froome reverts to 'normal' pedalling, but he is soon on Quintana's back wheel. Then, just 500 metres or so after his first high-altitude attack, he does it again, sprinting past the Colombian's left shoulder just before Chalet Reynard.

Quintana chases and bridges the gap. Once back together, the pair ride on, towards the summit. I leave the studio and head across the bleached rock for the finish line. On the road far below, Nieve and Contador ride together to try to limit their losses, but can do nothing.

Froome and Quintana close on the Simpson memorial, but – as was the case in 2000, when Armstrong and Pantani passed – there is no time for gestures, no cap- or helmet-doffing. With 1,300 metres to go, Froome lifts himself out of the saddle one more time. Quintana puffs out his cheeks and, after almost 12 kilometres on the Ventoux, riding at the front of the race, he cannot respond.

Now the outcome is clear: Chris Froome, on the mountain where fellow Briton Tom Simpson collapsed and died, is about to take the biggest, most controversial, stage win of his career.

For all the high-fives, back-slapping and fist bumps, Chris Froome was not the first Briton to win, wearing the yellow jersey, on the Ventoux. That ground-breaking moment had gone, almost unnoticed, nine summers earlier, when a different rider became the first Briton to win the Tour de France.

In 2006, in a virtuoso display of attacking riding that ranked with the Ventoux's greatest exploits and that went virtually unreported in the British press, Nicole Cooke rode solo over the summit, climbing up from Malaucène, to clinch victory in that edition of the women's Tour de France.

It took some persuasion and a succession of emails before Nicole agreed to meet me. At first, I was a little bruised to be lumped in with the hordes of exclusively male sportswriters who she so vehemently attacked in her eye-popping book, *The Breakaway*. But Nicole's emails made her convictions plain.

We – the male-dominated sports media – had collectively failed her, and women's cycling generally, by choosing to ignore her and her peers and instead to focus on the ongoing soap opera of doping scandals in men's cycling. In the process, she believed we'd driven women's cycling from the periphery of a financial model to the outer limits of sustainability. The dopers – and any of those in the media who'd been complicit, sympathetic or indulgent – were to blame.

Her emails both scolded and scalded me.

> . . . Those reporters and journalists, including yourself, failed to see what was so obvious to myself and others, and rather, spent time furthering a corrupt fiction whilst ignoring my exploits.
>
> My moment in the sun was taken for ever, by people who thought so little of my efforts because they were so wrapped up in writing eulogies for the corrupt.

Any apologies or talk of blaming it on 'the culture', what was known and unknown at the time, or on the lack of editorial space and the constraints of British libel law, fell on stony ground. 'The cheats win on the way up and on the way down,' she had said bitterly in *The Breakaway*. But then, given her experience, her treatment by the media, why should I not expect her to think that? And, if needed, there was further conclusive damning evidence that I remembered only too well.

When Cooke, in the yellow jersey of Tour de France leadership, was racing solo to a memorable win over the Ventoux, we – the British cycling media – were chasing Jan Ullrich, Ivan Basso and the others around a hotel car park in Strasbourg as Operación Puerto overshadowed the Grand Départ of the 2006 Tour. Nicole's triumph over the Ventoux, and the first-ever British win in the Tour de France, went unrecognised because of the obsession with doping and because of gender bias. She may have become the first cyclist since Tom Simpson to be nominated for BBC Sports Personality of the Year after her victory, but there's no doubt that she deserved better.

Just a cursory glance at her long list of career achievements – Olympic gold medallist, World Road champion, multiple national champion, World Cup winner, Tour de France winner, Giro d'Italia winner, Classic winner – and it was clear this was a résumé that outshone those of Bradley Wiggins, Chris Froome and Mark Cavendish.

Ironic, then, that as she achieved that solo victory over the Ventoux, wearing the yellow jersey, those same media hordes were whipping themselves into a frenzy as the start of the 2006 men's Tour dissolved into farce. Ironic, too, that when the 2006 Tour route had been unveiled the previous autumn with the usual pomp, in the Palais des Congrès, Paris, incoming Tour director Christian Prudhomme had said: 'The worst thing in sport today is suspicion. We can never eliminate doping, but to eliminate suspicion is possible.'

Cooke's win on Ventoux was one of the most spectacular ever seen on the mountain. Perhaps fittingly, given her outsider status, her victory focused on the recently ignored north face, rather than the TV-friendly south side, now so familiar from recent men's racing. What's more, Cooke didn't need to attack on the Ventoux. Barring a major turnaround, the race was already effectively won. 'I think up to that point I had a lead of around a minute,' she said. 'It wasn't a huge lead but with bonuses here and there . . .'

But she adopted a warrior's approach to the 115-kilometre stage over the Giant, from Valréas to Isle-sur-la-Sorgue, attacking, à la Merckx, from the foot of the climb. Even more surprisingly, she had never ridden the Ventoux before. 'My approach was pretty simple,' she told me. 'These are the moments you train for, these are the magic days, days that define your career and that you dream of when you're training in the winter and it's cold and wet.'

After retiring from racing in 2013, Nicole Cooke studied for an MBA. She now works in the City of London, close to St Paul's, and has also spent time working in Paris. When she's in London she cycles into work every day, but it's a far cry from the 180-kilometre training rides to and from Lake Garda that were once her stock in trade. We finally meet in an anonymous branch of an anonymous brasserie, close to her workplace and a short walk from St Paul's.

Even in retirement, she continues to be a thorn in the side of the cycling establishment and is a regular critic of the lack of support for women's cycling and the ongoing inadequacies of anti-doping regulations. She shakes her head wearily as we discuss her battles – before Jess Varnish, sexism and Sutton, and before the Bradley Wiggins TUEs and the tale of the errant Jiffy bag – with British Cycling.

Given her dominant form, victory in the 2006 women's Tour seemed probable, even before the Ventoux stage. Her attack on the long climb from Malaucène made victory inevitable.

'I was probably already going to win overall. There were two stages to go after the Ventoux stage and in that Tour I'd picked up the yellow jersey in the prologue and had led all the way through. So I did consciously want to make the most of the day as well as sealing the overall. We set up the team for that, to make a fast pace to the bottom of the climb and then it would be up to me to attack.'

But Nicole hadn't ridden the Ventoux before. 'I know the high Alps – the Col de Bonette, Col de Vars – really well. So it was a little bit of an . . . an exploration, a bit of a journey into the unknown!

'The risk was that I would blow up – and really blow – but at that point it felt like the worst that could happen would be that I'd get caught and have to manage the situation and not lose time before the finish. But there's always a risk. And it was hot, boiling hot, somewhere in the high thirties. I had pretty obvious tan lines afterwards.

'I attacked early, in the trees up from Malaucène, after about two kilometres. Once I'd made the move, everyone got into their pace, but the time gap steadily drifted out. After that, it was down to me, and my personal time trial, up the mountain.'

Attacking in the heat, so soon after the start of the climb – on the Ventoux of all places? That's very early, I say. That's definitely Merckx territory. You have to go back to the 1970s, maybe even 1950s, to find the last time someone achieved a similar exploit on the Ventoux . . .

'Yes, I know,' she laughs. 'But there was the prestige of the day, wanting to really stamp my authority on the race, but also that personal drive to put myself to the test. I felt I could ride it really well, and I wanted to see if I could do it.

'And in the context of that race and that field, the competition wasn't as strong as the field in that year's Giro, for example. I don't think I would have done it at the Giro – it was a combination of circumstances. There were other stages when it would have been a flawed tactic and when I would decide to wait.'

Did attacking that soon, on so fearsome a climb, spread panic among her rivals?

'I guess, probably – I hadn't thought of it in those terms, really, but I don't suppose anybody wanted to chase me all the way up the Ventoux. And the heat was a big factor. People don't want to chase on a hot day because it's so debilitating.

'At the start I looked back and could still see them, chasing behind me. Gradually it stretched out. Once I couldn't see them any more, I was getting time checks every two kilometres as the lead drew out.'

Nicole rode on, focused on the 21.4-kilometre climb, steeling herself through the gruelling sections at 12 per cent on the approach to Mont Serein ski station. 'There's a point – about halfway up – where the road is long, straight, steep, and that was where the team car pulled in behind me.

'I was riding against the distance markers so I knew how many kilometres there were to go. I'd trained in the mountains before the Tour, during the build-up, so I knew the importance of pacing myself.'

She rode through the junction to the ski station, past a crowd of spectators at the Chalet Liotard, and began the final section of the climb, through the pines, and on towards the ladder of hairpins snaking across the white rocks, the observatory towering over her.

'I can remember it was amazing at the top, but it all went so quickly. It was just, "Get over the top, then charge on." I took in a bit of the atmosphere and it would have been glorious if it had been a mountain-top finish. That was a bit sad in a way.'

There was little time to take in either her surroundings or the Simpson memorial, just below the summit.

'I really went for it on the descent. You might think that attacking so early was a risk, but I went pretty hard downhill as well. I was looking for the memorial – I did want to see it – but, bombing past at 80 kilometres an hour, the chances were slim.'

Again, such a tactic, particularly through the forest section from Chalet Reynard to St Estève, with its infrequent but tight bends and occasional switches in camber, is, at best, nerve-wracking.

The descent from Chalet Reynard to St Estève is high speed and there are some corners and a chicane with rocky outcrops, where it's easy to get it wrong. There are a few crosses and plaques on the way down, I point out. Nicole just shrugs.

'I'd never seen it before, but I still went full tilt down it. And the director in the car behind, he stuck with it. I could hear the car screeching through the corners behind me. We left everyone else, all the other vehicles, behind us ... I was a fearless descender at the time, but I'm older now!'

Her rapid descent further extended her advantage. 'I think I had about three minutes at the top and then around four by the bottom. But after "beasting" it over the mountain, I still had about 40 kilometres to go to the finish.'

Between Bédoin, at the foot of the Ventoux, and the finish among sleepy Isle-sur-la-Sorgue's network of waterways and antique shops, Cooke punched her way through the hot afternoon air and drew yet more time out of the chasing bunch. 'I didn't let up at all. I pushed hard all the way to the finish. There were some sections, straight road, in the baking heat, when I was just out there. It was only in the last 500 metres that I relaxed a bit and allowed myself to celebrate ...

'Everybody in the team was thrilled because the plan to take hold of the race had come off. My team-mates came in exhausted and saw me jumping around grinning. After the finish, we went off to a café close to the finish and had ice creams. It was one of the special days.'

Then, having sealed victory in the women's Tour, over the most feared mountain in France, you might have expected her to have sat back and waited for the media coverage, the column inches and the phone calls. But there were none.

'By then it was nothing new. The fun came on the Saturday when Puerto broke and that became a hot topic, which obviously had an effect on the wider perception of professional cycling. That then set in motion a series of events which, by the end of 2006, left our team without a sponsor.'

Only long-time Cooke diarist, Brendan Gallagher, then covering cycling for the *Daily Telegraph,* wrote anything particularly significant for the national press, and that was in September. That lack of coverage was compounded by Adrian Chiles's lame questioning when Cooke was interviewed by the BBC. 'Do you fall off your bike a lot?' a smirking Chiles asked of the crazed descender of the Ventoux and the first British winner of the Tour de France.

Nicole Cooke acknowledges that winning that 2006 women's Tour, against the backdrop of the scandal in Strasbourg, was a bittersweet experience. 'That takes nothing away from the day and the excitement of doing it. Doping scandals were in the background throughout my whole career so there was nothing new in that.'

By that time, she had become adjusted to the obstacles in her way. Redressing that balance, she says, was 'a work in progress throughout her career'.

'At the end of 2006, I had a really good team set-up and from the cycling side of things everything was looking good. By that point I was already looking to push the coverage of women's cycling. The Tour win didn't spark a new approach.'

Nicole also won the 2007 women's Tour, and battled to third place in 2008, but by 2009 the race was discontinued.

'My best experience of the women's Tour was in 2002, when it was still two weeks long. Every day in the first week was at least 160 kilometres and that included one stage over the Paris–Roubaix cobbles. That was what it was like when I first turned professional and that's where I'd like to see it get back to.'

Instead, there is now a one-day event – La Course – tacked onto the Tour de France. This also suffers from a lack of media coverage, despite being based around the route of the men's Tour, but, worse still, reeks of tokenism.

Does she directly attribute what has happened to the women's Tour de France to the ongoing ethical malaise in men's cycling?

'I think the UCI played a role in not providing a platform for women's racing to continue. They could have done a lot more.'

Like others, she lobbied then UCI President McQuaid to act in support of women's racing. 'It must have been 2005, when the kilometre was taken out of the Olympics. There was a lot of noise about it because of the petition for Chris Hoy. I was asked to sign it but I said no, but I would sign a petition for equal men and women's events at the Olympics.

'That was what I then took up with McQuaid. But it didn't go anywhere at all, it was just ignored. Again the UCI could have done a lot more.'

So, given her experience, is there not a role for her to play? She gives a measured 'yes', but admits too that she has had little contact with current UCI president – and former British Cycling Federation president – Brian Cookson.

'I think there's certainly a role,' she says hesitantly. 'But, having had 15 years of dealing with all the things that took the shine off my career, I was quite happy to step away from it for a while. That's what I'm doing now. There's other things to do. I'm weary of dealing with people who don't reply to emails or do the things they're employed to do.

'Coming back to cycling in some capacity is possible – I wouldn't discount it.'

Cooke is a big fan of the women's Tour in Britain. 'They're doing really well. I can see the legacy of banging the drum and creating change. That feels good. It's a vindication.'

A vindication of your success and that of those who followed in your wake . . .?

'. . . because British Cycling didn't support me. But I think from the start I wasn't willing to accept incompetence. Unfortunately, the reaction was not to respond or to engage.'

Those myriad problems between Cooke and the British federation fuelled resentment on both sides. 'The culture was that anything to thwart Nicole was encouraged,' she says.

Among the blockers, she says, was Shane Sutton, once Welsh coach to a teenage Cooke. 'He has qualities but he has to be kept on a very short lead and kept in check. He never had a handle over me and so was probably a little fearful of me and my dad's persistence in terms of holding him to account. He didn't like that. It felt like anything to get me out of the way was encouraged.'

But Sutton and Brailsford were presumably happy enough in Beijing, when Cooke took the Olympic gold medal in the women's road race?

'Oh, yes, the reflected glory was brilliant,' she smiles. 'They were delighted!

'It was painfully obvious at British Cycling that women were always treated as second class. Those were the attitudes of leadership. It was not in any way equal.

'That was a real turn-off to riders who were achieving results and still not getting selected. That was enough to send some people, with more options, elsewhere.'

What irks most, so she says, are all the missed opportunities. 'It wouldn't have taken much for British Cycling to have the best women's team out there. We could have had a decade of fantastic success. That's what's sad.'

And that – the success of a British women's Tour – might have saved the women's Tour de France, I suggest . . .

'Yes, perhaps, but the Tour de France demise on the women's side is more linked to the UCI not supporting the women's calendar.

'If the UCI were serious, they'd say anyone who works in cycling cannot have a doping past. Clear out a whole load of people and try to create something better.'

So she advocates zero tolerance too, then? Doesn't that mean, though, that you'd have hardly any teams and hardly anyone in the team cars?

'Well, the sponsors wouldn't necessarily go away. And once you've kicked out the rot, you'd even make cycling more attractive to people who are uncomfortable in corrupt circles. I think it would make it more attractive to the right sort of people. You'd easily fill spots on teams. You're still going to have a race and a new star at the end of it.'

By the time Nicole retired, her position as maverick, outsider and rebel was consolidated. The spats with British Cycling, Shane Sutton and Dave Brailsford were well known within the cycling milieu. They had briefed against her – claiming she was almost impossible to work with, not a team player, too closely controlled by her parents.

But her successes blew any criticisms away. In fact, the more obstacles were put in her path, the more determined she became. She epitomised the very best of British and expected the same of those around her, when riding for the national team.

When she retired she released a powerful and damning statement. It's worth revisiting, particularly in the light of Laura Trott's investiture as British national treasure. Cooke may have been enraged by the lack of recognition for her own achievements, but perhaps there is some solace for her in being an agent of change.

My father wrote ... and asked for championships to be established for girls. The result was that the following year, the BCF put on a superb set of British track championships ...

From 1998 on, there have been Youth track events for girls and later, as they saw them succeed, they put on Junior events as well ... Now all the budding young stars like Jo Rowsell and Laura Trott can see an aspirational pathway for the girls, just as there has been for the boys, that simply did not exist when I started out on my career.

And doping? Unlike others, protesting that they saw no evil, heard no evil and spoke no evil, and wouldn't countenance it, Cooke says she confronted it, put her hand in the fire – but, instead of buckling, she had the character to walk away.

I have had days where temptation to start onto the slippery slope was brought in front of me. I was asked what 'medicines' I would like to take to help me, and was reminded that the team had certain expectations of me ... and I was not living up to them with my performance. I said I would do my best until I had to drop out of the race, but I was not taking anything.

Pressure was put on me but I was determined, and fortunate. I had a very good team-mate who was in a similar predicament and she took the same stance I did. Team-mates that say 'No' are priceless. I would have been very naive to think that I would not encounter moments like this.

I am appalled that so many men bleat on about the fact that the pressures were too great. Too great for what? This is not doing 71 mph on the motorway when the legal limit is 70. This is stealing somebody else's livelihood.

And what about my old Texan sparring partner and all the other alphas?

> When Lance 'cries' on Oprah and she passes him a tissue, spare a thought for all of those genuine people who walked away with no reward – just shattered dreams. Each one of them is worth a thousand Lances.

Looking down from the summit of Mont Ventoux, Dave Brailsford, who'd steered Wiggins and Froome through the catfights of 2012, who'd built Team Sky from scratch, who'd battled to take British Cycling out of the era of the gallant but underfunded and underprepared loser, could barely contain his excitement. Alongside him, a select group watched Froome's solo climb to the top of the mountain that afternoon in July 2013. His wife Michelle, future UCI President Brian Cookson, and, most notably, Greg and Kathy LeMond, making a return to the Tour after exile during the Armstrong years, looked on.

Triple Tour winner LeMond had stayed away from cycling for many years, scarred by his feud with Armstrong and wary of a milieu that had long been dominated by the Texan. A bitter critic of cycling's doping culture for more than a decade, he was an obvious port of call for an immediate reaction to Froome's extraordinary performance. Journalists crowded around, eager to hear his verdict.

But if some expected scepticism, LeMond wasn't biting. 'I don't think that every time a rider has a great ride people should be saying, "He's a doper." I really don't like that. You usually have one rider that's the strongest. If the others are half a per cent off, then they're out the back.'

But LeMond was blunt in his assessment of Brailsford's refusal to share Froome's performance data over concerns of what Team

Sky's principal had called misinterpretation and 'pseudo-science'. 'That's bullshit. That's what they said about drug controls. You'd never look at it [power output] as a positive [test], you'd look at it together with blood profiles.

'I am not to going to make hypothetical ifs and buts,' LeMond continued, 'but as part of the profiling, you profile your watts. That's instead of having hypothetical watts, which is pretty accurate to maybe three, four per cent, but that could be a difference of saying positive or negative. If you don't have anything to hide, give it [the data] to everybody.

'I think there's a natural tendency among riders today to be guarded or defensive. But it's the opposite that needs to happen.'

And what about the comparisons with Armstrong in 2000, already being made, even before Froome had crossed the line? That one was easy for Greg to answer: 'Froome's got a lot more natural talent than Armstrong, that's for sure. That's not a doubt.'

A few weeks before Christmas 2015, a distinctive white Jaguar with a personalised number plate, is one of a handful of luxury cars sitting in the courtyard of the Rosewood hotel in Holborn as dusk gathers over central London. In the opulent lounge, Dave Brailsford and I are taking tea. In fact, in his case, coffee, although it's hard to understand why a man with this much energy would need a caffeine boost.

Brailsford is a workaholic, an obsessive, driven to succeed. This is not a myth fuelled by great PR or propagated by embedded journalists. Anyone who has spent time with either Team GB or Team Sky will testify to that. But, of course, there is a price for all of this success. I don't know how often he is at home, with his family. Given that he admits he spends most of his time working, not often would be an educated guess.

He has followed the path of his father, John, a fanatical and accomplished mountaineer, who would drive the family to the Alps, drop them in a campsite and then disappear into the mountains for weeks on end. It's almost impossible to visualise Brailsford on the school run, in Waitrose or Sainsbury's, at a school play, walking the dog. Maybe when he's not in the Team Sky bus poring over performance analytics, or at the dinner table with his staff in yet another anonymous hotel, he longs for those moments. It's just hard to imagine it.

There have been plenty of past problems between us, particularly over Team Sky's 'zero tolerance' policy, the hiring and firing of certain individuals, the TUEs. We've shown each other our inner chimps. He's accused me of 'having it in' for him, both on the phone and to my face; I've responded by saying 'I'm not doing your PR'. Relations are strained.

Most of the time, even in the aftermath of a draining and tense Tour de France, we've agreed to differ. Despite that, until late 2016, he would always talk. Until then, we could still meet and chat over a cup of coffee; until then, he didn't do blacklists, as such. Now, however, those opportunities to talk are dwindling. Increasingly throughout 2016, his answers were evasive, and circuitous and dismissive.

Once blacklists take shape, you are in trouble. There are signs that Team Sky has drafted one – Paul Kimmage seems obviously to be on it, while others hover on the periphery. Michelle Froome, too, would appear to operate one. Team Sky's media handlers wouldn't know this, as they weren't around back then, but blacklists are what Armstrong and his entourage used to operate. Blacklisting, certainly in cycling and probably everywhere else, is associated with having something to hide. They are counterproductive and divisive.

I first met Brailsford before the Athens Olympics, when the fruits of lottery investment and the streak of detached ruthlessness – which he'd employed to drag British Cycling from a creaking old boys' network to a far slicker and more professional outfit – were becoming evident. He knows France well and a love of the Alps runs in the family. 'Dad is a connoisseur in terms of France, so I think the first time I'd have heard of the Ventoux would have been him telling me about it.'

John Brailsford, he explains, loved the Dolomites and the Chamonix regions of the Alps. 'He ended up writing guide-books on the Écrins region and was really into his cycling too, so he knows all the famous climbs in the area.'

But his father wasn't a big fan of the Pyrenees. 'They were a little too green and not really high enough. I think the Alps and the Dolomites were a bit more epic. But,' he says, 'Dad used to talk about this massive Mont Ventoux . . .'

Brailsford used to holiday in the Alps when his father was guiding. 'But I remember one year, when I was about 14, or 15, we drove over from the Alps to the Pyrenees, to go and do some riding on the Tourmalet. As we were driving down, we could see Ventoux from a distance. Dad said, "There it is" – and after that I started to read about it.'

Unlike Christian Prudhomme, however, Brailsford rates the Ventoux and Alpe d'Huez as the two most iconic and recog-nised climbs in the sport. 'Maybe some of the smaller Classic climbs fit that too, but in stage-racing terms I think they're the two, maybe with the Tourmalet.

'Ventoux's an intimidating climb. There are several things – the ferocity and difficulty of the climb itself, the length of it and then the climate that goes with it, the heat and then usually the wind, once you come out of the forest . . .

'But then,' he enthuses, 'you've got the history – and it's so rich in history. Obviously from a British point of view, the Tom Simpson story is always part of the history. If you can get your name down as a winner on the Ventoux, then you're among the legends. Any stage over the Ventoux is always a big stage.'

Brailsford's fascination with the Alpine climbs, fuelled by his father, has been lifelong. 'We had these books that were published with all the cols of the Alps – they had these beautifully hand-drawn profiles with all the gradients – and we ticked off the routes as we did them.

'Now you see all the profiles online everywhere, but back then it was quite something to study these old school maps with the percentages for each kilometre. So we'd look at these beautiful profiles and say, "Oh, we have to go and do this one."

'We were looking at the Ventoux and I just thought, "Bloody hell – I wouldn't mind having a crack at that …" Funnily enough, Dad went and rode the Ventoux a couple of times, but he and I never rode it together.'

More than 30 years later, Brailsford stood at the summit of the Ventoux, watching a distant figure pedal steadily across the moonscape to win stage 15 of the Tour de France. For both Brailsford and Froome, it should have been a celebration of their most spectacular success. But even before Team Sky's leader crossed the line, the suspicions of doping had gone viral.

Brailsford now says that such concerns hadn't even entered his mind. 'I guess when you're watching a performance like that, on that mountain, you're so engrossed – watching to see if your plan is executed – and it either is, or it isn't.'

So was Froome's now infamous and decisive attack, immediately before the false flat leading to Chalet Reynard, planned?

'I wouldn't say it was planned – it was very much that he was going to attack. He was keen to attack far enough out to give himself a big advantage, and he was confident. He was up for it.

'The way the stage panned out played into his hands. The opportunity arose and he just seized it, although maybe a little bit earlier than he was planning.

'There's that classic piece of footage, when he's in a low gear, he comes around a corner which is relatively flat – which you can't see on telly – but he didn't change gear, he stayed in a relatively small gear but he just increased his cadence.

'It looked impressive,' Brailsford says with understatement. 'Everybody got very excited about that. It couldn't have gone any better. It was textbook. As he was coming up, I was thinking about where I wanted to be, to see him cross the line. So I stood on this wall, thinking, "Brilliant – people will always remember this. This is an extraordinary performance."

'I was thinking, "He deserves this", and I was also allowing myself to get lost in the moment and getting quite emotional about it all. I was remembering all the work he'd done to get there, thinking about all the positive things. The thought that people would question it genuinely didn't enter my mind.'

As Froome climbed through that last horrendous bend to the Ventoux's summit, to seal the stage win, Brailsford, watching from beyond the finish line, was exuberant, punching the air and jumping for joy. Within moments, though, he was turning the same thin air blue, as, in the wake of Froome's solo win, the media huddled around him and the doping questions began.

'Yeah, I can remember that,' he says.

'Chris crossed the line and then ...' – in the calm of the Rosewood's lounge, Brailsford slams his fist into the palm of his hand for emphasis – '... bang!'

When I first started covering cycling, stage races like the Tour, the Giro and the Vuelta were heavily populated by long, flat stages, designed to generate opportunities for the sprinters and rouleurs to shine, not to mention the 'pack-fill' who dominated in the peloton. The division of opportunities was clear: there would be a series of flat, or at worst, rolling stages, in which the team leaders were expected to keep their powder dry, sit in the bunch, avoid trouble and await the mountains and time trials.

But the Grand Tours of European cycling are not like that any more. Four or five days of sprinting have been deemed dull, uneventful, bad for TV ratings. At the same time, the rise of riders as accomplished as Peter Sagan, who can climb, time-trial competently and sprint, has hit the big-name sprinters – the Cavendishes and Greipels – of the peloton hard.

It hasn't gone unnoticed by those 'pure' sprinters that even 'flat' stages are no longer flat and that their opportunities are few and far between. For riders like Cavendish, it has ended the days of multiple stage wins in the Giro or the Tour. 'I'm sick of red spots – so, so sick of them,' Cavendish said in July 2015, referring to the red spots signifying categorised climbs on the route du Tour.

Asked, on stage seven of the 2015 Tour, when he expected the next sprint finish, Cavendish's German rival, André Greipel, scratched his head as he contemplated a further two weeks of climbs. Eventually, the German responded. 'I think the Champs-Élysées will be a sprint for sure,' he said. Nor is Cavendish keen on the Vuelta a España, describing the number of mountain stages in the race as 'stupid'.

'No one wants to go to the Vuelta any more unless they crashed out of the Tour de France,' he said. Based on his hissy fit at the top of the Giant last time the Tour tackled it, he doesn't like the Ventoux much either. But then, like Jean-Louis Pages, you'd probably realised that.

As the routes of three-week stage races become more and more demanding, the modern stick-thin peloton has become crammed with excellent climbers, all engineered towards high performance on increasingly explosive courses. That is why leaving it to those climactic kilometres across the moonscape has become leaving it too late on Mont Ventoux. Performance analysts will tell you that by the time you pass Chalet Reynard, the wind is too unpredictable, the gradient too slight and the time gaps that much harder to achieve.

Far better, then, to attack in the still heat of the forest, where a high, grinding pace on the long, straight, airless ramps will exhaust the front group and force so many riders into submission. Chris Froome detailed that change in thinking in his book *The Climb*, ghostwritten by David Walsh.

> I had spoken to Contador about Ventoux. I said to him: 'It's going to be a big day for us in the Tour.'
>
> He nodded and had a little think. 'Yeah, yeah, it's a tough climb, but in the final [section] it's always headwind and it's difficult to make a selection.'
>
> That conversation lodged in my brain until I was two-thirds of the way up Ventoux. Richie Porte had done the work and had laid it all out. I could launch myself now to the top of Ventoux.
>
> . . . Contador hadn't expected anything here.

Miguel Indurain had understood that too, even back in 1994, as he led the front group in pursuit of the distantly toiling Eros Poli. The Spaniard's attack came in almost the same spot – seven kilometres from the summit and just before Chalet Reynard – as Froome's now-infamous acceleration 19 years later. But in 1994, Indurain's turn of speed merely splintered his group; in 2013, Froome's acceleration detonated it.

If Froome's hamster legs, both provocative and comical at the same time – '*comme un Mobylette*,' they snorted on French TV — raised the spectre of doping, both motorised and pharmaceutical, yet again, they proved fatal to his rivals. All the dancing in the world couldn't save Alberto this time.

The morning after Froome's spectacular stage win, Dave

Brailsford pulled on his Team Sky kit, climbed onto his Pinarello and set off from his hotel in Orange to ride the Ventoux. 'I've ridden it a lot with Team Sky,' Brailsford said. 'Whenever we're close we'll go up it, even if it's a recce. So I've ridden it a lot lately, quite often on one of our rest days in and around that area.

'If we're close, Tim Kerrison and I will always get up and go. I ride my bike a lot with Tim. We're pretty keen.'

That morning Brailsford and coach Kerrison met Alastair Campbell at the top. 'He was coming up from the other side – I think he set off first,' Brailsford says.

Brailsford and Campbell, long-standing friends, mulled over the previous afternoon's victory and what it might mean.

Earlier that morning, Brailsford and Froome, already paying a high price for his victory on the Ventoux, had faced the press. 'I can understand the questions,' said Froome, who found himself besieged as soon as he emerged from his room, 'but I'm also one of those people who have been let down, who's believed in people who've turned out to be cheats and liars, but I can assure you, I'm not.'

A little later, as the hotel dining room filled with media, Team Sky's beleaguered press officer, Chris Haynes, got the ball rolling in a short and tense press conference. As they defended themselves, not really against specific itemised accusations of doping but more against a general atmosphere of scepticism, both Brailsford and Froome looked aggrieved.

'I know what I've done to get here and I'm extremely proud of what I've done,' Froome said. 'To compare me with Lance . . . Lance cheated, I'm not cheating. End of story.'

But Brailsford's weariness and frustration finally took over. 'You're all asking the same question,' he said. 'I'm getting asked the same question by a hundred people, so why don't you collectively – you're all in the same job – get yourselves together, have a meeting, get yourselves organised and you tell me what we could do so that you don't have to ask that question . . .'

This proved too much for Froome, who stifled a laugh. Brailsford was off and running, though. 'I know what we do but I haven't got a magic wand,' he says. 'It's a rest day, it's ten o'clock in the morning and I'm trying to defend somebody who's done nothing wrong.'

But the old ways of thinking had become ingrained. Froome's display of dominance had come on the Ventoux of all places, the mountain most associated with cycling's perpetual struggle to exorcise its demons. When the race reached Gap, 48 hours later, the French media were in attack mode. What had started in the Pyrenees as aggressive questioning – 'Look me in the eyes and tell me you're clean,' French TV presenter Gérard Holtz had said to Froome after his stage win at Ax 3 Domaines – had, in the aftermath of the Ventoux, become an inquest.

So in Gap, Brailsford appeared on the live post-race chat programme, while Holtz – who had never batted an eyelid at outrageous performances before or during the Armstrong years – again played at chief inquisitor. This was, to paraphrase one description of Geoffrey Howe's attacks on Margaret Thatcher, like being savaged by a dead sheep, albeit a highly coiffed one.

Introducing Brailsford sardonically, with a knowing smile on his lips, as 'Monsieur Tolérance Zéro', Holtz mocked Froome's prowess on Ventoux. Froome, he smirked, had ridden '*Comme un Mobylette . . .*' Like a scooter. That phrase again.

'We're all fans of cycling,' Holtz says, 'but when we see Chris Froome climb the Ventoux like he's on a scooter, we all ask questions. When we see Chris accelerate like that, we all ask questions. Do you understand why people say, "That's not possible?"

'It's normal to have to answer those questions after everything that happened last winter,' Holtz said, referring to Armstrong's confession. 'Last winter we really heard about the depth of the problem. We have a responsibility to try to improve that situation.'

Brailsford responded calmly in French. 'I understand, but I've seen him do exactly that, very specific, twice a week, in training. I've seen him do it often.'

Then he added: 'Honestly, when I saw more detail of his performance afterwards, I believed that he could have climbed Ventoux faster.'

In hindsight, his final comment may not have helped defuse the tension.

So here's the thing – my thing – about Team Sky. It has a lot to do with context and with my own experience of covering cycling. Both are relevant: otherwise it may seem as if, to use Brailsford's own words, I've 'got it in' for them.

We are absolutely right to expect the highest levels of probity from Team Sky; I expect less, for example, of Team Astana. That is not because of some notion of British 'fair play', or because Team Sky is British, but because since its inception Team Sky has set itself high standards of accountability, transparency and ethical conduct. They have insisted that we expect this of them.

'No doping will ever take place,' Team Sky pledged. 'Zero tolerance.' This was set out as a guarantee, a guarantee that, in the environment they inhabited, I believe was impossible to maintain. I don't see why Team Sky shouldn't have been expected to adhere to those standards, three, five, ten years down the line.

If you guaranteed that level of propriety, post-Generation EPO, post-Lance, if you presented yourself as the 'cleanest of the clean', then you had better follow through. If not, then you deserved what you got. Most, wearied by all that had gone before, from Pantani to Puerto, Festina to Armstrong, welcomed Team Sky's high-minded positioning; in fact, I'd go as far as to say that they craved it. Team Sky was forgiven the earnest pretentiousness – the mood lighting in the team bus, the thin blue line, the daytime and evening dress codes – because people wanted to believe in what they were saying.

For most of the 1980s and the 1990s, there were only a handful of English-speaking riders in European cycling. At the Tour, there'd be a couple of Australians, a handful of oddball Americans and a token maverick Brit – a Millar (or two), a Yates or a Boardman. When I first started writing about cycling it was hard work getting editors interested in taking stories about foreign stars named Miguel, Gianni, Johan or Toni – no matter what they had won (or how cartoonish a portrait I drew). Then came Lance and his Hollywood success story. In 1999, all that mattered was that an English-speaking cancer survivor had won the Tour de France. His story drew chief sportswriters like bees around honey. Any misgivings were trampled underfoot by the stampede to his door.

Back then, I still believed the mantra that doping was 'dangerous' – that a man who'd had cancer would not dare dope because of the risks to his health. I didn't yet fully understand just how skilfully and effectively doping could be manipulated, with the right doctor and the right budget, even for a former cancer sufferer. That July, I argued with Pierre Ballester, of *L'Équipe*, who insisted Armstrong was doping and was angered by my naivety. And the real significance of Christophe Bassons' mid-race breakdown after Armstrong's bullying, the omnipotence of the *omertà*, eluded me. In hindsight perhaps I knew but refused to acknowledge it.

There is no doubt that the journalists who covered the Armstrong era, and also the many subsequent scandals, have a more jaundiced perspective. They are more sceptical of remarkable performance. That is because many of them erred on the side of caution and sat on the fence, losing credibility through their unwillingness to embrace the suspicion that swirled around the American for so long.

It was a harsh lesson: the fine cord of mutual respect between reporter and athlete that had long been a characteristic of sports-writing, and, forged on the long days on the road, that was particularly evident in cycling, was abruptly cut. I can still hear Raphaël Géminiani telling me, all those years ago, as I jogged towards a Portaloo in Vaujany, that '*cyclisme est une grand famille!*' Maybe, given all the time spent thrown together, it once was, but it's now become a highly dysfunctional one.

By the time the Cofidis scandal swallowed up David Millar's career in the spring of 2004, I was no longer naive. We talked regularly, and as his immersion in the scandal deepened, I understood Millar was caught up in the same vortex and was lying to me, well before his arrest and subsequent confession. In the aftermath of his admission, David and I worked together on his first book, *Racing Through the Dark*. It was a cathartic experience for him. He devoted himself to the project, fever-ishly generating thousands of words, and pouring his creative energies into it.

But after making that journey I knew it would be wrong to get 'close' to a rider ever again. As doping scandals proliferate across sport, it is imperative to be detached.

So I say stick to business and don't blur the lines. Stick to business, because no matter how much you may be drawn to individuals, no matter how charismatic they may be, that's what professional sport has become.

There is no point in Team Sky personnel ever railing against those who question them or pore over their performances. The team has made, and continues to make, strategic errors in terms of their medical and anti-doping policy, their core values of accountability and transparency and particularly in terms of their management of media relationships.

None of that proves that they have been doping. But they have to accept that there are now very significant reasons why people are uneasy. Only a part of that is the legacy of the Armstrong years: part of it is also down to their own decisions, their obfuscation and lack of clarity. Remove the history, pre-Team Sky, and there would still be doubts.

Take, for example, Bradley Wiggins' golden six months of 2012, which spanned March to August and included multiple prestigious stage-race wins, Tour de France victory and an Olympic gold medal. This unprecedented success was achieved during a period when medical consultant Geert Leinders, now banned for life for doping offences earlier in his career, was a retained consultant with Team Sky.

I can't think of another team that has ever, collectively, been under such scrutiny in any sport. But despite their public proc-lamations of openness and transparency, of their willingness to answer every question, that has not been the case, particularly in the hothouse environment of the Tour de France, where, it can be argued, a cool head is most needed. Every New Year, they meet with the media in a series of briefings, some informal, some more structured, and attempt to wipe clean the slate. This is a welcome initiative but every Tour de France still ends in bitterness and recrimination because of unflattering media coverage.

I would have liked to interview Chris Froome for this book, but, despite repeated attempts to arrange a conversation about his 2013 win on the Ventoux, it was not possible.

It appears that I have since been blacklisted by him, or at least by Michelle Froome, who manages his media contacts, because of stories I wrote in July 2015. In two pieces – one appearing in *The Times* (described by Kimmage at the time as the 'official

Waiting for the peloton, high on Ventoux, July 1987.

Dawn on Ventoux, huddled under blankets.

Running on empty on the final bend.

Hugo Koblet, the original *pédaleur de charme*, was as well known for his grooming routine as for his success on his bike. (Offside)

Louison Bobet battles it out with Ferdi Kübler on the lower slopes of Ventoux in 1955 on the way to his third successive yellow jersey. (Offside)

Pierre Dumas fighting to resuscitate Jean Malléjac after the Frenchman's collapse in the forested section of Ventoux's south side. (Offside)

The charismatic Raphael Géminiani is greeted by adoring fans in Monaco during that 1955 Tour. (Getty Images)

13 July 1967: one final laugh in Marseille's sweltering Vieux Port for Tom Simpson and Barry Hoban before they set off for the Ventoux. (Getty Images)

Simpson on the climb up Ventoux. With the financial pressures mounting, he knew he had to put in a good performance, despite the extreme heat and an upset stomach. (PA)

A young Eddy Merckx takes a breather on the beach at the 1967 Giro d'Italia. (Offside)

Nicole Cooke's lone attack on Ventoux's north side went almost unnoticed in the British press, but sealed victory as she became the first Briton to win the Tour de France. (Getty Images)

Tyler Hamilton, photographed after the publication of his book *The Secret Race*, remembers he had 'the best legs I ever had' on Ventoux in 2000. (Offside)

Marco Pantani edges clear of Lance Armstrong at the summit of Ventoux during the 2000 Tour de France. (Getty Images)

Not so mellow: Armstrong during his conciliatory meeting with former French professional Christophe Bassons in December 2013.

(Offside)

The climb through the forest from St Estève to Chalet Reynard can be oppressive and claustrophobic in the heat. (PA)

Chalet Reynard, a key landmark on the southern ascent at 1,426m, with almost 500m of climbing still ahead. (PA)

While the summer can bring extreme heat during the Tour, the 2016 Paris–Nice race came past Chalet Reynard with snow on the ground. (Getty Images)

Ventoux becomes a desolate, cold place – especially when the Mistral blows. (PA)

Chris Froome reinforces his dominance of the 2013 Tour de France as he closes on stage victory at the summit of Ventoux. (Getty Images)

Froome's desperate sprint up Ventoux towards the finish line after crashing in 2016 has already become legendary. (PA)

Dave Brailsford about to challenge the race jury after Froome's crash in July 2016. After all his successes with British Cycling and Team Sky, Brailsford found himself under intense scrutiny as the year ended. (PA)

organ of Team Sky'), the other online for *Men's Health* – I explored the rationale for the continuing trolling of Froome over his ride on Mont Ventoux in 2013. That had been fuelled by a video on YouTube displaying performance data from that day.

The performance data appearing onscreen alongside the footage was touted as conclusive evidence that his ride on the Ventoux in 2013 bore comparison with Armstrong's in July 2000 – that his power outputs, his heart rate were, effectively, 'mutant'. This naturally pressed the 'cheat!' button and generated a lot of white noise. A Twitter storm and oblique suggestions by Team Sky of the hacking, and others the leaking, of his performance analytics only fuelled the Froome-gate frenzy that had begun to build after he had won the first summit finish in the Pyrenees.

However, even now, I am not convinced that the video, while unnerving, conclusively 'proved' anything, beyond the watery nature of the UCI's anti-doping policy, the tawdriness of Twitter trolling and the prevalence of the resulting faithlessness among so many who loved the Tour. Yes, Froome's performance on the bastard Ventoux in 2013 was extraordinary, but did this video provide definitive, irrefutable proof that he had cheated?

And did Froome in 2013 really bear comparison with Armstrong in 2000? Did Merckx in 1970, for that matter, bear comparison with outstanding climbing performances in 1957?

What had happened in sports science and cycling technology in the intervening 13 years? And what, if anything, had changed on the Ventoux?

There were three key factors that favoured Froome against Armstrong: the road surface, the wind and the tactical situation. In 2000, the surface on the climb from Bédoin, particularly above Chalet Reynard, was a rougher aggregate, cracked, pitted and frost-damaged. That created a 'heavy' surface with greater rolling resistance. The road was resurfaced and much improved by 2013.

In 2000, the Mistral was blowing so hard, particularly at the summit and across the final kilometres of the climb, that the Tour organisation opted not to build their usual finish line banners and presentation podium. In contrast, when Froome won in 2013, there was barely any wind at the summit. I have ridden the climb on both surfaces and was at the summit of Ventoux on both of those days.

Froome in 2013 found himself in a different tactical situation to Armstrong. Froome's decisive attack – like Miguel Indurain's in 1994 – came just before Chalet Reynard. Beyond Chalet Reynard he rode a high tempo with Nairo Quintana until he dropped him. Thirteen years earlier, Armstrong was controlling tentative attacks into a buffeting Mistral, until Pantani's moves five kilometres from the summit. The pair traded violent accelerations until they settled into a rhythm, prior to their bitter denouement.

All of that said, the instinctive scepticism persisted, the speculation over doping or hidden motors continues. So where did the deep-seated mistrust of Team Sky come from? Why was the Ventoux such a touchstone for judging Froome?

Beyond the predictable knee-jerk counter-accusations tossed at the sceptics – the trolls were resentful of Froome's success, the French didn't like foreigners, the conspiracy theorists had no understanding of sports science and performance analytics and so on – Team Sky's attempts to build trust had been damaged by some key failings.

The team's zero-tolerance policy had been flawed from the outset as they had recruited staff from a pool of professionals in which it was impossible to guarantee propriety. Nobody, beyond the team itself, believed that 'zero tolerance' was possible. Their ethical stance had been undermined by a series of confessions of past involvement in doping by key members of their coaching and medical staff, who had initially been vetted and given a clean bill of health. This suggested that their vetting process was unreliable.

The team's judgement of 'reputational risk' could be questioned, given the recruitment of personnel such as Leinders and others, including Bobby Julich and Steven de Jongh. Their relationships and histories had been subject to speculation even prior to the team's formation. That insight was easily available.

The zero-tolerance stance had been further undermined by an admitted use of TUEs (therapeutic use exemptions), allowing them to apply to the UCI's medical committee to use prohibited products, in extenuating circumstances. Well before the furore over Wiggins, the team applied for such a TUE for Chris Froome, in April 2014, when he was allowed to use glucocorticosteroids to treat what was described as a chest infection prior to the Tour of Romandie.

Already behind in his build-up for that year's Tour de France, Froome had pulled out of the previous weekend's Liège–Bastogne–Liège and needed to test his form in the Swiss race. The argument that he should rest until his health had recovered, as adhered to by other World Tour teams within the MPCC, was rejected by Team Sky. Froome was granted a TUE, took the corticosteroids, rode in Romandie and won the race.

Team Sky defended their position, saying: 'We follow the rules and ride clean.' Many countered by arguing that, while the UCI decision to grant a TUE was within the rules, Team Sky's ethical stance of zero tolerance had been compromised, that Froome should have been rested, but that such considerations had been overruled by performance objectives. Subsequently, I exchanged direct messages with Michelle

Froome, who took me to task over comments I had made regarding this TUE. 'Chris pulled out of LBL [Liège–Bastogne–Liège] to give him some more time to recover. He was not ill, he did not have a chest infection; his asthma was exacerbated due to a prior infection.'

Yet the Team Sky website had stated at the time that Froome had a mild chest infection and Brailsford had described him as 'ill', while Froome had been reported in the national press as saying: 'I have had a chest infection.'

Michelle Froome responded: 'Both of Chris's TUEs were for exacerbated asthma. Cortisone is not used to treat chest infections – it's an anti-inflammatory. It helps open the airways.

'Chris couldn't breathe without wheezing after the prologue at [the Tour of] Romandie and they applied for an emergency TUE for an asthmatic reaction.'

At the climax of the 2015 Tour de France, as the race headed through the Alps, Froome was again unwell. This time, however, just a year after the Romandie TUE, Froome said he had refused – on moral grounds – to apply for a TUE. 'I didn't feel having a TUE in the last week of the Tour was something I was prepared to do,' he told the BBC in early 2017, adding: 'It did not sit well morally with me.'

There have been other contradictions. The team's response to questioning over its use of the legal but controversial painkiller, tramadol, has been confusing. In 2013, then team doctor Alan Farrell said that tramadol was 'an effective painkiller when it's used in a clinically appropriate scenario. Certainly in our team we would have used it in the past but only when justified.'

In April 2014, as his book *Shadows on the Road* was published, I interviewed former Team Sky rider Michael Barry. 'I used tramadol at Sky,' he said, adding that he saw some Sky riders using it 'frequently' in races.

However, the MPCC – the teams within the French-created Movement for Credible Cycling, the same teams who believed that a rider should be rested, rather than use a TUE – wanted tramadol banned by WADA (World Anti-Doping Agency). Team Sky, despite Christian Prudhomme's public support for the collective, remain resolutely separate from the MPCC.

Jan Mathieu, the team doctor for the Lotto Belisol team, had said: 'Tramadol is a really strong painkiller. It is dangerous for your concentration and you can become addicted to it.' Others also spoke out against painkiller abuse, including Taylor Phinney, the American rider. 'Some people find it surprising that riders would take painkillers or caffeine pills in races, but it is actually really common,' Phinney said in 2012.

'That stuff can make you pretty loopy. I don't even want to try it as I feel it's dangerous. You have to ask, "Why are you taking a painkiller?" Essentially, you are taking a painkiller to enhance your performance.'

In his book, Barry described tramadol as being 'as performance-enhancing as any banned drug I had taken' and added that 'some riders took tramadol every time they raced'. 'The effects are noticeable very quickly,' he said. 'Tramadol made me feel euphoric, but it's also very hard to focus. It kills the pain in your legs and you can push really hard. After I crashed in the Tour de France I was taking it, but I stopped after four days.'

He then added, disconcertingly echoing the histories of Malléjac, Rivière, Simpson and so many others: 'Tramadol allows you to push beyond your natural pain limit.'

After the interview with Barry was published, Team Sky issued a statement: 'None of our riders should ride whilst using tramadol – that's the policy. Team Sky do not give it to riders whilst racing or training, either as a pre-emptive measure or to manage existing pain. We believe that its side effects, such as dizziness and drowsiness, could cause issues for the safety of all riders.'

The statement added: 'We also feel that if a rider has the level of severe pain for its appropriate use they should not be riding.' Yet that level of pastoral care would seem at odds with the willingness to apply for TUEs for team leaders Wiggins and Froome.

The last, most provocative point, revolved around Froome's alleged visits, in the company of Richie Porte, to Philippe Maire's bike shop in Cagnes-sur-Mer, close to Nice. Maire had been a strong amateur rider, whose own aspirations for a pro career had fallen short. But he was friend and mechanic to the Côte d'Azur-based big names, counting Armstrong among them. In April 2014, written answers Armstrong had been compelled to give as part of a lawsuit filed by Acceptance Insurance named Maire as one of those who delivered performance-enhancing drugs to him.

Maire's reputation as one of the best mechanics on the Côte d'Azur ensured that other professionals based in Nice and Monaco also visited him. But Maire was also cited by Tyler Hamilton as the 'Motoman' of legend, the handyman and drugs delivery boy to Armstrong during his seven-year streak. Owen Slot and I interviewed Maire for *The Times* in July 2013. He denied Hamilton's claims, but then revealed that Froome and Richie Porte had made visits to his shop. He added that any further visits had subsequently been prohibited by Brailsford.

Froome and Porte's visits, Maire said, happened prior to Team Sky's creation of a service course – a workshop and equipment store – in Nice. According to Maire, the visits had been at the instigation of his old friend – and Armstrong's – Sean Yates, sports director at Team Sky during Wiggins' golden year of 2012.

In response to Brailsford's exhortations after the Ventoux

stage, asking – understandably – that the media move beyond posing the same question in a hundred different ways, Owen Slot and I then sent an email to him asking for clarification on some points, including Maire's claim that Froome and Porte had visited his shop. These were the questions, sent to Brailsford on two occasions in July 2013, that Owen and I drafted towards the end of that summer's Tour de France.

1. If Chris Froome was doping in secret would you/Team Sky know? Nigel Mitchell [head of nutrition] told us that, except for urine testing to check hydration levels, there is no regular blood profiling/testing done within the team itself. What data do you have to be 100 per cent certain that you know what goes into his body?
2. When you share your data, how can we be sure that it is genuine? Could you not concoct data files with false data?
3. As Sky has been around for a few years now, there has been a natural staff/rider turnover. If you were a doping team, by now there would be whispers/rumours circulating (as with Armstrong). When employees leave Team Sky, what sort of confidentiality agreements do they have to sign?
4. If a rider/riders tested positive, what repercussions would there be from your sponsors? Are there contractual penalties written into riders' contracts and the contract with Sky and other sponsors?
5. Philippe Maire, allegedly Motoman, claims that Chris and Richie were frequent clients of his bike shop in Cagnes-sur-Mer. Is this true? Why did they visit him? Were you aware of this? Maire claims that you told them to stop seeing him. Is that true? If yes, why would you have told them this?

6. Can you clarify Team Sky's policy on needle usage? Are IVs or recuperative IVs ever used? Do the UCI ever check the hotels or team buses for this?

7. Do any of the Sky riders use tramadol? The MPCC urges non-use of tramadol. Is that one reason why Sky won't join the MPCC?

8. Last year, when Sky's riding style was criticised, it was explained that in a clean world, you wouldn't see dramatic accelerations at the end of long stages. But that is what we are seeing now – and yet we are also told that, physiologically, Chris hasn't changed dramatically since last year. Why is he able to ride in this way then?

9. One of the reasons the questions still remain is the zero-tolerance team clear-out last autumn is not convincing. Why did Sean Yates leave? Did you have any misgivings over his ethical stance or history? Dario Cioni failed a haematocrit test – was that covered in your questioning? Are you convinced he never doped? Likewise Servais Knaven, who was with TVM and T-Mobile at times of team doping crises?

We thanked him for his time and looked forward to hearing from him. Brailsford didn't reply.

And the enduring collective value of the MPCC? Well, Brailsford's misgivings on that score at least proved well founded. The MPCC's resolve was tested in July 2015 when Astana's Lars Boom tested positive for cortisol, two days before the 2015 Tour started. Under MPCC rules, Boom should have been withdrawn by his team, rested for eight days and thus not started the Tour. But, as the deadline for substitute riders had been passed, that would have left Astana a man short for team leader Vincenzo Nibali's defence of his 2014 Tour title. Faced with the choice of undermining Nibali's ambitions even before the race began, or exile from the MPCC, Astana didn't hesitate for a moment. They turned their backs on the MPCC and Boom started the race.

Perhaps Team Sky should be flattered. As I said, people hold it to high standards: they expect less, much less, of Team Astana.

Midway through the 2015 Tour, I was tired from a long drive towards the Alps. After filing my copy, I went to bed early. About half past midnight, my phone rang, once, twice, each time with a bad signal. The third time, much clearer, there was a woman's voice in my ear, shrill, high-pitched, angry. 'Jeremy? This is Michelle Froome . . .'

A week earlier, unsolicited, she had started messaging me during that summer's Tour, initially about her husband's reluctance to wear the yellow jersey after race leader Tony Martin had crashed out, then regarding the bottle-throwing incident between Vincenzo Nibali and Froome on the same stage, sending me a very poor-quality image, in which a bottle-clutching arm is raised.

Now, however, with her husband a few days from overall victory, she was raging against the media, targeting my work and that of others, as well as some on Twitter and some working for rival teams. My story on Philippe Maire was the last straw. Now she said she couldn't even bear to come near to the Tour, to visit her husband.

I tried to remain calm. 'Then maybe you shouldn't come, Michelle,' I said. 'Maybe it's too toxic.' That word again – the word that always best captured the Armstrong years and the mistrust and suspicion that hung in the air, constantly.

After what she had said about my own stories detailing why there was such scepticism towards Froome, I asked if her husband could clarify to me if he had in fact visited Maire for legitimate reasons. I suggested that, as she managed his press relations, she might facilitate me speaking to him the next morning. I knew this was unlikely, however, as the Froomes had already tried to enforce a copy-approval agreement on all interviews after his first Tour win. The next morning, when a voicemail landed, it wasn't Froome, but a press officer from Team Sky. I called him back.

'It's about your piece,' he said, referring to the story I'd written for *The Times* that week, setting out the French suspicions towards Froome. He wanted to take issue. He and I talked at length as I crawled through the traffic jams on the A7, south towards Lyon and on towards the stage finish in Valence. It wasn't the first time I'd been cold-called by the team after a critical story had been published. Other senior figures within Team Sky had vented down the phone in the past.

But this conversation was less confrontational. I stood by what I'd said, pointing out that I had put both sides, that I'd made it clear that it was simplistic to compare Froome's Ventoux ride in 2013 with Armstrong's in 2000, but I also reaffirmed my view that Team Sky's use of a TUE had been glib and contrary to their positioning of zero tolerance. I defended the mention of Froome's visits to Philippe Maire's bike shop, first detailed in *The Times* in July 2013.

'Those visits were not suspicious!' he said, while also acknowledging that the visits to Maire's shop had taken place. He told me that, yes, they had occurred but they had been entirely innocent. I countered by saying that if they had taken place then there might a question of judgement to be addressed. 'That story was first published two years ago,' I said. 'It's been out there since then.' And we'd sought clarification in 2013, I pointed out, recalling the email that we had sent Brailsford at the time requesting his version of events, that he had not replied to.

Given Maire's close relationship with Yates – 'my best friend', the Frenchman had told us – it seemed quite likely that Yates, who has always denied any connections with doping, had recommended his French mechanic friend to his two team leaders. Asking questions about the exact nature of Froome and Porte's relationship with Maire was both logical and legitimate.

When I got to Valence that lunchtime, the atmosphere in the pressroom was foul. I wasn't the only journalist who'd been contacted by an angry Michelle Froome in the past 24 to 48 hours. Instead of answering essential questions, Team Sky had turned to attacking those who asked them. In the heat of battle, just when they needed to demonstrate them most, Team Sky had deserted their launch values, of accountability and transparency.

This was a depressingly familiar scenario from the Armstrong Era, the Tour de France as Groundhog Day. Too many of us had been here before, blacklisted, cold-called, bullied and manipulated, during the Armstrong years. These were the 'old' ways; this was how the *omertà* worked.

The Ventoux video, the alleged hacking of detailed information, the supposed bias of some journalists, both for and against, the anger of the Froomes and Team Sky, the weary suspicion of the French and the knee-jerk retaliation of a chauvinistic British media, some of whom had not lived through the Lance Era, had fermented into a familiar atmosphere.

Two years after Armstrong's confession, the air was toxic again.

'The better we do, the more questions we get asked,' Dave Brailsford says.

'What we want to try and prove is that we can genuinely do this – we want to make unbelievable things believable,' he reiterates. 'But it's such a challenge . . .'

Had Brailsford felt protective of Froome after the controversy over his victory on the Ventoux?

'Yeah . . . I think I was. I felt it was unjust and I still feel it is unjust.

'I was happy for him, for what he'd done. But then, pretty quick, you realise, "Jesus, he's going to get hit pretty hard – he's going to have to deal with all this shit." That's what got my back up.

'If I thought he was doing something wrong, if I didn't believe him, I wouldn't be doing this. And I do believe him, one hundred per cent, and I do think he's doing it the right way.

'The idea that "this is not fair" whirls around inside your head. There's a dynamic, oscillating all the time, between "Come on, you need to answer these questions, it's the right thing to do" through to "This is bollocks".

'In the end it came back to the whole question of data again – that's why the demand for numbers raised its head. Nothing was going to take away from the pleasure of the performance, and you've got to enjoy it otherwise why do it?'

Then there's all the other stuff – the media pressing around the bus, in your face, doubting their own interpretations, desperate not to be fooled again, dredging up innuendo and rumour but also unsure what to write . . . this is uncharted territory, I say. Nobody said it was easy . . .

He nods. '. . . and it's a separate challenge, really. When it comes to that separate challenge, the thing that we started to engage more with was whether we should release the data and, if we do, what would happen then.

'There are two ways of approaching it. You either gather the facts, do it properly – look at the facts and on the balance of what you have, the balance of probability, you form an opinion. That's one way.

'The second way is that you decide on your opinion, then you gather the facts and then you make sure that the facts are interpreted in a way that reinforces your opinion.

'I'm all for the first approach,' he says, 'but not for the second. There are too many people taking the second approach and lacking scientific rigour, looking for evidence that will back an opinion.'

The pseudo-scientists, you mean?

'Yes – they don't test the rigour of the evidence first; they don't make sure it stands up. They can't see through those separate distinctions.'

But isn't dealing with that, however infuriating and frustrating it may be, however misinformed or cynical, the key element in the team's brief – isn't that the transparency and accountability part of Team Sky's original mission? Isn't that the cornerstone?

'Everybody's interested in comparing – there's nothing wrong with that. We're interested, too, but do it with the right information – do it in a rigorous way. Draw your conclusions afterwards, not before.'

Surprisingly, he does think that it is possible to compare current and past performances on the Ventoux. 'I think you can, but only if it's rigorous. Let's really look at the conditions, what was going on in the peloton at the time, what was the temperature at the time, what was the length of the stage – let's go to town on it all – then you can have an informed opinion about it.

'But really, ultimately, unless you have everybody fresh, riding from the bottom to the top, on the same day, then you can't draw any real conclusions. I get that comparisons are fun, but it has to be done in the context where there's no margin for error.'

The abuse, the scepticism, the mockery and questioning – surely that takes its toll?

'My job is to be robust and resilient enough to take that on board and to try to protect the team from it. It doesn't take a genius to see that if you want to pull a load of people together, to motivate them, you find a common enemy.

'All the stuff that comes at us just galvanises everybody. In many respects it makes my job easier. Everybody's pumped up because they feel under attack. It's a siege mentality – you can start to use language which is quite emotive. That really worked for us in 2015, when Chris was getting such a hard time. I was thinking, of that very emotionally charged situation, "How can you use this to try to get a better performance?"'

In the end, for better or worse, he admits that Team Sky unleashed their inner chimps.

'We decided to close ranks and say: "Fuck 'em all – we're going to win this race, we're going to pull together." Everyone was up for that.'

Even, says Brailsford, the most affable team personnel, such as coach Rod Ellingworth. 'When you've got someone like Rod, a very personable, popular, likeable guy, saying, "I'm not taking this shit," that's a big behavioural change. When they saw that, it galvanised everybody and brought the group together.

'So you can use it for your own benefit, although I wouldn't say it was optimal. You'd prefer to be in a situation, at some point in the future, where people see a performance and go: "Wow, that's amazing – well done."'

He returns to his baseline, to where we started. 'We want to make the unbelievable believable,' he reiterates.

There's a resigned smile. 'It feels a long way off, though.'

An hour ahead of the peloton racing in the 2016 Paris–Nice, I sit waiting at Chalet Reynard, listening to race radio. Here, in the lee of the mountain, with the peloton approaching from the north, the reception isn't so good, but I can just about hear the time checks.

'*Huit minutes pour les échappées,*' after just over 20 kilometres, the radio says ... Then, '*Dix minutes pour les échappées,*' this time after 30 kilometres. I can't catch any of the names in the breakaway apart from the immediately recognisable '*Boooom*' of Lars Boom.

There is hazy sunshine at Chalet Reynard, but the temperature is struggling. The deep snow banks of the previous week have almost melted away. It's almost spring, but not quite. A pair of Brits at the café – one wearing kit from Edgware Road Club and the other Rapha CC's melancholic all-black – drink coffee and swap stories. They have followed the race from the frozen, icy hills of the Beaujolais, down to the watery spring sunshine of the Ventoux.

Inside the café, the log fire is burning and the rotisserie turning. Yet despite a queue of hungry fans at 11.50, the kitchen remains firmly closed. '*A midi!*' insists the owner tetchily as, one by one, punters ask if they can eat. '*Nooooon . . . pas avant midi!*'

Far below, as the break's lead grows to 11 minutes, the chase is on, as Team Sky and Tinkoff Saxo move to the front of the peloton. The loss of the Mont Brouilly finish 48 hours earlier, due to snow, has robbed race favourites Alberto Contador, Geraint Thomas and Richie Porte of a key rendezvous. Instead, Michael Matthews – the Australian equivalent to Peter Sagan, able to climb and sprint – rides on in yellow.

The breakaway leaves Bédoin behind and, as the climb begins, André Greipel is one of the first to crack. He is distanced even before St Estève, on the slope leading through the hamlet of St Colombe. In the peloton other sprinters soon follow suit and, by St Estève, Tyler Farrar, Tom Boonen and Marcel Kittel are losing contact. Unexpectedly, Andrew Talansky, the volatile hope of American cycling, is also among them.

But this is the Ventoux: a ruthless indicator of who's been naughty and who's been good during the winter break, even as early as March. Some of those left behind will make up for lost time: after the freezing descent from Chalet Reynard to Sault, there are still 120 kilometres to race, across country to the finish in Salon-de-Provence. So the crowd stands around, stamping their feet to keep warm, biding their time, cheering the occasional race vehicle that comes past, eavesdropping on race radio.

The breakaways eventually appear, wrapped up against the cold, but breathing hard. The climb has done its job, reducing them down to a handful. Boom is long gone and the peloton is now closing fast. The Movistar team lead the field past, but they remain bunched together, Contador, Thomas and Porte in their midst, riding at brisk training pace. This is nothing compared to the intensity expected in July, when the race returns for the Tour de France.

The stars roll past, followed by the long line of team cars. The convoy turns right, accelerates and disappears back into the forest and then turns towards the valley again, descending towards Sault and the Plateau d'Albion.

Race radio crackles again. Greipel has abandoned.

On 14 July 2016, the Tour de France returned to Mont Ventoux.

To the sound of a distant dustcart, beeping, banging and rattling its way through the sunrise, I woke up next to Richie Porte. The Australian was in the neighbouring room in my hotel, Le Clos de l'Aube Rouge, in an anonymous suburb of Montpellier. We'd crossed paths on the gloomy corridor the night before, acknowledging each other with a cursory nod. After the wind-blown stage from Carcassonne to Montpellier, BMC Racing team's leader was turning in for an early night, just as I was heading out in search of a late dinner.

As we passed each other, there was a flicker of recognition in his eyes, based perhaps on some vague memory of his hackles rising in response to a question about his improved performances after his 2013 victory in Paris–Nice. But maybe not: maybe it was my imagination. Perhaps by now any rider who'd won a race in Team Sky colours had become so accustomed to that line of questioning, the constant innuendo, that it was quickly forgotten, water off a duck's back.

By the next morning, he probably thought I was stalking him. We exited our rooms at almost the same moment, me appearing in the corridor as he locked his own door, both grunting in recognition once more and me then following him – at a respectful distance, mind – down the same gloomy passage, through the lobby and to the hotel's breakfast room.

Richie is an odd fish. It's hard to shake the idea that, with his talents, a more forceful character would have achieved greater results. But he struggles to impress, his voice a flat monotone and his demeanour often one of boredom. He always appears a little distracted. But he must love cycling because on his 29th birthday he rode 400 kilometres around Tasmania in a single day, with fellow pro Cameron Wurf, sustaining himself with Coke, iced coffee and cheese and Vegemite rolls.

I've seen him really animated just the once, hurling abuse at former team-mate and training partner Froome as they crossed a finish line during the 2016 Critérium du Dauphiné, moments after Team Sky's leader and his team-mates had blocked Porte's path and cost him a top-three finish in the Alpine race. I didn't catch all of what was said, as a breeze blew across the mountains and the crowd, such as it was, cheered the riders home, but as the pair free-wheeled past us, I was pretty sure I heard Porte bellow a stream of obscenities. We jogged after him, anticipating a Cavendish-style meltdown of helmet-hurling and microphone-mashing. But no: ten minutes later, Richie had calmed down, got off the bus and assured us that everything between him and Chris was just fine.

Back in Montpellier, I walked through the lobby towards the

breakfast room. Two or three armed gendarmes, in bullet-proof vests, their right hands on their holsters, hung around edgily in the reception area. Post-*Charlie Hebdo*, post-Bataclan, this was the Tour's new normal and a sight I was becoming increasingly used to as the race wore on. France's most-loved sporting event was on terror alert. A police car parked outside, adjacent to the BMC Racing team bus, monitored the hotel entrance.

I sat down to breakfast a few tables from BMC's management, where Jim Ochowicz – with almost two weeks of the Tour still to come – was talking through plans for the team's end-of-race party in Paris. Porte, the first of his riders to appear, paused to say good morning before strolling on to the private annexe where he and his team-mates ate undisturbed.

Today, Ventoux day, was a big moment for Porte, a potential moving day. He had lost vital time on the second stage of the race, stalled by a puncture on the climb to the finish in Cherbourg. On that occasion, he hadn't calmed down before speaking to the press and his fragile self-belief was all too visible. 'It was a disaster but what can you do?' he blurted, before venting about sustaining his hopes, not of overall victory, but for a stage win. Since then, BMC had been working to rebuild his morale. Now they would find out how effective their reboot had been.

It was a big day for me as well. For the first time in over a decade, I'd opted to take up a place on the press motorbike offered up to the media. Years ago, when the riders washed their own kit each evening and slept in musty dormitories, and Dr Dumas rode pillion, many journalists covered major races, such as the Tour, from motorbikes. This was long before the Tour became a motorshow, long before race car parks were crammed with branded-up Octavias, Scenics, Méganes and even the occasional Maserati Ghibli.

The great pontificators of cycling journalism once rode

pillion, like Dumas, stopping at a mid-stage buffet and nodding off against their driver's back on long, hot stages through the flatlands, donning mackintosh and flat cap for storm-wracked stages through the Alps and Pyrenees. They spent hours chin-stroking their way through 600 words and a bottle of Brouilly or Morgon, sometimes even at the same dining table as the riders. They read their copy down the line, from a phone box or a hotel lobby. They didn't have to do podcasts, webchats, live radio, blogs, tweets, or Instagram sunsets (hashtag cliché). They certainly didn't write about doping.

Now, following an initiative from the Tour's *service presse*, they can do that again – the pillion passenger part, that is, not the chin-stroking. Taking a seat on the motorbike was a chance to get closer to the peloton, to experience the weather, the bumps and gradients in the road, the wind in my face. After years spent driving to the pressroom and finding a place in a crammed sports hall or gymnasium, as close to a plasma screen as possible, I wanted to experience that again. Luckily, nobody else wanted to take the remaining available pillion seat on the stage from Montpellier to the Ventoux.

I cadged a lift to the start with the fresh-faced team from Danish newspaper *BT*, covering only their second Tour. We headed into town, parallel to the race route, me encouraging them to drive the wrong way down tram tracks as we struggled through the road closures to the start. 'Don't worry, it's the Tour – there won't be any trams today,' I said airily as a tram appeared around a corner and rolled alarmingly quickly towards us.

Already, the wind that had marked the previous afternoon's racing and decapitated the eagerly awaited finish on the Giant was blowing hard. A viciously gusting Mistral sent spirals of dust spinning into the blue sky at the start village in Montpellier's Champ de Mars gardens.

The stage had been scheduled to climax at Ventoux's summit, but after the recent introduction of the extreme-weather protocol, ASO were wary of taking risks. Faced with 100-kilometre-an-hour winds, the Tour organisation had to consider the worst-case scenario – that the protocol was invoked mid-stage and the summit finish abandoned. So Prudhomme and his team opted to bring the finish line down the mountain to Chalet Reynard.

The decision was met with disappointment and derision from some. Prudhomme, however, insisted that there was no choice. 'We can't set up two finish lines. We're not going to play poker by saying, "Let's see tomorrow whether we put it higher or lower,"' he had explained the previous evening in Montpellier.

Prudhomme didn't respond well to one journalist's suggestion that cycling was getting soft. 'I think it was the right decision, the decision of a responsible organiser, to protect both the riders and the public.'

Already in March 2016, ASO had cancelled a stage of Paris–Nice, invoking the new extreme-weather protocol (EWP) as sleet settled on the roads around Mont Brouilly. The introduction of the EWP had been accelerated by indecision at two recent Italian races, Milan–San Remo in 2013 and Tirreno–Adriatico in 2015. On both occasions, as heavy snow fell on the peloton, there had been heated debate over whether to continue racing. The parameters of the newly introduced EWP were developed to end the conficts between riders and race organisers. The EWP had been welcomed by some but also criticised by others.

As Team Sky's Rod Ellingworth pointed out, the days of suffering through blizzards and freezing rain were probably over. So, in all probability, were the days of extraordinary exploits, such as Bernard Hinault's victory in the snowbound 1980 Liège–Bastogne–Liège or Andy Hampsten's attack, mid-blizzard, on the Gavia climb, during the 1988 Giro d'Italia.

'Things move on,' Ellingworth said. 'We spend a lot of money on riders, and their health and safety is key to the team. So I don't think there's any team who would have wanted to carry on on Mont Brouilly.

'If you did get riders injured badly in those conditions, you'd think, "Why didn't they stop the race?"

'So carrying on is a big risk. Everybody knows that and everybody knows that cancelling the race is a big deal too. I don't think there's an ideal solution.'

Not everyone was so sure. Allan Peiper, a survivor of the 1988 blizzard on the Gavia and now a sports director at BMC, was conflicted. 'If I look back, I was proud to go over the Gavia that day,' the Australian said, as we stood in warm sunshine in Nice, a few days after the Brouilly stage had been cancelled. 'I was last over the top of the Gavia, and I finished 39th on the stage and rode all the way to the finish. It was something to go through, a rite of passage. Maybe that's lost now because of the growing professionalism of the sport.'

Did Peiper think that some riders needed to man up a bit?

'I can think that, but I can't say it. I come from a different generation.

'I came to Europe and lived in an old butcher's shop, stealing spinach from a stall at the side of the street, so how can I tell riders to toughen up? It's like two different worlds.'

Peiper's schooling as a professional was in Flanders, where the icy winters hardened him. 'But global warming has changed things,' he said. 'I remember in the winter of 1985 to 1986. There were two weeks in Belgium when it was minus 15, and I trained nearly every day, around Geraardsbergen, where the roads were salted.

'I was used to riding in those conditions but those days are gone: we don't have that weather any more. We haven't really had a wet Paris–Roubaix in 20 years, so the riders are not as used to those conditions.

'You get the first hint of rain in Belgium and the riders are travelling to Spain to train. The mentality has changed.'

As a young rider, Peiper experienced bad weather on the Ventoux. 'I defended the white jersey in Paris–Nice on the Ventoux in March 1985. It had been snowing then, too, and the snow was at least a metre thick on the side of the road.

'We made it to Chalet Reynard where the finish was – Sean Kelly won and took the leader's jersey. It wasn't raining or snowing but it was freezing.

'But I hate the Ventoux, just hate it. It's a bastard of a climb. I've ridden it a couple of times in the past few years – in fact, a couple of years ago I got up in an hour and 32 minutes, which is pretty quick for my age.

'But,' Peiper said, 'every time I go back I wonder, "What *am* I thinking . . .?!"'

I pulled my helmet on and climbed aboard the Kawasaki motorbike. Laurent, my driver, had done 13 Tours on a motorbike, in the race. Nothing, it seemed, fazed him. He'd grown used to having team cars brush his knee as they eased past to deliver a fresh bidon or five to their domestiques. We chatted a little before we set off. He didn't do this every July for the money, he said, but out of his lifelong love for cycling and particularly for the Tour.

As soon as we rolled out of Montpellier, the wind was tugging at us, buffeting the bike, pulling cypress trees out of shape, blowing flags on campervans taut. Soon, race radio crackled into life. A breakaway of 13 had formed, including André Greipel, the German sprinter whose hopes of leading the race to the revised finish at Chalet Reynard were non-existent.

Laurent let the break ride past. We slipped in alongside, riding just off the back wheel of the last rider, leaning into the curves as the group sped on, hitting a steady 40 kph on the flat but reaching 60 kph when the Mistral changed direction and became a tailwind. We followed for a while then pulled over and waited what seemed an age – almost a quarter of an hour – for the peloton. Eventually, with the familiar dark jerseys of Team Sky massed at the front, and a skeletal figure in yellow tucked in behind them, the peloton breezed past.

Then we were off again, speeding to the rear of the huge group of riders, massed shoulder to shoulder across the road. As the team in pole position in the overall standings, Team Sky's lead car wore a red number '1', and led the convoy of support cars in their wake.

Riding at the back of the peloton, alongside his Astana team car, was recent Giro d'Italia winner, Vincenzo Nibali. The chance of any Tour glory long gone and his mind now firmly set on the Rio Olympics, Nibali had turned domestique. I watched as the 2014 Tour winner stuffed water bottle after water bottle down the neck of his jersey before elegantly speeding back up to the peloton.

I glanced across at sports director Nicolas Portal in Team Sky's number '1' car. Cradling the road book's stage profile on his lap, he sent instructions to his riders, barking orders into his short-wave radio. Moments later, as the peloton approached the Bouches-du-Rhône where the Mistral was blowing hardest, the pace suddenly lifted. We too picked up speed, barrelling through Tarascon and gunning our way towards St Rémy-de-Provence, showering sparks as we grazed the kerb, the trees at the roadside bent over, the gusting winds battering the peloton and moving the Kawasaki around.

Huge gaps appeared between the huddled groups of riders as the wind split the field. I watched them, hunched over their bikes, battling to hold on, until, one by one, they lost contact with the wheel ahead of them. Fabio Aru, slated as one of Froome's main rivals, now riding on a punctured tyre, braked to a halt and slid off his bike, only to remount, in the blink of an eye, on a team-mate's machine. Before I could even turn to watch his pursuit of the bunch, Aru, mouth agape, was back alongside us, riding at 60 kilometres an hour and shepherded by three of his team as they chased down the yellow jersey group up ahead.

Finally, the Ventoux's bleached summit came into view. On the lumpy, bumpy climb past Gordes and climbing up from the lavender-filled valley of the abbey of Sénanque, the breakaway clung on to its lead, Greipel still hanging on through the warm afternoon. We hurtled downhill, past Venasque and on towards Bédoin. Laurent, conscious of the fast-approaching race, accelerated past the now fracturing break, and motored on towards the foot of the climb at St Estève.

As we began the climb through the forest, the crowds were thick, but not intimidating, not even at 'Froome's Corner', the spot where, in 2013, he had suddenly accelerated clear of his rivals before winning the stage. The cynicism that greeted Froome's turn of speed that day hadn't dissipated. As Laurent leaned the Kawasaki through the corner, I spotted two fans dressed as speed cameras.

We threaded our way through the crowds and then into the barriered-off section leading to the finish. Laurent dropped me just behind the line and we shook hands. Then we both set off in search of a TV screen to watch the final moments.

The TV coverage of those closing moments has already become classic, unforgettable footage, totally in keeping with the Ventoux's timeless capacity to generate high drama. The images of Porte slamming into the rear end of a stalled motorbike, of three riders on the floor, of a leering crowd taunting the yellow jersey in the Tour de France, as they watched him running, not cycling, on Mont Ventoux, have a Hogarthian quality. This was bedlam on – and off – a bike.

No wonder, that when he finally rolled across the line, Froome was shaking his head in disbelief. Moments later, Dave Brailsford, his face like thunder, marched past me and headed straight for the referees, the UCI race jury and commissaires. Moments before, he had been sitting, with Alastair Campbell, in the Team Sky tour bus – the 'Death Star' – parked a couple of hundred metres away, watching his bike-less team leader jogging up Ventoux.

'It was like a real "what the fuck?" moment,' Campbell recalled. 'There had been the shortening of the route because of the weather, and then that. I thought Chris showed remarkable calm.

'Dave and the other guys on the bus were pretty calm as well, considering. Dave was straight onto the notion that they would need to have a defence for all the different actions Chris took.'

It took over an hour to make a decision to reinstate Froome as race leader. Boos mixed with cheers as he finally appeared in front of a dwindling crowd for the podium presentation. My immediate reaction was that such a decision would generate even more anti-Team Sky sentiment. Yet even truncated, the Ventoux hadn't disappointed, although the whole drama was soon to be put into terrifying perspective.

The lingering image of Froome, wearing the yellow jersey and running up Ventoux, slotted seamlessly into the mythology of Kübler and Malléjac, Simpson and Merckx, Bernard and Fignon, Poli and Pantani. Ventoux was always dramatic.

We left Chalet Reynard and got back into the warmth of the car. The wind had eased a little during the afternoon, but now as the sky darkened and the temperature dropped, it was picking up again. Even though the summit hadn't been fit to race up to, the evacuation route for all race vehicles was over the top. We drove uphill, past discarded crowd barriers, tossed angrily across the vast scree by the Mistral. The wind buffeted the car yet harder. Further up, a line of campervans had paused, wobbling in the wind, hazards on, uncertain whether to continue.

'This really is a bit mad,' Pete Goding, sitting in the passenger seat downloading images from his camera, said, with some understatement. I drove on.

We rounded the famed final hairpin and the full force of the raging Mistral slammed into the side of the car. Lying on top of a motorbike, were two motorcyclists in helmets and leathers, clinging onto their machine. A clutch of cyclists crouched, shivering, against the vast bulk of the meteorological station. Hikers, desperate to get out of the wind, fumbled their way downhill on all fours, clambering over rocks and clinging to the black-and-yellow snow poles.

We paused in the lee of the wind at the foot of the Tintin rocket and then eased gingerly over the top. Just below the summit, a four-by-four's rear end was jacked up, off the ground, back wheels spinning, the caravan hooked to its towbar lying on its side, slowly dragging the car across the tarmac towards the edge of the road. A group clustered around the front end of the car, clinging to the open doors, battling to hold it in place.

Easing through the chaos, we began the descent. Within a kilometre or so, the wind had eased dramatically. By the time we reached Malaucène it was little more than a stiff breeze.

Later, Team Sky's Rod Ellingworth described the mayhem on the Death Star. The bus had been tilted over on one side at the summit, the alarms ringing frantically and terrified riders throwing themselves onto the floor. Alastair Campbell was another of those who drove over the summit. 'It was horrific,' he said. 'We ended up packing in a load of Spanish hitchhikers who were planning to walk over the top.'

It was very late when we got to the hotel, hidden away in the Drôme countryside. I checked Twitter before I fell asleep, but the Wi-Fi signal was so slow that my eyes were closing, even as I saw an AFP newsflash about a serious traffic accident in Nice, on the Promenade des Anglais. I woke early the next morning and headed downstairs, sitting under the giant plane tree in the courtyard, hoping to be brought coffee. The Wi-Fi signal was better there, but Twitter still refused to load.

Madame appeared and we exchanged greetings. '*Bien dormi?*' she asked, out of habit rather than interest.

Unfortunately, I hadn't, so I said so. It's the Tour, I explained, it messes with your sleep. She nodded.

'*Moi non plus,*' she said. There was a pause.

'It's just so awful.'

I looked up and saw there was a tear rolling down her cheek.

I shifted uneasily in my chair. 'What . . . what's happened?'

She wiped her eyes. 'In Nice, the killings in Nice.'

So she told me, about the madman driving through the crowds watching the Bastille Day fireworks, using his lorry like a battering ram, targeting pushchairs, mowing them down, killing 86 people. I sat, listening, stunned into silence, suddenly very awake.

We packed in a panic, paid our bill and got back into the car, trying to understand. Pete drove, fast, as I scoured for any updates online on terror and the Tour. We got closer to the autoroute and closer to a 4G signal. Twitter loaded and simultaneously the texts and messages came flooding in. The stage was cancelled – the Tour was stopping, or so some of them said. Or it might be stopping. Nobody knew for sure, not yet.

I checked with French colleague Julien Prétot. No news yet, he said. Prudhomme was talking to the Élysée Palace, to the President.

And then there was a voicemail from the newsdesk.

'How quickly can you get to Nice?' the message asked.

I called in. They asked again: 'How far are you from Nice?'

'Probably three, maybe four hours,' I said, suddenly dreading the instruction that might come, to turn around, head to the motorway, blast over to Nice; to doorstep broken families, red-eyed policemen, disbelieving relatives.

'That far? Hmm ... OK.' It's too far, I realised. They're not going to ask me to go.

'So what's happening with the race?'

'Prudhomme's making a statement,' I said. 'We're on our way.'

I jogged through the parked cars, past the Tour security crew and into the pretty main square in Bourg-Saint-Andéol. It was the earliest I'd been in a Tour start village for years.

Over at the ASO stand, Prudhomme, Cyrille Tricart and Jean-Louis Pages were deep in conversation. Prudhomme was frowning, focusing on tugging a black armband over the sleeve of his shirt. He caught my eye and nodded, unsmiling, in recognition. He'd dealt with crises before – Puerto, Landis, Armstrong. But that was doping. That was nothing compared to this.

All the staff were following suit, hastily pulling on black armbands. Then Prudhomme strode across the start village to the '*espace interview*', site of ad-hoc press meetings. We gathered around him, camera crews, boom mikes, iPhones. He composed himself and then started speaking: 'We have had a crisis meeting with the prefecture of the Ardèche and the gendarmerie. The Tour will continue.'

And then, a crack audible in his voice, he said: 'We want this day to be a day of dignity as a tribute to the victims.

'We asked ourselves if the stage should be cancelled, but after talking to the highest authorities in the state, we think that the race must continue.'

Abruptly, he turned away before taking his place alongside local police, dignitaries, race officials, in a minute's silence. Before I left the village I ran into Jean-Louis Pages, working his last Tour for ASO. 'I'm so sorry,' I said. 'This must be so hard to deal with.'

'For me, not really. It's tougher for the police. We follow their advice. We do as we're told.'

Jean-Louis introduced the Tour's gendarmerie liaison officer, Lieutenant Colonel Eric Luzet. 'We were in direct contact with the Élysée Palace,' Luzet said. 'It was decided to carry on with the Tour because it was important to continue to live normally.'

By now, with the sun climbing into the morning sky, the teams had all arrived, the time trial's early starters going through the motions, warming up in the shade of the canopies extending from each bus. I paused to say hello to an unsettled Rod Ellingworth, hanging around in front of the Team Sky bus. He had security on his mind. 'We're so vulnerable,' he said of the teams and of the Tour, 'even if they load the place with gendarmes. I've told my missus to skip coming to Paris after this. It's not worth it . . .'

But other than extreme measures – heavier security, snipers on rooftops, bag searches, tickets, even no public access – how can you protect 200 kilometres of open road?

'*Pas possible*,' Jean-Louis had said, before adding that it went against everything, the years of open access, that the Tour stood for. Instead, he said, you just have to do the best you can.

The snipers and the 'super-gendarmes', Luzet had said, were 'everywhere on the Tour'. 'They are here in case there is a particularly dangerous situation, such as a terrorist attack,' he'd told me.

I saw them a couple of days later, at another start village, in Moirans-en-Montagne. 'See those guys?' said Julien Prétot, nudging me and pointing to two figures perched on a clifftop, one holding binoculars, the other a rifle, scanning the crowd pressed against the barriers and milling around the riders.

There was a muted howl of protest from rival teams after Chris Froome had been restored as race leader following the debacle on the Ventoux. It wasn't immediate, because Nice overshadowed every other concern, but within 48 hours the resentment was simmering. One sports director accused the UCI of 'making the rules up as they go along', while Patrick Lefevere, general manager of the Etixx Quick-Step team, was even more critical. 'You think it was the UCI commissaires who decided about Froome being reinstated?' he said provocatively. 'The UCI has to be the boss – but it isn't.'

Lefevere said that there was no point in lodging a protest against the decision to reinstate Froome in the yellow jersey. 'They don't even listen,' he said.

I asked if they listened to Sir Dave Brailsford. 'Maybe,' he smiled. 'I have the impression that everybody is happy Froome is in yellow.'

Nairo Quintana's sports director, Eusebio Unzué, was also critical of the decision.

'If we have rules, we have to apply them fairly. It has to be equal, for all riders, for all teams, for all racers. The worst thing about all this isn't what happened, but the precedent they've established. What's going to happen the next time? Sure, it was exceptional, but there are crashes every day. That is part of cycling. You crash, you get up, you carry on.'

'It was not a good decision,' Marc Madiot, director of French team FDJ, told me. 'Froome is not popular in France and I don't think this decision did him any favours.

'Look, I don't think it was fair what happened to him, but the next day in the time trial he would have taken the race lead anyway. They didn't need to make a special case.

'There have been crowd problems on the Tour for a hundred years. If it had been somebody other than Froome, they wouldn't have done anything.'

Lefevere also suggested that Froome was, in some way, protected. 'You saw the other day, when the group of four, with Froome and Peter Sagan, went clear [on the stage to Montpellier].

'Okay, they were strong, but normally the peloton would chase and catch them. But the red car of the Tour organisation and five motorbikes were immediately in front of them. If you ever rode a bike,' Lefevere said, 'you'll know what I mean.'

Surely Froome's misfortune, many argued, was just that – bad luck? Punctures are bad luck; crashes can sometimes be bad luck. Being misdirected by gendarmes within sight of the finish line is bad luck. Level crossings dropping in front of the pursuing peloton as a break slips clear, that's more bad luck. It's all part of racing on the open road. If Froome's finishing time was to be adjusted because of the logjam on the Ventoux, how about all the others who had suffered bad luck, on a daily basis?

And there were other criticisms filtering through, revolving around the interpretation of UCI rules and regulations. Should Froome, for example, have been disqualified for running? Possibly, said some, if you followed the letter of the law, yes. Others said no, that riders have been seen making their way on foot – walking, jogging, running – in other chaotic circumstances, such as the Koppenberg climb in the Tour of Flanders, or the Arenberg forest in Paris–Roubaix.

Under the usual interpretation of UCI rules, riders always have to be with their bike, functioning or not, and should not use any other form of transport. The rules specify that 'attempts to finish without having completed the whole course on a bicycle' shall result in a fine and disqualification. In the 2015 Tour, when Argentinian rider Eduardo Sepúlveda panicked after his team car failed to see him stopped at the roadside, he hitched a 100-metre lift, mid-stage, in a rival team car to catch up and change bikes. He was disqualified from his debut Tour.

'Be consistent,' Unzué said. 'The UCI says we have rules for everyone, so apply those rules consistently. We need to know that the judges have a clear vision of how they will apply the rules.'

But soon Unzué was himself fending off accusations after Quintana was filmed threading his way through the chaos below Chalet Reynard and briefly grabbing onto a Mavic motorbike. 'Nairo had to grab the Mavic bike so he wouldn't get smashed against the barrier. He had to do it so he couldn't fall as a result of the crash. He was up against the barrier; he was trying to defend himself against something even worse.'

So as Froome was running up Ventoux, Quintana was taking a tow from a motorbike ...

'He came into that crash with Yates, and the Mavic bike had to stop, and Nairo nearly fell as well. He would have been knocked over ...'

There was yet another dimension to the debate, as Tejay Van Garderen bemoaned the lack of chivalry shown by some towards misfortune befalling the wearer of the yellow jersey. 'The gentlemanly thing to do,' the American said, 'would be to stop and wait and regroup. You saw a lot of that in the past but these days people just seem to want to take advantage of it.'

The polemic continued, but it was a half-hearted debate. The Tour bubble had already burst. The brutal truths of the real world had intruded. The party was over. That realisation had been written all over Prudhomme's weary face. And from that mournful morning in Bourg-Saint-Andéol, all the way to a stiflingly humid evening on the Champs-Élysées, nobody was really in the mood for a celebration.

It's the end of a long summer. Not for the first time, I'm hanging around the Team Sky bus hoping to speak to Dave Brailsford. This time the location is Gandia, Spain, as the 2016 Vuelta a España comes to an end. It's a hot September afternoon, team buses and cars parked haphazardly on the finish line, by the beach resort's small port, an hour or so south of Valencia.

I spot Brailsford. He's sitting on a bench on the quayside, sunglasses on, deep in a phone conversation, hand cupped, oddly, Mourinho-like, over his mouth. I scan the scene for camera crews, but there are none. Does he think someone is lip-reading?

We'd been meaning to talk since late July when he'd mailed me regarding a tweet I'd put out about Team Sky's budget, their *catenaccio* riding style and the Tour's musings over rider numbers in each team, all of which had been hot topics when Froome had won his third Tour. I maintain a respectful distance, waiting for him to finish the call. Next time I look, he's gone. Somehow, through the parked cars, the crowds milling around the team, I miss him. A few minutes later, the bus doors hiss closed and it moves off.

The next day, at the start of the Vuelta's pivotal time trial, I am hanging around once more by the bus. I try to speak to him again. We exchange texts. Something's come up, he says, and he can't talk.

It's the same next day in Benidorm, although this time there is another sighting, among the crowds at the start village. He is on another lengthy phone call, hand cupped over mouth-piece, shades on, body language a million miles from the bonhomie of Holborn. Eventually, he deigns to speak. 'Better be quick,' he says brusquely. I throw him some quickfire standard questions. Is a Tour–Vuelta double more possible for Froome than a Giro–Tour double? Did travelling to Rio impact on Froome's Vuelta? Blah–blah cycling speak, but enough for a story.

Two days later, the leak, fuelled by Russian hackery, of Bradley Wiggins' highly questionable TUE history becomes a tale of unexplained couriers and mystery Jiffy bags, and sparks a lengthy saga of fresh suspicion against Team Sky. This time, however, Brailsford's justifications are muddled and contradictory. He gets his facts wrong. He falters badly when trying to explain why a package was flown to Wiggins. He says he doesn't know what was in it. Froome, meanwhile, distances himself from his team boss.

The questions, spearheaded by Matt Lawton at the *Daily Mail* and Daniel Benson at cyclingnews.com, won't go away. Even David Walsh, happy to vouch for Brailsford and Team Sky in the past, turns on him and calls for his resignation.

There is obfuscation, fumbled communications and contradictory accounts, but this time there is no talk of pseudo–scientists. Wiggins stumbles anxiously through an interview on *The Andrew Marr Show*, mumbling about a 'level playing field', but later reverts to type, abusing the press in one of his final press conferences after racing in Ghent. The media are all stirring it, Bradley says, targeting the *Daily Mail* and describing journalists as 'cunts'. It's classic Wiggins, child-like and petulant until the end. And it doesn't address the issue.

Still, some depict his bravado as 'Brad being Brad', a man of the people setting the record straight, slagging off the malicious, malevolent *Mail*. But I just see entitlement and arrogance as a substitute for telling the truth.

What was in the bag, Brad? *What was in the bag?*

It's a question that won't go away and that Wiggins, his

retirement looming, won't answer. Now even a Parliamentary select committee wants to know. Meanwhile, the shadows lengthen and Team Sky and Brailsford twist on the end of a rope.

Portraits of Britain's most distinguished parliamentarians run the length of the wood-panelled first floor corridor in Portcullis House, Westminster. Thatcher, Douglas-Home, Major, Blair and Cameron stare loftily down from the walls. Outside, a December morning fog is wafting over the grey Thames. Dutifully, as packs of tourists gather for selfies on Westminster Bridge, the fog lifts and Big Ben's clock face sharpens a little.

In the corridor outside the Thatcher Room, where the Department for Culture, Media and Sport is convening the latest select committee investigating doping in sport, a knot of sports journalists is gathering. They are keen to follow the evidence of British Cycling president Bob Howden, former Team GB coach Shane Sutton and, finally, the driving force behind the British cycling revolution, knight of the realm, David Brailsford.

At around 11.15, Bob Howden takes his seat before the committee and is the first to give evidence. He is quickly out of his depth. He is told by one select committee member that the Wiggins story is 'a disaster for you and British Cycling'. MP after MP mocks Howden's inability to detail the contents of packages flown around Europe by British Cycling staff. 'I'm getting worried about our customs now!' Andrew Bingham snorts.

John Nicolson MP nods in the direction of the watching media, seated behind Howden. 'There are journalists behind you, laughing,' he points out. Committee member Nigel Huddleston voices what everyone is thinking. 'Are you up to this?' he says. 'If I was a corporate sponsor I'd be very concerned.'

The second act is Shane Sutton, for so long Brailsford's right-hand man, Wiggins' mentor and coach, and now centre stage. The questions about Wiggins' medical needs and that now-infamous Jiffy bag are put to him, one after another.

'There's a huge amount of autonomy given to the medical staff,' committee chairman Damian Collins says to Sutton. 'You'd expect the head coach to be party to those conversations ...' Sutton counters that he hadn't asked what the treatment for Wiggins was. 'I didn't ask any questions. My job was outside that of the medical team.'

There are long pauses after some questions, as if he is biting his tongue, swallowing his anger. But it doesn't help. His famously pugnacious temper shows itself in the end.

'You, sitting there, being British,' he tells the committee, 'you should be embracing the success they've achieved. They've all done it clean.'

Shane pauses. 'You've actually upset me there. I'm astounded that you would take that sort of tone with me. I'm upset you question the integrity of the team.'

Brailsford is the headline act. Dressed immaculately in a three-piece suit, crisp white shirt and cufflinks, he looks every part the calm captain of industry, unflappable, at ease. He settles into his chair and unbuttons his jacket.

I listen to Dave talking, as I've listened to him talk so many times before. I think of his journey, from the fan packing a van for Planet X, the driven business student, to his dream job at British Cycling, the gold medals won everywhere from LA, to Palma, to Athens, Beijing, and then the great homecoming to London 2012; of the moments he'd shamelessly jumped for joy on finish lines and, most of all, of Froome's win that day over-looking the Simpson memorial, up on the Ventoux.

Soon we learn what Brailsford believes the package couriered to Wiggins contained – an over-the-counter decongestant readily available in France, although not in the UK. It quickly becomes clear that, according to Brailsford, Team Sky flew a banal over-the-counter drug, costing a few euros, out to France to be delivered by hand by a British Cycling employee – a trip that took four days to complete – when it was readily available near by.

He takes some more questions. I am struck by just how far he has come in his attitude towards sports doctors. When Team Sky was created, Brailsford had identified his philosophy towards sports medicine as a significant break with the dubious practices of the past. 'I want British doctors who haven't worked in professional cycling before,' he told the *Guardian* in June 2009. 'The problem is that people come into professional cycling and compromise. We can't compromise.'

Now, he sat in Westminster detailing the structure of his medical team, their influence and their role in rider care. 'The issuing of a TUE is driven by the team doctor,' he says.

'But do you push back on the decisions of your medical staff?' Collins asks him.

Brailsford denies that his medical staff wield too much power and might need reining in. 'We have created a very clear policy on culture and anti-doping,' he says.

Yet a picture was emerging of a management structure that handed autonomy to medical staff, who blithely despatched products around Europe to be hand-delivered to their star riders. In the pre-doping-control era, the 'treatment' that so appalled Pierre Dumas had been left in the hands of soigneurs, or the riders themselves. That culture of self-medication, as Malléjac, Simpson and the earliest dabblings of Generation EPO demonstrated, had sometimes been disastrous.

As anti-doping established a presence, sports medicine did the same, enabling ethical competitors to stay within the rules, but allowing others, as we now know, to circumvent them.

Meanwhile, the year-round demands to perform intensified, all of which enhanced the influence of sports doctors and brought them from the wings to centre stage. Michele Ferrari's trajectory is, of course, the paradigm of this. A genius to some and a diabolical influence to others – and a man who Armstrong still says he loves. At the height of Armstrong's success, however, Ferrari was probably the most influential man in cycling.

Nearly three hours after the select committee session had opened, Brailsford remained defiant. 'There is no question of a cover-up,' he says. 'There was no intention to mislead in any shape or form.' But the committee still wants to see a paper trail.

Brailsford might have thought the matter had been put to bed. But his answers had only provoked more questions. Now nothing could stem the tsunami of suspicion that was coming Team Sky's way or the inevitability of further probing, both by the media and by Collins and his committee members.

At the heart of it all was Brailsford, all energy and ambition, whose supposed attention to marginal gains and microscopic detail suggested that he knew just how finely ground Froome liked his espresso, the thickness of paint on each of his riders' frames, and the preferred weight of down in Geraint Thomas's pillow. Yet nobody at Team Sky, it appeared, knew what was in Brad's bag.

In the aftermath of Wiggins' Tour win and London 2012, cycling in Britain had exploded in popularity. There was a vast reservoir of cash, some public, some private, buoying the collective that was British Cycling and Team Sky. But where one structure began and the other ended was never clear. Jiffy-gate revealed that the reservoir had morphed into a gravy train, characterised by British Cycling employees swanning around Europe working for Team Sky, swapping hats more often than Matt Damon in *The Adjustment Bureau*.

From the innovations in the Death Star, the altitude training in Tenerife, the marginal gains and the bespoke campervans, to the tacit suggestions that other teams were staffed by sporting simpletons and performance halfwits, Team Sky's mantra was that success had been built on a highly publicised culture of ingenuity and innovation.

Now many were joining the growing armies of trolls and pseudo-scientists that had been on the march since Froome's win on Ventoux, doubting Brailsford and his theory of marginal gains, wondering instead if they'd been fooled by the oldest trick in the book.

'We might, in that indeterminate period they call mourning, be in a submarine, silent on the ocean's bed, aware of the depth charges, now near and now far, buffeting us with recollections.'

The Year of Magical Thinking,
JOAN DIDION

The Light That Never Goes Out

On a grey November morning in the rural suburbs of Ghent, I walk up to the front door of Joanne Simpson's house and ring the bell. As I wait, I glimpse the plasma screen in her lounge through her front window, relaying the 2016 election results from America and the unmistakably ruddy complexion of a wide-eyed Donald Trump.

Joanne flings open the door. She is in her mid-fifties, petite, cheery and bespectacled, with her father's nose and immediate, ready smile. She looks fit, wiry and healthy. Perhaps that's no surprise, given she rides well over 300 kilometres a week and says that, in good shape, her best average speed from Bédoin to the summit of the Ventoux is 17 kilometres an hour. That sounds pretty quick to me. Then she tells me that she once topped 100 kilometres an hour as she descended to Malaucène.

As her partner heads off to work, Joanne fires up the coffee machine. The house, in a quiet cul-de-sac, is modern, ordered and neat. On the wall, there are some small watercolour paintings of cyclists, and a couple of black-and-white photographs too. One in particular catches my eye, of her dad, in his kit, crouched on a patch of grass. It's Tom being Tom, mugging for the snappers, picking a flower on the morning before he died.

Joanne built much of the kitchen and some other furniture herself. 'I'm a technical designer and a furniture maker, like Daddy,' she says. The workshop adjoining the kitchen houses a workstand, numerous tools and, on the wall, her dad's old saddle and other memorabilia. 'Most of what I have I treasure – the little things, his passport, the bike he won the Ronde with. You don't give things like that away.'

There's also a Pinarello bike, fixed to a turbo trainer. 'I've always had a bike, a racing bike,' she says, although Joanne only started riding seriously in her mid-thirties. 'Now I ride three times a week, about 120-kilometre loops each time, not the really long distances. So over 300 kilometres a week, but that's not extreme . . .' However, in the Flemish Ardennes, where she does most of her riding, such a distance counts for a lot. 'They're all the roads from the Ronde Van Vlaanderen – the Tour of Flanders. The Muur, the Koppenberg and so on. So 120 kilometres or so in that area – that's hard going.'

Joanne is a survivor. She has survived the trauma and the numerous aftershocks, within her family, of losing her father so young, in such a dramatic way. She also survived a major head injury that left her in a coma after she fell from her bike. And there's more: a week before flight MH17 was shot down over the Ukraine, Joanne flew that same route, from Amsterdam to Kuala Lumpur. 'It seems like I have so many lives,' she says.

Maybe you've got a guardian angel, I suggest. She smiles.

Joanne came off her bike when she tangled with some road furniture. 'I hit my head. My helmet cracked in three places.' Although now fully recovered, she has been left with some senses impaired. 'The noise impulses and the visual impulses in my brain don't go together. I can't handle visual and audio impulses together. I can't go to parties, I can't go into town. I can't work with machinery any more. I didn't drive for a year but I can now. But on the motorway I feel nauseous sometimes. That's why I wanted to meet here at home.'

Yet she is so fizzing with energy and enthusiasm, so expressive, that it's hard to tell anything might be wrong. Only sometimes, when she briefly loses her thread, does the aftermath of her accident show. Now, she says that she finds her old self on the bike. 'The accident damaged my life, but it hasn't impaired my riding on the bike. Everything works fine on the bike, it's really weird.

'I feel liberated when I'm on the bike, it's unbelievable. I can ride in the group and judge the wheels and the movement. But off the bike, my balance is gone.'

There's a pause.

'I should live on the bike,' Joanne says, in a moment of supreme irony, given that her father died, high on the Giant, gripping resolutely onto his.

Joanne Simpson was born nine months after the 1962 Tour de France. 'Nine months after the criteriums – and all those parties . . .!' she says with a Simpson glint in her eye. When her father died she was on holiday in Corsica with her mother. She was just four. The grieving was left to the adults. 'Grandpa and Mum went off and two months later Mum picked us up, with Nana. By then, everything, the funeral and all that, was over and done with.'

Later, her mother recalled the blur of activity in the hours after her husband's death on the Ventoux. 'Everything was organised for me to get to Avignon,' Helen explained in a Belgian TV documentary. 'I didn't know what to do – I was only 27 and I'd got two small children ... I didn't know if I wanted Tom to be buried in France or England. I had to make all these decisions, which was not easy.'

After Tom's death, Helen Simpson grew close to her hus-band's former team-mate, Barry Hoban, who had been one of his closest confidants in the British team riding the 1967 Tour. 'We just became good friends,' Helen Simpson said of her rela-tionship with Hoban, 'and eventually we got married, two years after Tom died.'

But Joanne admits she struggled to accept Hoban. 'Mum was *my* mum, you know – we had a special bond, I think. And I used to wonder what would happen if Daddy came back home.

'As a little kid, you're very naive and don't understand. Daddy had always been off racing so we were used to him being away. And in those days, kids weren't told the truth, they weren't told all the details.'

Joanne says that when she was a teenager, she was resentful of Hoban. '"You're not my father," I'd say to him,' she recalls.

'I've apologised to him millions of times. But he's the best father we could ever have had. It can't have been easy for him, looking after two kids that weren't his.'

As she grew up, shielded from the coverage of her father's death on the Ventoux, Joanne remembers that she had 'no idea what was going on'. 'We never saw a newspaper, we never heard people talk about it. Not ever. It was all hush-hush. We never had a sense of the controversy around Daddy's death, because nobody ever mentioned it.'

That was until Joanne was 17 and Helen and Barry decided to move back to Britain from Belgium. Joanne wanted to stay on and complete her studies in Ghent. It was a decision that opened the door to her father's world. 'I was in my last year of high school, and all my friends were in Ghent. I had the choice, and I said, "Of course I'm not going back." So I stayed and lived in digs in Ghent with Rosa Desnerck.'

The Desnerck family owned near-legendary bike shop Plume Vainqueur, or Plum as it is now. After sponsoring a professional team throughout the 1950s they then also took in fledgling Euro pros – including, at one point, a young Tom Simpson.

'Mum wanted me to be somewhere that was still part of cycling and at Rosa's there were other English-speakers – riders who wanted to come to Europe and get the experience. Gary Wiggins – Bradley's dad – was there, Eric Heiden too. All sorts of riders were in these digs. And that was when I started reading about my dad, and seeing the old newspaper stories.

'It was all new information to me, so I started asking my mum about it. "Mum," I'd say, "is this true?" But she was adamant it was all lies. I believed everything my mum and Barry told me. And if anybody mentioned doping, I got on my high horse . . .

'But then, when I got to my mid-thirties, which was when I started to fall in love with my racing bike, I started wondering. I was angry that I hadn't been told the whole story and then I was angry at Daddy . . . *Why? Why are you so stubborn?* But Mum says *I'm* stubborn like that – "You're just like your father," she says.'

After years of listening, with rising frustration, to the stories about her father's career, some true, some mythical and some contentious, Joanne is now taking action. Through lawyers, she is pursuing a copy of her father's autopsy. 'I just want the truth,' she says. 'I love the truth. Whatever the truth is, I want to know. Where did journalists get the information that Daddy was doped and had alcohol in his blood?'

I begin to detail the numerous exhaustive accounts and eyewitness descriptions, which document both the culture of the time and the prevalence of amphetamine abuse. Even Chris Sidwells, Tom Simpson's nephew, in *Mr Tom*, his biography of his uncle, says: '... like many before him and since, he began to use drugs – stimulants, because that's what they used then. Not often, but use them he did and I can't change that.'

But Joanne waves all that away. 'Prove it to me,' she says.

She has her own history of that day. 'One of Daddy's teammates, Colin Lewis, raided a café – I'm not sure if it was the Relais in Bédoin – and grabbed everything he could get. He then gave Coca-Cola to all the riders, then found Daddy and gave him the last bottle he had.

'But it was Cointreau ... Anyway Dad said, "Colin, give it to me – my throat's so dry." So he took two slugs of it and then threw it away. That's how the alcohol got there. I've no problem with that – I know how it happened.'

Incredibly, neither Joanne nor her mother has ever seen her father's autopsy report. 'I've asked Mum if I could see the autopsy report, because I'm sure in the report there are no lies. But she doesn't have it.' Once again Joanne's frustration takes over. 'I said to her, "Does this mean that you have *never, ever* read the report?" and she said, "No."

'So I asked, "Where does all the information come from then?", and she said, "I don't know – the journalists are liars." But I want the truth. That's why I want to see the autopsy.

'I can live with the truth. If that's the truth – that Daddy took amphetamines – then so be it. I don't have to defend him constantly.

'But you also have to see it in the context of those days. It's like 40 years ago everybody used to smoke. They used to think smoking was good for you!

'If the autopsy shows that he didn't have amphetamines, then they can't say that he died of doping. Then it's a heart attack. But if they were there, then I won't be accusing journalists any more, or defending him.

'I can live with the truth,' she repeats vehemently. 'Once I know the truth it won't hurt me any more. And I know the autopsy report will be the truth.'

The tension in relations between Tom Simpson and an impetuous Eddy Merckx, which, as Peugeot team-mates, had come to a head during that infamous 1967 Paris–Nice, left its mark on Joanne too. Even now, she describes her relationship with Merckx as 'funny'.

'Are Eddy and I friends? Well, now, yes – but, until recently, no. I've met him about 20 times in my life, but I always had to remind him who I was, to introduce myself. That was up until 2016.'

Merckx was the only professional to travel to Tom Simpson's funeral in the summer of 1967. But it's still taken the best part of 50 years for Joanne and cycling's most famous champion to get to know each other. 'I'm curious about Daddy's friends,' Joanne says. 'I still like to hear all the old stories. I don't want to hear, "Oh, your dad was a good bike rider . . ." I know that. I want to hear the naughty stories, or the funny stories.'

But through a mutual acquaintance, Joanne and Merckx started riding together in August 2016, as they prepared to mark the 50th anniversary of her father's death by riding up the mountain. 'We had a lunch together, a tête-à-tête of sorts. He's a lovely guy. I said to him: "Eddy, don't you think it's time for a Simpson and a Merckx to ride together again?"

'So he told me that he was riding in Herentals. "Come along, you're welcome," he said. He didn't have to ask twice. I turned up and we set off. Eddy was funny. He said: "Simpson – ride in front where I can see you! I don't want to get flicked again . . ."

'We spent the whole day together, riding, and then there was a barbecue afterwards. Eddy was reminiscing about Daddy, telling stories.'

Tom was popular wasn't he? I say.

'Very liked, I think,' Joanne says. 'He must have been a nice guy. I see all the pictures, messing about, the bowler hat, showing his playful side. I miss knowing him; I miss what I could have had.'

When Joanne joined the Cinglés du Mont Ventoux – the club of riders who have climbed all three ascents in one day – it was highly celebrated. 'I'd wanted to do it incognito, but the guys behind it said they were so honoured that a Simpson was taking on the "Cinglés" that they rode a few kilometres with me. I think I must have been the most "judged" rider ever to do it!'

Now, Joanne organises a ride on Ventoux every five years or so. 'The first time I rode up was in 1997 and then, in 2001, I rode from Ghent to the Ventoux.' Until she trained to ride the Ventoux in 1997, the mountain was almost a Simpson forbidden zone. For a long time, it was a taboo place, a no-go area that had caused the Simpson family too much pain. Joanne says that much was clear when she told her mother what she was planning. 'I said, "You know what, for Daddy's 30th anniversary, I'm going to climb the Ventoux and finish what he couldn't finish."

'When I told my mum, she was, "Oh, you don't have to do this, you don't need to prove anything" – even up to the day before . . . "It's the Ventoux," she said. "Please don't."'

Maybe that was more about their own memories, though, I suggest, about everything that they had been through. Whatever, Joanne was undeterred.

'I was riding up, thinking, "Bloody hell, Dad – this isn't easy." But then it was only 29 degrees when we went up; it wasn't 40 degrees or more, like when he rode it. But then as I got higher up, I thought, "You did choose a beautiful place to die. What a view – *what a view* . . ."'

'I wanted to finish the 1.3 kilometres that Daddy didn't finish. And I was so positive about it, and trained so hard, that I rode up and then said, "What's the fuss? What's the big deal?" So I thought, "Next time I'll ride down from Ghent." That's what we did. We rode in stages, riding about 125, maybe 145 kilometres a day, with some friends in a little group.

'We had a couple of rest days. The hardest part was Luxembourg and the Ardennes, all those 25 per cent climbs! You don't get climbs like that in France.'

After that trip, Joanne's commitment to maintaining her father's memorial grew. 'In 2007 I built the rest of the steps. But with all the permissions I needed from local councils, it took five years to do it.'

Stubborn and dogged, I say, just like your father. She smiles.

On the 50th anniversary of Tom Simpson's death on Mont Ventoux, the 2017 Tour de France will be far away, on the other side of the country. Joanne has been bitterly disappointed by ASO's lack of interest in reaching out to her family. 'I've had no contact with them. My experience of ASO, speaking as one of the Simpson family, is that they've ignored us, as if we're . . .' Joanne's voice trails off.

But Tom died competing in their race, I say. Joanne looks out of the window.

'July 2017 is Daddy's 50th anniversary, but the Tour ignores it because they don't want to be associated with it and with the "negative" image.' She is convinced, also, that the Tour chose 2016 for its most recent ascent of the mountain, rather than

2017, in a deliberate avoidance of the Simpson anniversary. 'Of course they did,' she says.

'It proves what I've always known all these years – they're ashamed. The Simpson name is a blemish. So I say good riddance.'

She has never met Christian Prudhomme, but in 1994, when Eros Poli took his famous stage win in Carpentras, Joanne and her mother were invited to the race as guests by then Tour director Jean-Marie Leblanc, himself a former rider and contemporary of Simpson. 'It was the first time we'd been invited. Jean-Marie knew my dad – but, as for the rest, they've never contributed to the memorial or the steps or anything like that.'

To raise the 15,000 euros to repair the steps to the Simpson memorial, Joanne collected money at the Ghent Six Day for five successive years. 'I didn't want sponsorship. So all the money came from the Belgian fans.'

One evening, Leblanc came into the velodrome in Ghent and dropped some cash into her bucket. 'He gave me five euros,' Joanne remembers. 'So I always say the Tour de France has given the family five euros towards the 13 steps up to the memorial.'

It's always the number 13, Joanne remarks. 'Daddy died on stage 13, on July 13; he was wearing number 49 – four and nine is 13 and it happened in 1967 – and six and seven is 13.

'There are 13 steps up to the memorial. There were two steps already and I added another 11 in 2007. At the time, I didn't even realise I'd built 13.'

Joanne is climbing the mountain in July 2017, on the day of the anniversary, leading a group, including Merckx and, she hopes, Greg LeMond, to the Simpson memorial and then on, to the top. 'I'm making the pace, leading the pack. It's more of an honorary thing, but I can see myself with all these 18-year-olds . . . Imagine if I'm only doing ten kilometres an hour!'

The Simpson memorial is one of the most visited in France, with a footfall that compares with the graves of Jim Morrison and Édith Piaf in Père Lachaise cemetery in Paris. 'Daddy was never a drama queen but he chose a good stage. When I go to the Ventoux, I sit on the steps up to the memorial and I think: "You chose a special place."

'Half the people who stop at the memorial don't even know that my dad ever won another race. They know that he died on the Ventoux – but they don't know that he won Flanders, or Paris–Nice or the World Championships. I sit there on the steps, Jeremy, and I hear what they say. Nobody knows who I am, but these people come up and you hear them say, "Oooh, look, this is where the alcoholic died" or, "This is where the doper died."

'Do you remember anything about it?' Joanne asks me.

I don't think so, I say, but then check myself because I can just remember the 1966 World Cup final. I watched that with my dad in a hotel in Glencoe. I remember the moon landings too, but Tom Simpson's death on a mountain in France . . .? I try harder. 'Maybe I can remember something,' I say. 'A newspaper headline, something on the news. When I see the footage, there's something familiar. But that's all.'

'That's all': the elusive Tom – always out of reach.

Every now and then, Joanne spends time up on the mountain. At around four or five o'clock, when the light changes and the temperature starts to drop, she will tidy up the mementoes scattered around the memorial. 'I keep the lovely bits and pieces, the touching stuff – the special stuff, the cards and things like that. But I like to make sure nobody sees me.

'Last time I went I found a cremation urn,' Joanne recalls quietly. 'We didn't know what to do, so we spread the ashes on the mountainside behind the memorial. I've kept the urn, though, I didn't feel I could throw it away.'

Joanne was at the memorial in July 2016, battling the Mistral on the day of the running *maillot jaune* incident. 'We'd been filming in the morning, but there was so much wind we had to come down. So we watched it in Mazan.' She was also there in 2009, when the Tour reached a climax at the summit of the Giant, with Lance Armstrong fighting to prevent Bradley Wiggins from leapfrogging him and taking third place overall.

Wiggins, who fought hard on the Ventoux to secure fourth overall – which, after Armstrong's later disqualification, subsequently became third – had a photo of Simpson taped to his top tube as he climbed the Giant. 'Tom will be watching over me,' Wiggins had said before the stage. Behind Wiggins came his Garmin team-mate David Millar, who threw his cap towards the monument as he rode by. Joanne, standing watching the riders pass, caught it. A note on it read: 'To Tommy, RIP, David Millar.'

'I've kept it safe, up in the loft,' she says. 'I've never met David Millar, but I have some respect for him.'

Yet, unlike in 1970, or in 1994, none of the Tour's officials paused to pay their respects. Only Marc Madiot, the sports director of Française des Jeux and former professional rider, stopped his car, pausing for a moment to leave a bouquet of flowers on the memorial.

It's the hour of the '*apéro*' in the south of France. I sit looking out over Marseille's Vieux Port, sipping an ice-cold beer in the wood-panelled, smoke-stained bar at La Caravelle. Things haven't changed much in here since Tom Simpson rode away from the start line, a stone's throw away, on 13 July 1967.

The heat of the afternoon has begun to fade, but even with a gentle sea breeze blowing through the open windows, the languid air is stifling. Outside, it's still sweltering as the early-evening promenaders stroll past. The picture windows overlook the fishing boats and yachts, bobbing against a backdrop of old and new apartments. Dominating the horizon, across the city, is the hilltop basilica of Notre-Dame de la Garde, one of the most recognisable buildings in France.

Marseille is an exotic city, cracked and broken in many places, grand and seductive in others. It is disparaged by some, depicted as seedy and dangerous, but I love the combination of rough and smooth, the collision of modernist and vintage, of French and North African, and the unerring heat of its long summers.

The modernist blocks that overlook the city are ranged on the series of hills rolling down towards the sea. Some are still no-go ghettos, while others, closer to the coast and now sold as designer apartments with sea views, ring the old town. Zinedine Zidane, arguably the city's most famous son, emerged from one such ghetto, the notorious Castellane district of bad estates and grim blocks. From the very top of the tallest of these you can see north, over the hills, beyond the brasseries and fountains of Aix-en-Provence and the wooded hump of the Luberon range, and, on a very clear day, even as far as the bleached summit of the Giant.

Since it was named European capital of culture in 2013, Marseille's 'front of house' – the Vieux Port, the Corniche and the areas around the university and the Prado – have been tidied up. My friend François Thomazeau, a veteran chronicler of cycling and of French life, lives close to the Vieux Port. '2013 did change things a bit,' he says. 'It sped up the completion of the Terrasses du Port area which is a success – maybe not commercially yet; it is a little bit too posh for Marseille's population.'

François says that the Marseillais have developed 'a real sense of pride at rediscovering how beautiful the city can be'. 'And the tourists keep coming,' he notes wryly, 'which is quite unexpected for us.'

But he acknowledges that the rise of the right wing, allied to the spate of terror attacks across France, is increasing tensions in the city, but adds that he's never seen 'blatant expressions of racism in the streets'.

Yet for all the investment, Marseille remains fragile. 'We just need more jobs,' Thomazeau says, 'and Olympique de Marseille winning games again . . .' But, as an outsider, conscious of the city's reputation, you don't have to walk too far from the Vieux Port into the old town to feel the tension in the air. This part of Marseille, only a short distance from the quayside brasseries and luxury hotels, is full of noise and heat and spice.

The heat on the morning of 13 July 1967 was already getting to some. As the teams arrived for the start of that day's Tour de France stage, Pierre Dumas was already anxious. According to *L'Équipe*, the Tour's doctor had spoken to the newspaper's journalist, Pierre Chany, at the Hôtel Noailles the previous evening. 'Dumas was worried,' Chany wrote, 'and said something I'll never forget: "It's going to be awfully hot tomorrow. If the guys start taking stuff, we could have a dead man on our hands."'

Joanne Simpson calls her father 'Daddy' throughout our long conversation in Ghent, her relationship with him frozen in time, a faint memory of a bike race, of embrocation on tanned legs, of a strong hand holding hers and a winning, ready smile, from half a century ago.

She says she has no memory of that fateful day in July 1967. 'It's all hearsay, all the stories my mum told me and Barry told me and other people. But I can't remember anything. I don't remember the last time I was with him. There's nothing.'

The rain falls outside the window as the Belgian winter warms to its task. Joanne looks puzzled by the memories. 'At the moment he died, we were in Corsica, on the beach.' She remembers the plot of land, near Bonifacio, and the dreams for a better life there. 'Apparently,' she recalls a story she must have heard a hundred times, 'we came back home from the beach and the whole village of Pianottoli-Caldarello – and my mum's parents were there too – the whole village was there and they were all crying.'

I visualise her walking through the lengthening shadows of a hot Corsican evening, clutching her mother's hand, taking in the pitying stares of the villagers, knowing but not yet understanding that she will never see her father again. It wasn't until she was a teenager that the anger came, the anger at being kept in the dark and the anger at her father for being 'so stubborn'.

And then, as a tide of frustration washes over her, Tom is with us, in her kitchen, as she berates her lost father.

'Why didn't you stop? You were sick . . . It was 42, 40 degrees up there . . .

'Still you go on! Why? You had two children at home. Why do you have to push your body so far?'

She pauses.

'Then, much later, you hear about the money. Everything is about money.

'The director from Salverani [the team that Simpson planned to ride for in 1968] said, "Your pay will depend on your results in the Tour de France." So it was all about money.'

The good life that Simpson had planned – the holiday development in Corsica, the new home just outside Ghent – 'It had a Salverani kitchen,' Joanne notes – never became a reality. And, as Joanne talks, I feel myself getting drawn back into the mythology of Simpson and the Ventoux; the grainy footage of the tiny figure laid out on the white rocks, the half-remembered anecdotes, the tales and counter-tales that, for better and for worse, have grown taller with the passing of time.

And I think how infinitely heartbreaking it must be for Joanne, sitting before me, mind racing and eyes brimming, to be unable to grasp the reality of who her father was and of what happened to him on that fated 13th day.

'Do you miss him?' I ask her again.

She stares at me.

'How can you miss what you never had?' she says.

And suddenly, her eyes fill with tears.

On a warm spring day in May 2017, I visited Joanne at home again. Her search for the definitive truth about what happened to her father, 50 years earlier, high on the Ventoux, had reached a dead end. She shows me the letter from the Centre Hospitalier Henri Truffaut in Avignon: 'French law authorises the destruction of medical records 25 years after death,' it reads, 'or 30 years in some cases. The dossier for Monsieur Thomas Simpson has thus been destroyed at some point between 1992 and 1997 . . .'

As I take in the letter's stark meaning, Joanne takes it from my hands and carefully places it back into an envelope.

VIII

White sky above me, the drum inside my head, pounding.

'Push me,' I tell them, even as I know I can't go on.

'Push me.'

And then they're all standing over me as I lay me down on Mont Ventoux, beautiful, bastard, baking Ventoux.

'Come on, Tom,' they say. 'That's enough now, Tom.'

But I've had it anyway. I know that now. I can't go any further.

This is it for me. This'll have to do.

Faces hover over me. Harry's crouched beside me.

Then there's a Frenchman's voice too, shouting, all disbelief and rage and desperation.

White sky fading, drum slowing.

Helen.

I can see Helen. She's on the beach, smiling, sunshine on her shoulders, the children swimming in the sea. They look so happy.

Give yourself a break, Tom, she says. No more pain.

The drum has stopped.

~

From the *Yorkshire Post*, 14 July 1967

TOMMY SIMPSON, aged 29, Britain's former World Professional Road Race Champion, died in hospital at Carpentras, France, last night after being overcome by heat exhaustion in the Tour de France Cycle Race, says a Reuter report from southern France.

Simpson, Britain's best known racing cyclist, abandoned the Tour on the steep slopes of the 6,000ft Mount Ventoux. He had been in seventh position in the overall placings after 12 stages of the Tour.

Simpson was born in Durham, but lived at Harworth, a mining village, near Doncaster, for most of his life. He went to the Continent in 1959 to seek his fortune as a professional rider, and was possibly at the peak of his racing career.

He was the first Englishman to wear the yellow jersey as overall leader in a Tour de France, and his triumphs in the road racing field have become a legend in British cycling.

Simpson had been going well on the early part of the Ventoux climb, but with less than a mile to go to the summit he slumped over his cycle and fell off.

The British team car went to his aid and Simpson, though obviously in great distress, gasped: 'Put me back on the bike.'

He was helped back on the machine, but then collapsed again. He had difficulty with his breathing and was given oxygen before being picked up by the helicopter and taken to hospital.

Known abroad by countless thousands of cycling fans as

'Mr Tom', he first came to the forefront of top-class racing in 1961 when he won the Belgium Classic, the Tour of Flanders.

From that time on his racing made history all along the line. He won many classic races for the first time by an English rider, and he won the World Professional Road Title in 1965.

At his semi-detached council home in Festival Avenue, Harworth, last night, Tommy's father, Mr Thomas Simpson, said: 'This has come as a tremendous shock and my wife is in a state of collapse. We are considering whether or not to travel to France.'

The first news his parents had of the tragedy was when they switched on the television to see if he had improved on his overnight position in the race. Tommy moved to the village with his parents when he was 12 and because his father could not afford to buy him a bicycle of his own Tommy took a job as a butcher's rounds boy so he could have regular use of a machine.

Married in 1961, Tommy made his home in Ghent, Belgium, and had bought a house in Tickhill ready for his retirement from racing. He has two children, Jane and Joanne.

Brian Robinson, of Mirfield, former professional cyclist and the first Briton ever to win a stage of the Tour, was a close friend of Simpson's. He said last night: 'Tommy was in his prime; he was well liked as a man for his character and his ability. I know the place well where Tom died. It is a hill of death.'

The four remaining members of the British team decided last night to continue the Tour. The team manager, Alec Taylor, said: 'I knew Tommy very well and I am sure that this is what he would have wanted.'

Mr Taylor said Simpson's widow would leave Corsica, where she and her children had been on holiday, to fly to Marseilles today.

A minute's silence will be observed in Simpson's memory before the Tour resumes today.

A post-mortem report said Tommy Simpson had taken amphetamines.

Autumn

I set off for the mountain once more, with half a lifetime spent writing about cycling, for better or worse, behind me. Things are different now, different from the first time, 30 years ago. I have no delusions about how fast I can climb the Giant, no dreams of a quicker time. Now, I just want to ride to the top, to cross the crucible again, to see the view from the summit, one more time.

I park the car just outside Bédoin, change my shoes and put the bike together. Ten minutes later, I begin riding towards the mountain. It's sunny but it's cold too, and I didn't sleep well. Yet today I want to ride as high as I can and then keep riding, all day, until exhaustion envelops me, until it's all I can do to drive home and slump in front of the fire.

I've pulled on a collage of kit, an eclectic mashup of lost and found, treasured and tainted, the bits and pieces of a life working in cycling. I am wearing a pair of Ray-Ban Wayfarers I found discarded on the seat of a yellow cab in Brooklyn; a Mellow Johnny's racing cap, bought in Austin; cycling shorts with VCRC, the name of David Millar's gentlemen's club, on the thigh; a Cinzano jersey, long zip, that I have grown to love; an old *Procycling* gilet, and ancient Shimano shoes, as comfortable as old slippers, the Velcro fastening frayed and distressed.

This time I'm riding alone.

I didn't ever expect that, the alone part. I always thought that

that same group, plodding up and over the Ventoux in the July of 1987, getting prizes under false pretences, would come together again. We're not, though – not on, or off, the bike. We've been caught and then overtaken by time – distanced by kids and commitments, break-ups and bereavements, careers and cancers. I miss them, like I miss my dad, who I never took to the Tour and now wish more than anything that I had.

Dad didn't like cycling, but he liked mountains. Before the Ventoux, before the Croix de Chaubouret above St Étienne, before the Izoard, Galibier and all the others, came the Sunday morning sorties to the Horseshoe Pass in North Wales. One Sunday, Dad drove behind us all the way, overtaking nervously from time to time, then pulling over, just ahead of us, as we rode out of Llangollen, before getting out and fiddling with his camera.

When we left him for the last time, he'd stood in the doorway of the house, in his gardening trousers, holding a mug of stewed tea, waving goodbye. Not so long after that, my mum was gone too, reduced to a terrified shadow of herself by hateful, hateful Alzheimer's.

When we finally closed up their house, we found a box of old photos at the bottom of her wardrobe. They were mostly out of focus, or with a finger blurring the edge of the lens. But there were some taken of me, with my blue Chas Roberts bike, beaming at the top of the Horseshoe Pass. And there were others of us all, arm in arm, at the top of the Ventoux.

The moon waxes and wanes, the summers get more fleeting. We get older and wiser. We learn that our days in the sun, empowered, brilliant days, high on a mountainside, the world at our feet, are finite.

What was it they have all said of this mountain? What was that talk of exorcism, redemption and catharsis? I try to remember as I get nearer to the forest.

The gradient bites and my speed dips.

I wish they were all here still, rather than taken away, out of time, long before I was ready. My parents, those absent friends, even Tommy in that stupid bowler hat, glint in his eye, having a laugh, putting on a brave face on that baking morning in Marseille. I wish he was here still, just so that he could wipe Joanne's eyes and hold her hand again.

I climb steadily, in low gear and with heavy heart, past the cherry orchards and the vineyards, on towards St Estève, turning into that familiar bend and its familiar pain.

I stand on the pedals and climb upwards one more time, on towards the steepest slopes of the Giant.

Acknowledgements

Thanks most of all to my family for their unflagging support during the writing of this book.

Sincere thanks to my agent, David Luxton, who has been a calm and supportive influence. Thanks to all at Simon & Schuster and particularly my editor Ian Marshall, who has been both supportive and patient. He's needed to be.

Thanks also to many interviewees, friends, facilitators, foes and informants, but particularly Peter Cossins, Pete Goding, OJ Borg, Owen Slot, Joanne Simpson, Francois Thomazeau, Tyler Hamilton, Nicole Cooke, Jonathan Vaughters, Dave Brailsford, Eros Poli, Pier Bergonzi, Éric Caritoux, Rod Ellingworth, Betty Kals, Christophe Bassons, Charly Wegelius, Christian Prudhomme, Julien Pretot, Lance Armstrong, Freya North, Bonnie Ford, Alastair Campbell, Matt Dickinson, Matt Lawton, Matt McGeehan, Tom Cary, Paul Kimmage, Jean-Louis Pages, Simon Clancy, Tim Moore, Kenny Pryde, Stephen Farrand, Ed Pickering, Gilles Le Roc'h, Daniel Benson, David Millar, Simon Mottram, Rupert Guinness, Daniel Friebe and Andrew Hood, plus the very many others from all those press rooms in all those towns.

I've had numerous riding, wining and dining partners over, around, and in the shadow of the Ventoux. Andrew Hodge was first and foremost, with Peter Waxman, Martin Sagar, Mark Hindley and Stuart Gillespie in our slipstream. Then came others, including James Poole, David Luxton, Ian Banbery, Paul Godfrey, Sarah Banbery, David Poole, Sarah Wharton, Steven Hunter, Cara Wilson, Duncan McPhee, Rachel Roberts, Ellis Bacon, Lionel Birnie, Deirdre Rooney, Bryn Lennon . . .

Some waited for me at the top of the climbs, while others were waited for. Others just killed time, waiting in a bar, or even picked me up from one. Like me, they all loved the mountain, the gorges and the hills of the Vaucluse and the Drôme.

Bibliography

Guy Barruol, *Le Mont Ventoux: Encyclopédie d'une montagne provençale* (Alpes de Lumière, 2007)

Michael Barry, *Shadows on the Road: Life at the heart of the peloton, from US Postal to Team Sky* (Faber & Faber, 2014)

Christophe Bassons with Benoît Hopquin, *A Clean Break: My story* (Bloomsbury, 2014)

Philippe Brunel, *An Intimate Portrait of the Tour de France: Masters and slaves of the road* (Buonpane Publications, 1996)

Les Carnets du Ventoux, various editions (Les Editions du Toulourenc)

Jeff Connor, *Wide Eyed and Legless: Inside the Tour de France* (Simon & Schuster, 1988)

Jeff Connor, *Field of Fire: The Tour de France of '87 and the rise and fall of ANC-Halfords* (Mainstream Publishing, 2012)

Nicole Cooke, *The Breakaway: My Story* (Simon & Schuster, 2014)

Daniel Coyle, *Lance Armstrong: tour de force*, (Collins Willow, 2005)

Le Dauphiné, *50 ans de Critérium du Dauphiné Libéré* (Editions le Dauphiné)

Gérard Delestre, *Paris-Nice 1933–1999: Anthologie de la 'Course au Soleil'* (Editions SPE-Barthélémy, 2001)

L'Équipe, *Cols Mythiques du Tour de France* (L'Équipe)

L'Équipe, *Le Ventoux Sommet de la Folie* (L'Équipe)

Laurent Fignon, *We Were Young and Carefree* (Yellow Jersey Press, 2010)

William Fotheringham, *Put Me Back On My Bike: In search of Tom Simpson* (Yellow Jersey Press, 2002)

Daniel Friebe, *Eddy Merckx: The cannibal* (Ebury Press, 2012)

Philippe Gaumont, *Prisonnier du Dopage* (Grasset, 2005)

Tyler Hamilton and Daniel Coyle, *The Secret Race: Inside the hidden world of the Tour de France: Doping, cover-ups, and winning at all costs* (Bantam Press, 2012)

NG Henderson, *Fabulous Fifties* (Kennedy Brothers)

Bernard Hinault, *Memories of the Peloton* (Springfield Books Limited, 1989)

Paul Howard, *Sex Lies and Handlebar Tape: The remarkable life of Jacques Anquetil* (Mainstream Publishing, 2008)

HR Kedward, *In Search of the Maquis: Rural resistance in southern France 1942–1944* (Oxford University Press, 1994)

Sean Kelly with David Walsh, *Sean Kelly: A man for all seasons* (Springfield Books Limited, 1991)

Greg LeMond and Samuel Abt, *The Incredible Comeback of an American Hero* (Stanley Paul, 1990)

Isaac Levendel, *Not the Germans Alone: A son's search for the truth of Vichy* (Northwestern University Press, 1999)

Steffen Lipp, *Mont Ventoux* (Édisud, 1989)

Robert MacFarlane, *Mountains of the Mind: A history of a fascination* (Granta, 2003)

David Millar in collaboration with Jeremy Whittle, *Racing Through The Dark: The rise and fall of David Millar* (Orion, 2011)

Miroir du Cyclisme, *Tour de France: Les Vainqueurs* (Vaillant Miroir Sprint)

Bernard Mondon, *Les Grandes Heures du Tour de France au Ventoux* (Editions Equinoxe, 1998)

Richard Moore, *In Search Of Robert Millar: Unravelling the mystery surrounding Britain's most successful Tour de France cyclist* (HarperSport, 2007)

Richard Moore, *Slaying The Badger: LeMond, Hinault and the greatest ever Tour de France* (Yellow Jersey Press , 2012)

Tim Moore, *French Revolutions: Cycling the Tour de France* (Yellow Jersey Press, 2012)

Caroline Moorhead, *Village of Secrets: Defying the Nazis in Vichy France* (Chatto & Windus, 2014)

Matt Rendell, *The Death of Marco Pantani: A biography* (Weidenfeld & Nicholson, 2006)

Bjarne Riis, *Riis: Stages of light and dark* (Vision Sports Publishing, 2012)

Stephen Roche with David Walsh, *The Agony and the Ecstasy: Stephen Roche's world of cycling* (Stanley Paul, 1988)

Stephen Roche, *Born to Ride* (Yellow Jersey Press, 2012)

Chris Sidwells, *Mr Tom: The true story of Tom Simpson* (Mousehold Press, 2000)

Tommy Simpson, *Cycling Is My Life* (Stanley Paul, 1966)

Rik Van Walleghem, *Eddy Merckx: The greatest cyclist of the 20th century* (VeloPress, 1996)

Jean-Paul Vespini, *La Legende du Ventoux* (La Provence)

Richard Virenque, *Ma Vérité* (Editions du Rocher, 1999)

Past editions of magazines including *Velo, Miroir du Cyclisme, Cycling Weekly, Cycle Sport, Procycling* and numerous others.

Glossary of names

Amaury Sports Organisation (ASO) – Paris-based owners of all major French races, including the Tour de France, and biggest promoter in world cycling

Lance Armstrong – fallen icon and confessed doper, stripped of seven Tour de France wins, after a lengthy investigation by USADA (US Anti Doping Agency)

Bedoin – gateway village to the famous southern ascent of Mont Ventoux, known as 'race' or 'Simpson' side

Jean-Francois Bernard – Mont Ventoux stage winner in 1987 Tour de France

Louison Bobet – three-time Tour de France winner and stage winner over Mont Ventoux

Dave Brailsford – founding father of the British Cycling 'medal factory' and team principal of Team Sky

Johan Bruyneel – former professional rider, subsequently sports director to Lance Armstrong, sanctioned for doping offences

Éric Caritoux – former Tour of Spain winner and French national champion, resident of Flassan

Chalet Reynard – ski station bar and café on the southern ascent of Mont Ventoux

Cingles du Mont Ventoux – select club of riders who have completed all three ascents of Mont Ventoux in one day

Nicole Cooke – former Olympic and world champion, first British Tour de France winner and stage winner over Mont Ventoux

Fausto Coppi – revered double Tour de France winner and five times Giro d'Italia champion, who died of complications following malaria, in 1960

Critérium du Dauphiné – Alpine stage race, formerly the Dauphiné Libéré, now owned by ASO and a critical warm-up race for the Tour de France

Drôme – the county, or *département,* north of Mont Ventoux and the Vaucluse, between the Rhone valley and the French Alps

Pierre Dumas – Tour de France doctor from 1952 to 1969, who revived Jean Malléjac on Mont Ventoux in 1955 and fought to resuscitate Tom Simpson, higher up the mountain in 1967

L'Équipe – legendary French sports newspaper, owned by ASO, and traditional mouthpiece of the Tour de France

Étape du Tour – ASO-owned high-end mass participation sportive ride staged every July over the route of one of that year's key Tour stages

Laurent Fignon – Paris-born double Tour de France winner who died of cancer in 2010, also remembered for losing the 1989 Tour by just eight seconds

Chris Froome – Kenyan-born Team Sky leader, triple Tour de France winner and stage winner on Mont Ventoux in 2013

Charly Gaul – former slaughterman turned mountain goat, renowned for his climbing abilities, winner of the 1958 Tour, including a stage win on Mont Ventoux

Raphael Géminiani – iconic 1950s star and personality, known for his volatile character, aggressive riding style and defiant nature

Tyler Hamilton – Massachusetts-born mountain climbing team-mate to Lance Armstrong, stage winner on Mont Ventoux, who subsequently confessed to serial doping

Hugo Koblet – charismatic Swiss rider known as the *pédaleur de charme*, Koblet won the 1951 Tour but was killed in a car crash in 1964

Ferdi Kubler – Kubler won the 1950 Tour but is remembered as well for a frenzied assault on Mont Ventoux which left him in a state of near-delirium

Floyd Landis – 2006 Tour winner, later stripped of victory, and key witness in the USADA anti-doping investigation which led to the downfall of Lance Armstrong

Greg LeMond – triple Tour de France winner and first Anglophone to win the Tour

Malaucene – gateway village to the northern ascent of Mont Ventoux

Jean Malléjac – French rider who collapsed during the 1955 Tour and was revived by doctor Dumas

Iban Mayo – Basque cyclist and holder of the record for the fastest ascent of the south side of Mont Ventoux, later banned for two years for doping

Eddy Merckx – five-time Tour de France winner, former team-mate to Tom Simpson and stage winner on Mont Ventoux in July 1970

David Millar – British ex-professional and winner of stages in all three Grand Tours of France, Italy and Spain, banned for doping between 2004 and 2006

Mont Serein – ski station and village below the summit of Mont Ventoux's north side

Marco Pantani – deceased Italian icon and mountain climber, former winner of the Tour and Giro, still revered in Italy despite numerous allegations of doping

Gaston Plaud – former professional and sports director of Peugeot-sponsored team from 1959–73

Eros Poli – heavyweight *super-domestique* rider and unlikely winner of the Mont Ventoux stage in the 1994 Tour de France

Jean Robic – diminutive winner of the 1947 Tour de France, renowned for eccentric style, gurning expressions and mercurial temperament

St Ésteve – site of the critical bend on Mont Ventoux's southern climb that signals the steepest section of road

Sault – gateway village at the foot of the Ventoux's eastern ascent to Chalet Reynard

Chris Sidwells – nephew of Tom Simpson and author of *Mr Tom: the true story of Tom Simpson*

Helen Simpson – wife of Tom Simpson, later Helen Hoban, after marrying his former team-mate, Barry Hoban

Joanne Simpson – daughter, with sister Jane, of Tom Simpson

Tom Simpson – former world champion and BBC Sports Personality of the Year, who collapsed and died close to the summit of Mont Ventoux in July 1967

Vaucluse – home county or *département* of Mont Ventoux, sited between the Drôme and the Bouches du Rhone

Jonathan Vaughters – former cyclist and confessed doper, key figure in the USADA investigation into Armstrong, now team manager

Richard Virenque – Mont Ventoux stage winner, convicted doper, now a television presenter and pundit

David Walsh – *Sunday Times* journalist and author

Index

Agen, 56
Agostinho, Joaquim, 103, 114
Aigues Mortes, 20
Alazards, 16
Albert, Monsieur, 21–2
Alcala, Raul, in Tour 1994, 146
Allée de l'Oulle, 59
Allée des Platanes, 42, 111, 146
Alpe d'Huez, 11, 24, 60, 63, 160,
    184
  as iconic climb, 216
Altig, Rudi, 108
Amaury Sports Organisation
    (ASO), 23, 25, 26, 101, 156,
    174, 246
amphetamines, *see under* doping
Anderson, Phil, 46, 137
  in Tour 1994, 146
The Andrew Marr Show, 260
Andy (friend), 37–9
Anquetil, Jacques, 106
  'Judas' accusation against, 54
  in Tour 1958, 73–4
Arenberg forest, 257
Armstrong, Lance, 43, 81, 118, 123,
    149–71, 173, 176–8 *passim*, 185,
    224, 232
  author's conversations with,
    152–5, 157–70, 189–92
  bike shop of, 150
  and cancer, 150, 152, 224

and chemotherapy, 150, 152
Cooke on, 213
crowds celebrate downfall of,
    197
and Dauphiné, 62
and Ferrari, 188, 264
first Tour de France win of, 149
first Ventoux race of, 169
Froome compared with, 214,
    221, 227, 228, 236
golf played by, 152
and Hamilton, 169–71, 187–90,
    191
jeered, 187
last Ventoux race of, 190
lifetime ban on, 154
and long distance, 199
and Pantani, 34, 117, 120, 151,
    152, 161, 162–5, 177
and *Roi du Mont Ventoux* film, *see*
    Roi du Mont Ventoux
and *Sunday Times*, 166
and therapy, 191
in Tour 1999, 171
in Tour 2000, 34, 113, 161–4,
    177, 228, 236
in Tour 2002, 117
in Tour 2009, 154–5, 190–1, 277
in Tour 2010, 190
trophies of, 192
and Vaughters, 184

Armstrong, Lance – *cont.*
  Walsh's 'Witchfinder'-like
    pursuit of, 197
  and Wiggins, 190
  and Winfrey, 158, 213
Armstrong, Max, 192
Aru, Fabio, 249–50
Aubisque, 121, 176

Baggio, Roberto, 144
Bahamontes, Federico, in Tour
  1958, 74, 75
Ballester, Pierre, 224
Barry, Michael, 230, 231
Bartali, Gino
  and climbs, 62
  in Tour 1951, 57, 58
  in Tour 1952, 66
  as Tour 'royal', 58
Bassons, Christophe, 155, 224
Bataclan, 244
Bauvin, Gilbert, in Tour 1952, 65
Bay of Marseille, 20
BBC Sports Personality of the
  Year, 23, 108, 203
Beaucaire–Tarascon, 57
Beaumes-de-Venise, 89
  to Valréas, 173
Beckett, Samuel, 86–7
Bédoin, 18–19, 25, 27, 28, 31, 82,
  94, 141
  becomes Tour's second ascent,
    60
  and Cingles du Ventoux, 31
  first road to summit from, 21
  focal point for crowds, 28
  Poli favours, 147
  and Simpson, 33
  to summit, thousands of
    spectators on, 73
  and Tom Simpson *randonnée*, 41,
    43

Bellier, Pierre, 16
Beloki, Joseba, 117
Benoît, Adolphe, 22
Benson, Daniel, 260
Bergaut, Louis, in Tour 1958, 75
Bergonzi, Pier, 164–5
Bernard, Jean-François 'Jeff', 46,
  47, 48, 129, 140
  enthusiastic hunter, 20
  resignation of, 111
  and *Roi du Mont Ventoux* film, *see*
    Roi du Mont Ventoux
  in Tour 1986, 128
  in Tour 1987, 20, 115, 127,
    130–1
Bidot, Jean, in Tour 1951, 58
Bidot, Marcel, 66, 67, 73–4
Bingham, Andrew, 261
Bistrot de Lagarde d'Apt, 90
Blair, Tony, 32, 133–4
Blauvac, 82, 94
Blondin, Antoine, 121
BMC Racing team, 242, 244
Bobet, Jean, 15–16
  memoir of, 54–5
Bobet, Louison 'Zonzon', 15, 29,
  60
  in brother's memoir, 54–5
  in Dauphiné 1955, 66
  death of, 71
  and doping, 71
  Gaul's resentment towards, 73
  illness of, 66–7
  'Judas' accusation against, 54
  reputation of, for moods and
    anxiety, 59
  in Tour 1951, 57, 58–9
  in Tour 1953, 66
  in Tour 1954, 66
  in Tour 1955, 66–7, 69, 70–1
  in Tour 1958, 71, 73–4
  as Tour 'royal', 58

Boifava, Davide, 110, 116–17
Bontempi, Guidy, 47
Boom, Lars, 234, 241
Boonen, Tom, 241
Borg, OJ, 132–3
Born to Ride (Roche), 112
Botero, Santiago, 117
Bouches-du-Rhône, 83
Boulevard Albin Durand, 42
Bowie, David, 101
Brailsford, Dave, 64, 197, 198, 200,
    211, 213, 214–18, 220–3, 230,
    236, 237–40, 251, 259–60 (*see
    also* Team Sky)
  and Campbell, 32
  clarification questions sent to,
    232–4
  driven nature of, 214
  and Maire, 232–3
  and select committee, 261, 262–3,
    264
Brailsford, John, 214–15, 216, 217
The Breakaway (Cooke), 201–2
Briançon, 59, 67
British Cycling, 204, 210, 213
Brive, 56
Brunel, Philippe, 193
Bruyneel, Johan, 167, 169, 178,
    185, 188
BT, 245
Burtin, Alex, 69

Cabelle col, and Tom Simpson
    randonnée, 41
Café Vendran, 14
Calzati, Sylvain, 176
Campbell, Alastair, 31–2, 133–4,
    221, 251, 252
Campbell, Rory, 32
Cannondale-Drapac team, 172
Caritoux, Éric, 16, 33, 84, 132–42
  threats against, 138

Caritoux, Jean-Claude, 140
Caritoux, Kim, 141
Caritoux, Nathalie, 141
Carpentras, 32
  and Tom Simpson *randonnée*, 41,
    42, 45
Cavendish, Mark, 27, 203, 219
  in Tour 2012, 65
Cazeneuve, Georges, 26
Cazeneuve, Thierry, 26
Chalet Liotard, 24, 58, 206
Chalet Reynard, 11, 12, 65, 103,
    136, 160, 176, 227, 228, 240–1
  finish line moves to, 246
  to St Estève, 207
  to Sault, 19, 241
  Sault to, 42, 46
  and Tom Simpson *randonnée*, 41,
    42–3
Champ de Mars, 245
Champelle lavender farm, 19
Chany, Pierre, 279
Chapeau Rouge bakery, 91
Charlie Hebdo, 244
Château–Chinon, 98
Chez Camille, 132–3
Chiles, Adrian, 208
Christophe, Eugène, 141
Cinglés du Mont Ventoux, 31,
    273
Cioni, Dario, 234
Cipollini, Mario, 148
  in Tour 1994, 143
Circuit du Ventoux, 22
Cirque du Litor, 55
Clement, Pope, 32
The Climb (Froome), 220
Coe, Seb, 157
Cofidis scandal, 225
Col des Aires, 82
  and GFNY, 35
Col d'Aubisque, 55

Col de la Croix de l'Homme
    Mort, 90
Col de Fontaube, 91
Col de l'Homme Mort, and
    GFNY, 35
Col de Macuègne, 82
    and GFNY, 35
Col de la Madeleine, 33–4
Col du Négron, 90
Col de Perjuret, 75
Col de la Péronière, and GFNY,
    35
Col des Tempêtes, 13, 33, 43, 198
Col de Turniol, 112
Collins, Damien, 262
Comité des Fêtes in Carpentras,
    41
Comtat Venaissin, 32–3
Contador, Alberto, 175, 220, 241,
    242
    in Tour 2013, 199, 200–1
Cooke, Nicole, 201–12
    on Armstrong, 213
    and British women's tour, 210
    career achievements of, 203
    on doping, 212
    and lack of media attention, 208
    and lack of support for women's
        cycling, 204
    and Olympic gold, 210
    in Tour 2002, 208–9
    in Tour 2006, 201–8
    in Tour 2007, 208
    in Tour 2008, 208
Cookson, Brian, 209, 213
Coppi, Fausto, 10, 15, 37
    in Bobet memoir, 54–5
    and brother's death, 55
    and climbs, 62
    and doping, 59
    in Tour 1951, 55, 56, 57, 59
    in Tour 1952, 60, 62–3, 64, 65–6

Coppi, Serse, in Tour 1951, 55
cortisol, see under doping
La Course, 209
Coyle, Daniel, 189
Cram, Steve, 157
Crédit Agricole team, 179, 180
Critérium du Dauphiné (formerly
    Dauphiné Libéré), 22, 24, 25,
    26, 75, 169, 170, 173, 176, 178,
    184–5, 187, 188–9, 243
    early visits of, to Ventoux, 62
    Tour de France goes hand in
        hand with, 66
Crow, Sheryl, 185
CSC team, 188
Cycle Sport, 53

Daily Mail, 260
Danielson, Tom, 183, 184
Dauphiné Libéré, see Critérium du
    Dauphiné
Dauphiné Libéré, 62
Day Ahead, 164
de Caunes, Antoine, 63
de Caunes, George, 63
de Gribaldy, Jean, 135–7
de Jongh, Steven, 229
de Vivie, Paul:
    epic ride of, 21–2
    round trip undertaken by, 22
    'Velocio' nom de plume of, 21
Déchevaux-Dumesnil, Suzanne,
    86
Delgado, Pedro, 112, 137–8, 139
Denson, Vin, 106
Department for Culture, Media
    and Sport, 261–4
Déprez, Louis, in Tour 1951,
    56
Desnerck, Rosa, 270
Didion, Joan, 266
Dietzen, Reimund, 138

Diouf, Antoine, 89–90
Dockray, Ken, 95, 96
doping, 71–2, 125, 157, 178,
    183–4, 212–14, 230
  and amphetamines, 42, 55, 59,
    71, 75, 122, 123, 140, 142,
    271
  and cortisol, 234
  and EPO, 113, 142, 158, 159,
    168, 170
  fear of Ventoux quelled by,
    185–6
  and Festina scandal, 115, 140,
    156, 187
  Hamilton's book on, 189–90
  investigation into, 173, 183, 184,
    198
  and Operación Puerto, 156, 203,
    208
  select committee investigates,
    261–4
  Simpson's daughter's concerns
    about, 271–2
  and Sky's zero-tolerance policy,
    150, 215, 223, 228–9, 234,
    236
  suspicion of, goes viral, 217
  and Tour de France, 42, 55, 59,
    71, 75, 115–16, 117, 122–3,
    142, 155–7, 167–8, 170, 187,
    203, 217, 218 (see also
    Armstrong, Lance)
  and tramadol, 230–1, 234
Drôme, 1, 18, 24, 86, 121
Dumas, Pierre, 69, 71, 75–6, 122,
    123, 244, 263, 279
Durand, Albin, 88–90

Ellingworth, Rod, 240, 246–7,
    252, 255
Ellis, Doug, 180–1, 183
Entrechaux, 93

Enzer, Marcel, in Tour 1962, 75
EPO, see under doping
L'Équipe, 10, 28, 46, 56, 70, 75,
    121, 193, 224, 233, 279
Étape du Tour, 34–5
  'carnage, chaos and catastrophic',
    34
Etixx Quickstep team, 256
Eurotrash, 63
Expo Cycles Bedoin, 28–9
extreme-weather protocol (EWP),
    245–6

Fabulous Fifties, 53, 55
Faema team, 102
Farrar, Tyler, 241
Farrell, Alan, 230
FDJ team, 256
Ferme St Hubert, 85
Fernández, Alberto, 137–9
Ferrari, Michele, 188, 263–4
Festina scandal, 115, 140, 156,
    187
Festina team, 113, 115, 140, 156,
    187
Fignon, Laurent, 15, 42, 47–8,
    112, 134, 135, 137, 139, 140
  death of, 47
  memoir of, 47, 48
  in Tour 1983, 47
  in Tour 1984, 47
  in Tour 1989, 127
Flassan, 16, 34, 132–4
  and New Labour project, 133–4
Flèche Wallonne, 68
Fontaube, 82
Fotheringham, Alasdair, 176–7
Fotheringham, William, 23
French National Championships,
    141
French Revolution, 33
Friebe, Daniel, 105

Froome, Chris, 10, 33, 106, 175, 203, 221, 226–30
  Armstrong compared with, 214, 221, 227, 228, 236
  asthmatic problem of, 230
  author interview refused by, 226
  author's feature articles on, 226
  bike-shop picture of, 28
  Brailsford feels protective towards, 237–8
  and Campbell, 32
  and clarification questions sent to Brailsford, 233–4
  and Dauphiné, 62
  Holtz mocks, 222
  jeered, 187
  'like he's on a scooter', 222
  and Maire, 232–3, 235, 236–7
  museum hopes to acquire bike of, 29
  Porte's exchange with, 243
  resented success of, 228
  restored as race leader, 2016, 256–7
  and *Roi du Mont Ventoux* film, 109
  and therapeutic-use exemptions (TUEs), 229–30, 232
  in Tour 2012, 65
  in Tour 2013, 109, 199–201, 213, 217–18, 220, 221–3, 226–7, 228, 236, 250
  in Tour 2015, 187, 230, 235
  in Tour 2016, 251, 256–7
  and yellow jersey, reluctance to wear, 235
Froome, Michelle, 200, 213, 215, 226, 229–30
  media criticised by, 235–6
Fuentes, Eufemiano, 188
Furka, 21

Gabelle col, and Tom Simpson *randonnée*, 41, 42
Gabriel, Jacques, 22
Galerians, 31
Galibier, 21, 24–5, 65
Gallagher, Brendan, 208
Gárate, Juan Manuel:
  and *Roi du Mont Ventoux* film, *see Roi du Mont Ventoux*
  in Tour 2009, 199
Garmin team, 183, 190, 197–8
Gaul, Charly, 10, 72–3
  and doping, 75
  hermit period of, 72–3
  museum hopes to acquire bike of, 29
  in Tour 1955, 67
  in Tour 1958, 73, 74–5
  in Tour 1962, 75
Gavia, 130, 246, 247
Géminiani, Raphaël 'Gem', 53–4, 60–2, 225
  and Bobet, 59
  on Gaul, 73
  Robic's fracas with, 65
  in Tour 1951, 57, 58
  in Tour 1952, 60, 62–3, 64, 65–6
  in Tour 1955, 68
  in Tour 1958, 73–4, 75
  as Tour 'royal', 58
GFNY world series, 2015, 35
Gherardo, 20–1
Giacotto, Vincenzo, 102
Giraud, Robert, 85–6
Giro d'Italia:
  1957, 73
  1967, 126
  1969, 122
  1970, 88
  1984, 139
  1988, 130, 246
  1989, 128

1994, 143
1999, 162
2006, 205
and doping, 122
Goddet, Jacques, 97, 126
Godeau, Roger, 87–8
Goding, Pete, 197, 252, 253
Gorges de la Nesque, 34, 82
    and GFNY, 35
    and Tom Simpson *randonnée*, 41
Greipel, André, 219, 241, 242
    in Tour 2016, 248, 250
Grozeau, 58
Guardian, 263
Guerinel, Jean-Michel, 28–9
Guimard, Cyrille, 103

Hamilton, Tyler, 160, 161, 184–6,
    232
    and Armstrong, 169–71, 187–9,
        191
    and doping, 185–6, 189
    and Fuentes, 188
    and Maire, 232
    on *60 Minutes*, 189
    in Tour 2002, 187
Hampsten, Andy, 46, 130, 246
Harworth Cycling Club, 49
Haynes, Chris, 221
Heiden, Eric, 270
Hemingway, Ernest, 86
Henderson, Noel, 53–4
Heras, Roberto, 117, 162
Herrera, Luis, 46
Hézard, Yves, 130
Hinault, Bernard, 36–7, 47, 112,
    128, 137, 139–40, 246
    retirement of, 127
    in Tour 1986, 127, 140
Hincapie, George, 185
Hoban, Barry, 42, 107, 195, 269,
    270

Hoban (formerly Simpson), Helen,
    42, 78, 95–6, 269, 270
Hoban, Helen, 273, 275
    and autopsy report, 271
Holtz, Gérard, 222
Hotel du Mont Ventoux, 14
Hotel du Theatre, 42
Howden, Bob, 261
Hoy, Chris, 209
Huddleston, Nigel, 261

Indurain, Miguel, 142
    and Dauphiné, 62
    in Tour 1994, 220, 228
InGamba, 147, 148
Inside Team Sky (Walsh), 197
International Cycle Sport, 53
Isle-sur-la-Sorgue, 83, 207
    Valréas to, 204

Jalabert, Laurent, 142
Jorgensen, Rob, 236
Julich, Bobby, 229

Kals, Betty, 29–31, 33, 43
Kelly, Sean, 135–6, 137, 248
    bike-shop picture of, 28
Kennaugh, Pete, in Tour 2013, 199
Kerrison, Tim, 221
Kimmage, Paul, 197–8, 215, 226
Kinnock, Neil, 134
Kitching, Ron, 53
Kittel, Marcel, 241
Knowlson, James, 86
Koblet, Hugo, 50, 60
    in Bobet memoir, 54–5
    and climbs, 62
    glamorous image of, 60
    in *Miroir du Cyclisme*, 57
    'pédaleur de charme' sobriquet of,
        56
    in Tour 1951, 56–7, 58, 59–60

Kreuziger, Roman, in Tour 2013, 199
Kübler, Ferdi, 15, 25, 60
  in Bobet memoir, 54–5
  and climbs, 62
  death of, 70
  in *L'Équipe*, 70
  in *Miroir du Cyclisme*, 36
  quits, 10, 69
  recollections of, 69–70
  in Tour 1950, 68
  in Tour 1955, 68, 69
  in *Vélo*, 68

La Vie Claire team, 128, 129
  in Tour 2002, 186
Lacets de Montvernier, 27
Landis, Floyd, 152, 189
Las Cuevas, Armand de, 169
Laurent (driver), 248, 250
Lauritzen, Dag Otto, 46
Lawton, Matt, 260
Lazaridès, Apo, in Tour 1951, 58
Lazaridès, Lucien:
  in Tour 1951, 58–9
  as Tour 'royal', 58
Lazzerini, Lino, 28
Le Cycliste, 21
Le Guilloux, Maurice 'Momo', 129–30
Le Pen, Jean-Marie, 89
Le Pen, Marine, 89
Leblanc, Jean-Marie, 275
Leblanc, Luc, 142
Lefevere, Patrick, 256, 257
Legeay, Roger, 179
Leinders, Geert, 226, 229
LeMond, Greg, 34, 127, 128–9, 213–14
  in Tour 1986, 127, 128
  in Tour 1989, 127
  in Tour 2000, 34

LeMond, Kathy, 213
Lennon, Bryn, 17–18
Les Baux, 10
Leuillot, Josette, 60–1
Lévitan, Félix, 122
Lewis, Colin, 271
Liège–Bastogne–Liège, 68, 136, 229, 246
Livingston, Kevin, 150, 161
Loriol-du-Comtat, 22
Lotto Belisol team, 231
Lure mountain, 91
Luzet, Eric, 255

McFarlane, Robert, 3
McQuaid, Pat, 156, 159, 209
Madeleine, 82, 94
  and Tom Simpson *randonnée*, 41
Madiot, Marc, 46, 256–7, 277
Madonna di Campiglio, 162
Magni, Fiorenzo, in Tour 1951, 57
Maija, Alvaro, 146
Maire, Philippe, 232–3, 235, 236–7
Maison Forestière Jamet, 114
Malaucène, 16–17, 18, 22, 24, 25, 26, 27, 28, 31, 57, 62, 120, 141
  and Cingles du Ventoux, 31
  and Tom Simpson *randonnée*, 41
  training camp in, 181
Malléjac, Jean:
  collapse of, 68–9, 71–2, 76, 123
  and doping, 71–2, 157
  in *Miroir du Cyclisme*, 36
  in Tour 1955, 68–9, 71–2, 76, 195
Mangeas, Daniel, 129
Marathon du Mont Ventoux, inaugural, 22
Marie, Thierry, in Tour 1994, 143
Marseille, 67, 85, 195, 277–9
Martin, Tony, 235

Mathieu, Jan, 231

Matthews, Michael, 241

Mayo, Iban, 160, 176–7, 189
Ventoux record held by, 176

Mazan, 42, 277

Mellow Johnny's, 150, 153, 155

Memories of the Peloton (Hinault), 36

Men's Health, 226

Mercatone Uno team, 148

Merckx, Eddy, 24–5, 29, 37,
97–106, 125–6, 163, 227
author's interview with, 101–6,
110
and doping, 122–3
injury to, 10, 104
and Joanne Simpson, 272–3
and long distance, 199
and *Roi du Mont Ventoux* film, *see*
Roi du Mont Ventoux
on Simpson death, 122, 126
and Simpson memorial, 97, 104
Simpson's near-feud with, 98,
272
in Tour 1969, 101, 103
in Tour 1970, 23, 97–8, 102–6,
109, 110, 115, 120
in Tour 1972, 120–2

Milan–San Remo, 246

Millar, David, 173, 175, 183, 225,
277

Millar, Fiona, 31, 32

Millar, Robert, 137

Miroir du Cyclisme, 36, 39, 57

Mr Tom (Sidwells), 271

Mistral, 9, 13, 14, 34, 39, 54, 228,
245–6, 248–9, 252, 277

Mistral, Frédéric, 85

Mitchell, Nigel, 233

Moirans-en-Montagne, 255

Mollans-sur-Ouvèze, 92

Mont Brouilly, 241, 246

Mont Serein, 17, 58
ski station at, 24, 206

Mont Ventoux (*see also individual
features*):
absence of, from Dauphiné, 26
appearance of, 1
'bastard of a climb', 248
BBC film of, 132–3
Bobet's description of, 15–16
clichés describe ascent of, 15
climbing on, 20
cycle racing becomes established
on, 22
and de Vivie's ride, 21
'death climb' and 'death zone'
epithets applied to, 15
early cycling on, 21
and extreme-weather protocol
(EWP), 245–6
fatalities commonplace on, 16
first to climb, 20
first Tour de France rider to
reach summit of, 58
and GFNY, 35
hairpins on, 11, 18, 134, 175
'hardest climb in France', 160
and heatstroke, 34, 35
hunting on, 19–20
as iconic climb, 216
landscape dominated by, 1, 19,
182
a 'majestic theatre', 47
meaning of name of, 13
in mid-1980s, 36
in *Miroir du Cyclisme*, 36, 39
and Mistral, 9, 13, 14, 34, 39, 54,
228, 245–6, 248–9, 252, 277
at night, 33
north side, 18, 23–4, 27, 45, 91,
92, 121, 141, 203
other-worldly nature of, 15
Petrarch's account of, 20–1

Mont Ventoux – *cont.*
   poster lauds delights of, 13–14
   significant part played by, 55
   Simpson memorial on, 39, 97,
      104, 201, 274, 275–7
   south side, 11, 24, 73, 91, 97,
      141, 203
   summit, first recorded bike ride
      to, 22
   summit, first road from Bédoin
      to, 21
   on TripAdvisor, 14, 20
   violent storms on, 92–3
   'Windy' sobriquet of, 13 (*see also*
      Mistral)
Montelimar, 34
Montpellier, 55, 56
Moore, Richard, 128
Moreau, Christophe, 142
Moser, Francesco, 139
Motorola team, 146
Mottet, Charly, 46, 112
Moulin de César, 93
Mountains of the Mind (McFarlane), 3
Mouvement pour un Cyclisme
      Crédible (MPCC), 229,
      230–1, 234
Movistar team, 242
Mur de la Peste, 85
Mura, Gianna, 117
Museeuw, Johan, bike-shop
      picture of, 28

Nencini, Gastone, in Tour 1960,
      77
Nesque river, 19
Nibali, Vincenzo, 234, 235, 249
Nice terror attack, 253–6
Nicolson, John, 261
Nieve, Mikel, in Tour 2013, 199,
      200–1
Nîmes–Gap, 128

Novitzky, Jeff, 166

Ocaña, Luis, in Tour 1972, 120–1
Ochowicz, Jim, 244
Olympic Games:
   1956, 50
   1984, 147
   2004, 215
   2005, 209
   2008, 210
   2016, 249
Operación Puerto, 156, 203, 208
Orange, 32
O'Reilly, Emma, 154
Ouvèze, 92–3

Pages, Jean-Louis, 27, 219, 254,
      255
Pantani, Marco, 73, 151
   and Armstrong, 34, 117, 120,
      151, 152, 161, 162–5, 177
   death of, 117, 163
   and doping, 117, 122, 157
   museum hopes to acquire bike
      of, 29
   public humiliation of, 162
   and *Roi du Mont Ventoux* film, *see*
      Roi du Mont Ventoux
   in Tour 1994, 18, 143
   in Tour 2000, 34, 113, 161–4,
      177
Paris–Nice, 82, 120, 136–7, 160
   1932, 22
   1967, 98–9, 272
   1970, 110
   1985, 248
   1993, 169
   1994, 60
   2016, 240–2, 246
   cancelled stage of, 246
Paris–Roubaix, 52, 88, 110, 136,
      247, 257

Parra, Fabio, 46
Pascal, Richard, 61
Peiper, Allan, 247–8
Pellenaars, Kees, 56
Peter (friend), 41, 44–5, 47, 90
Petrarch, 20–1
Peugeot team, 98, 106
Peyresourde, 77
Phinney, Taylor, 231
Pingeon, Roger, in Tour 1967, 126
Place de la Comédie, 55, 57, 144
Plateau d'Albion, 90–1
Plaud, Gaston, 98
Poli, Eros, 142–8
    downhill race speed of, 18
    and long distance, 199
    size and weight of, 10, 142, 145,
        146
    in Tour 1994, 10, 18, 142–8,
        220, 275
Pont de Rognonas, 57
Portal, Nicolas, 249
Porte, Richie, 220, 232–3, 237,
        241, 242–3
    in Tour 2013, 199
    in Tour 2016, 244, 250
Poulidor, Raymond, 29, 121, 196
Prétot, Julien, 253, 255–6
Procycling, 53
Prost, Alain, 34
    in Tour 2000, 34
La Provence Sportive, 22
Prudhomme, Christian, 23, 24, 25,
        203, 216, 231, 246, 258, 275
    and Nice terror attack, 253,
        254–5
Put Me Back on My Bike
    (Fotheringham), 23
Puy de Dôme, 60

Quick-step, 101
Quintana, Nairo, 175

in Tour 2013, 198–9, 201, 228
in Tour 2016, 258

Racing Through the Dark (Millar),
    225
La Repubblica, 117
Reynolds, Harry, 78
Riccò, Riccardo, 152
Riis, Bjarne, 142, 157, 188, 226
Rivière, Roger, in Tour 1960, 75,
    77
Robic, Jean 'Biquet':
    and climbs, 62
    Géminiani's fracas with, 65
    in Tour 1947, 63
    in Tour 1952, 64, 65–6
Robinson, Brian, 78, 284
Roche, Stephen, 46, 112, 137
Rocher du Cire, 85
Rodríguez, Manolo, in Tour 1951,
    58
Roi du Mont Ventoux, 108–20
    passim
Rolland, Antonin, in Tour 1955,
    67, 71
Rolland, Pierre, 182
Rooks, Steven, 137
Route des Cèdres, 31
Route du Sud, 181
Routes du Ventoux, 28
RoyalDine cafeteria, 41
Rumeau, Christian, 137, 138–9

Sagan, Peter, 219, 241, 257
St Colombe, 10, 21, 241
St Didier, Mondial Cups, 41
St Estève, 161
    bends leading to, 19
    brutality of bend at, 10–11
    Chalet Reynard to, 207
    as decisive point, 160
    road surface at, 74

St Raphaël-Géminiani., 51
St Rémy-de-Provence, 32
Sarrians, 88
Sault, 19, 27, 28, 31, 90, 134, 141–2
  to Chalet Raynard, 42, 46
  Chalet Reynard to, 19, 241
  and Cingles du Ventoux, 31
  and Tom Simpson *randonnée*, 41,
    42–3
Sciandri, Max, in Tour 1994, 146
The Secret Race (Hamilton, Coyle),
  189–90
Sénanque abbey, 250
Sepúlveda, Eduardo, 257–8
Sestrières, 60, 63
Shadows on the Road (Barry), 230,
  231
Sidwells, Chris, 271
Simeoni, Philippo, 155
Simpson, Helen, *see* Hoban, Helen
Simpson, Joanne, 266–77, 279–81
  and autopsy report, 271–2
  and father's memorial, 274,
    275–6
  head injury to, 267–8
  and Merckx, 272–3
Simpson, Tom, 15, 216
  anniversary of death of, 20th, 41
  anniversary of death of, 30th,
    273
  anniversary of death of, 50th,
    23, 27, 272, 274–5
  attempts to revive, 39
  BBC Sports Personality of the
    Year, 23, 108
  at Bédoin, 33
  and Corsica, 99, 124
  daughter seeks autopsy report
    on, 271–2
  daughter's interview concerning,
    268–77, 279–81
  death of, 1–2, 22–3, 29, 37, 39,

    72, 82, 97–8, 123
  and doping, 125, 157
  and draft-dodger accusations, 51
  fan club of, 96
  first Tour de France of, 77
  funeral of, 98
  hand injury of, 106, 107
  at Harworth Cycling Club, 49
  kidney infection of, 107
  memorial to, 39, 97, 104, 201,
    274, 275–7
  Merckx's near-feud with, 98
  in *Miroir du Cyclisme*, 36
  and number 13, 275
  randonnée (sportive) marks
    anniversary of, 41–5
  in Tour 1960, 77–8
  in Tour 1961, 95
  in Tour 1965, 106–8
  in Tour 1967, 125–6
  in Tour of Flanders, 95
  and Tour's parent organisation,
    23
  Vaughters on, 183
  world champion, 22, 108
  Yorkshire Post obituary of, 283
Simpson, Tom Sr, 49, 51, 284
Six Day race, 140
60 Minutes, 189
Skil team, 135, 136, 137
Slaying the Badger (Moore), 128
Slot, Owen, 232–3
Soulor, 55
Spanish Pyrenees, 176
Stabholz, Camille, 132–3
Stelvio, 11
Stephens, Neil, in Tour 1994, 146
Sunday Times, 166
Sutton, Shane, 210, 211
  and select committee, 261–2

Talansky, Andrew, 241

Tapie, Bernard, 127, 128–30
Tapie, Dominique, 129–30
Taylor, Alec, 284–5
Team Astana, 223, 234–5
Team GB, 214, 261
Team Sky, 65, 150, 197–8, 213,
    214, 220–1, 223, 225–6,
    228–35 *passim*, 237, 241, 249
    (*see also* Brailsford, Dave)
  author's tweet concerning, 259
  mistrust of, 228
  and select committee, *see under*
    Brailsford, David
  statement of, on tramadol, 231–2
  strategic errors of, 225
  and therapeutic-use exemptions
    (TUEs), 236
  zero-tolerance policy of, 150,
    215, 223, 228–9, 234, 236
Terrasses du Ventoux café, 93
therapeutic-use exemptions
    (TUEs), 204, 215, 229–30,
    232, 236, 260, 263
Thévenet, Bernard, 26, 29
  in Tour 1972, 24, 27, 121
Thomas, Geraint, 241, 242
Thomazeau, François, 278–9
Times, 226, 232, 236
Tinkoff Saxo team, 241
Tirreno–Adriatico, 246
Tom Simpson *randonnée*, 41–5
Tomorrow We Ride (Bobet), 54–5
Torti, Emilio Croci, 69
Toshiba team, 127, 130
Toulourenc, 82, 83, 91, 92–3
Tour of Flanders, 95, 257, 267
Tour de France, 217
  1947, 63
  1950, 68
  1951, 55–8, 62
  1952, 60–1, 62–5
  1953, 66

1954, 66, 68
1955, 29, 36, 39, 66–72, 76, 123,
    195
1958, 29, 71, 73–5
1960, 77–8
1961, 95
1962, 75
1965, 29, 106–8
1966, 122
1967, 3–5, 23, 33, 71, 98, 123,
    125–6, 269, 279
1969, 101, 103, 122
1970, 23, 24–5, 29, 97–8, 102–6,
    109, 110, 115, 120
1972, 24, 26, 27, 29, 120–2
1976, 26
1983, 47
1984, 47
1986, 127, 128, 135, 140
1987, 20, 41, 46–8, 109, 115,
    127, 130–1
1989, 127
1994, 10, 18, 142–8, 220, 228,
    275
1998, 113, 140, 156, 187
1999, 115, 171
2000, 34, 109, 113, 161–4, 185,
    228, 236
2001, 180
2002, 109, 115, 117, 186, 208–9
2006, 201–8
2007, 208
2008, 208
2009, 35, 109, 154–5, 190–1,
    199, 277
2010, 190
2012, 65, 190, 226
2013, 109, 197, 198–201, 213,
    217–18, 220, 221–3, 226–7,
    228, 236, 250
2014, 64
2015, 27, 187, 230, 234–5, 257–8

Tour de France – *cont.*
2016, 242–6, 248–59, 275
2017, 274–5
'boring', 160
in Britain, 210
commercial interests take over
from national in, 64
and La Course, 209
Dauphiné goes hand in hand
with, 66
and doping, 42, 55, 59, 71, 75,
115–16, 117, 122–3, 142,
155–7, 167–8, 170, 203, 217,
218 (*see also* Armstrong,
Lance; doping)
and extreme-weather protocol
(EWP), 245–6
and Festina scandal, 113, 115,
140, 156, 187
first British win in, 203
first mountain time trial of, 73
first TV coverage of, 63
French riders dominate, 48
and hypothermia, 34
and individual time trial, 40
and infighting (1958), 73–4
King of the Mountains
classification of, 68
memorabilia from, 28–9
and Nice terror attack, 253–6
and Operación Puerto, 156, 203,
208
and post-terrorism security,
243–4
and Robic–Géminiani fracas
(1952), 65
and *Roi du Mont Ventoux* film,
108–20
and Simpson anniversary, 274–5
women's, 2002, 208–9
women's, 2006, 201–8
women's, 2007, 208

women's, 2008, 208
Yorkshire as feature of, 25–6
Tour of Romandie, 229, 230
Tour of Spain, *see* Vuelta a
España
Tour of Valencia, 164
Tour of Ventoux, 82
Tour de Yorkshire, 63
Tourmalet, 24, 216
Tours du Sud-Est, 22
tramadol, *see under* doping
Tricart, Cyrille, 254
TripAdvisor, 14, 20
Trott, Laura, 211
TUEs (therapeutic-use
exemptions), 204, 215, 229–
30, 232, 236, 260, 263
Twitter, 23, 70, 172, 227, 235, 253,
259
Tygart, Travis, 166, 167

Ullrich, Jan, 117, 162
Union Cycliste Internationale
(UCI), 122, 155–6, 157, 159,
189, 209
and Froome, 257
and rules interpretation, 257–8
and women's cycling, 209, 211
United States Anti-Doping
Agency (USADA), 154, 184
Unzué, Eusebio, 256, 258
US Postal Service team, 161, 162,
170, 178, 185, 188

Vaison-la-Romaine, 32, 35, 93
Valréas:
Beaumes-de-Venise to, 173
to Isle-sur-la-Sorgue, 204
Van Den Bossche, Martin, 105–6
van Est, Wim:
Soulor fall of, 55–6
in Tour 1951, 55–6

Van Garderen, Tejay, 258
Van Genechten, Richard:
  in Tour 1954, 68
  in Tour 1955, 68
Vandevelde, Christian, 183, 184
Vanwalleghem, Rik, 126
Vaucluse, 1, 19, 22, 28, 35, 83, 97, 132, 135, 174
  in WW2, 86–7, 88, 89–90
Vaughters, Jonathan, 75, 160, 169, 197
  author's conversation with, 171–84
  and doping, 178
  and Rhône wines, 173–4
  in Tour 2001, 180
  in Tour 2002, 187
  Ventoux record set by, 176, 177, 178
Vélo, 68
Velon, 172
Velo101 website, 35
Vendran, Raoul, 14
Ventoux, *see* Mont Ventoux
Ventoux Sports, 41, 42
Verbruggen, Hein, 159, 189
Villes-sur-Auzon, 34, 84
Vinokourov, Alexander, 178
Virage du Bois, 10, 19
Virenque, Richard, 142
  and doping, 115–16
  and long distance, 199
  museum hopes to acquire bike of, 29
  and *Roi du Mont Ventoux* film, *see* Roi du Mont Ventoux
  in Tour 2002, 115, 187
Voeckler, Thomas, 63–4
Voet, Willy, 140
Vuelta a España, 87, 133, 134, 136, 137–9, 140, 219, 259

Wadley, Jock, 53
Waiting for Godot (Beckett), 87–8
Walsh, David, 165–6, 197–8, 220, 260
We Were Young and Carefree (Fignon), 47
Whittle, Mr (author's father), 12, 287
Whittle, Mrs (author's mother), 12, 287
Wiggins, Bradley, 183, 203
  on *The Andrew Marr Show*, 260
  and Armstrong, 190
  media criticised by, 260
  and Olympic gold, 226
  and select committee, 261–2
  and therapeutic-use exemptions (TUEs), 204, 229, 232, 260
  in Tour 2009, 277
  in Tour 2012, 65, 190, 226
Wiggins, Gary, 270
Winfrey, Oprah, 158, 213
World Anti-Doping Agency (WADA), 231
World Cup 1966, 276
World Cup 1994, 144
World War Two, 55, 85–7, 88–9
Wurf, Cameron, 243

Yates, Sean, 226, 232, 236, 258
The Year of Magical Thinking (Didion), 266
Yorkshire, as Tour de France feature, 25–6
Yorkshire Post, 283

Zabel, Erik, 157
Zabriskie, Dave, 183, 184
Zidane, Zinedine, 278
Zimmermann, Urs, 135